THE ETHICS OF ARTIFICIAL INTELLIGENCE IN EDUCATION

THE ETHICS OF ARTIFICIAL INTELLIGENCE IN EDUCATION

Toni Linder
Ann Smith

Kruger Brentt
Publishers

2025

Kruger Brentt Publishers UK. LTD.
Company Number 9728962

Regd. Office: 68 St Margarets Road, Edgware, Middlesex HA8 9UU

ISBN: 978-1-78715-408-7

For information on all our publications visit our website at http://krugerbrentt.com/

PREFACE

The Ethics of Artificial Intelligence (AI) in education represent a dynamic intersection shaping the future of learning environments worldwide. As AI technologies increasingly permeate educational settings, ethical considerations become paramount in ensuring that these innovations benefit students, educators, and society as a whole while upholding fundamental values and principles.

At its core, the integration of AI into education revolves around enhancing learning experiences, optimizing administrative tasks, and personalizing educational content to meet individual student needs. AI algorithms analyze vast amounts of data to provide insights, recommendations, and adaptive learning pathways tailored to each student's learning style and pace. This personalized approach holds the promise of improving learning outcomes and engagement, but it also raises ethical concerns related to privacy, fairness, and transparency.

One of the foremost ethical challenges in AI education pertains to the collection, storage, and use of student data. AI systems rely on extensive data inputs, including personal information and learning analytics, to function effectively. Ensuring robust data privacy policies, obtaining informed consent, and safeguarding sensitive information from unauthorized access are essential ethical imperatives. Educators and policymakers must navigate the delicate balance between leveraging data-driven insights for educational benefits while mitigating risks associated with data breaches and privacy violations.

AI algorithms used in educational contexts must be rigorously tested and monitored to mitigate biases that could lead to discriminatory outcomes. Bias can arise from skewed training data, algorithmic design flaws, or unintended correlations that perpetuate inequalities based on factors such as race, gender, or socioeconomic status. Ethical AI design principles advocate for transparency in algorithmic decision-making processes, promoting fairness and equity in student assessments, admissions, and educational interventions.

Human-centered AI design emphasizes the importance of incorporating ethical considerations into the development and deployment of AI technologies in education. This approach prioritizes human values, well-being, and educational goals while empowering educators to maintain oversight and control over AI-driven interventions. By fostering collaboration between technologists, educators, and stakeholders, human-centered AI design aims to create inclusive and supportive learning environments that uphold ethical standards and promote positive educational outcomes.

Accountability is crucial in ensuring responsible AI deployment in education. Clear lines of responsibility must be established to address issues of algorithmic decision-making, system errors, and the impact of AI on educational practices. Transparent communication about AI capabilities, limitations, and potential risks fosters trust among educators, students, and parents, enabling informed decision-making and ethical governance of AI technologies in educational settings.

Preparing educators and educational leaders to ethically navigate AI technologies is essential for their effective integration into teaching and learning practices. Ethical professional development programs emphasize digital literacy, critical thinking skills, and ethical decision-making frameworks tailored to AI use in education. By empowering educators with the knowledge and tools to evaluate, implement, and monitor AI technologies responsibly, ethical professional development supports ethical AI practices that prioritize student well-being and educational integrity.

Toni Linder
Ann Smith

CONTENTS

Preface v

Introduction 1

Introduction to Ethics and Artificial Intelligence in Education 1

The Ethical Dilemmas of AI in Education 2

Part-I: Understanding AI in Education

1. **AI and Machine Learning in Education** 5

1.1 Defining Artificial Intelligence and Machine Learning 5

1.2 The Evolution of AI in Education 25

1.3 AI Applications in Educational Settings 27

2. **The Promise and Potential of AI** 31

2.1 Advantages and Opportunities of AI in Education 31

2.2 Improving Learning Outcomes with AI 34

2.3 Personalization and Adaptively in Education 59

3. **Ethical Foundations** 69

3.1 Ethical Theories and Frameworks 69

3.2 Ethical Principles in Educational AI 117

3.3 The Importance of Ethical Decision-Making 121

Part-II: Ethical Considerations and Challenges

4. **Data Privacy and Security** 127

4.1 Data Collection and Student Privacy 127

4.2 Securing AI-Generated Educational Data 148

4.3 Ethical Data Use and Ownership 150

5. **Bias and Fairness in AI** 155

5.1 Recognizing Bias in AI Algorithms 155

5.2 Mitigating Bias in Educational AI *178*
5.3 Fairness and Equality in Learning Opportunities *182*
6. Transparency and Accountability..........185
6.1 Explaining AI Decision to Stakeholders *185*
6.2 Responsible AI Development and Deployment *188*
6.3 Ethical responsibility in AI Systems *192*
Part-III: Human-AI Interaction in Education
7. Teacher and Student Perspectives..........199
7.1 Educators Views on AI Integration *199*
7.2 Student Experiences with AI-Enhanced Learning *201*
7.3 Ethical Considerations from Educational Stakeholders *205*
8. AI and Educational Ethics..........209
8.1 Ethics Education for AI Developers and Users *209*
8.2 Fostering Ethical Behavior in AI-Driven Learning *212*
8.3 Building Ethical AI Communities *216*
Part-IV: Ethical Guidelines and Policies
9. Regulatory Framework and Policies..........223
9.1 National and International Regulations *223*
9.2 Guidelines for Ethical AI Adoption *247*
9.3 Challenges in Enforcing AI Ethics Policies *251*
10. Educational Institutions and AI Ethics..........255
10.1 Developing Ethical AI Policies in Schools and Universities *255*
10.2 Implementing Ethical AI Practices in Institutions *257*
10.3 Case Studies of Ethical AI in Education *259*
Part-V: Future Directions and Ethical Innovations
11. Emerging Trends in Educational AI..........265
11.1 AI-Powered Assistants and Chatbots *265*
11.2 AI in Assessment and Grading *266*
11.3 Ethical Implications of Emerging Technologies *268*
12. Collaboration and Ethics..........271
12.1 Partnerships for Ethical AI in Education *271*
12.2 Multidisciplinary Approaches to AI Ethics *273*
12.3 International Collaboration on AI Ethics *275*

Conclusion **279**
Summary of Key Ethical Considerations 279
The Future of AI Ethics in Education 280
Final Thoughts and Reflections 282
Glossary of Terms **283**
Resources for Further Reading **285**
Index **287**

INTRODUCTION

INTRODUCTION TO ETHICS AND ARTIFICIAL INTELLIGENCE IN EDUCATION

Ethics and artificial intelligence (AI) in education is an emerging field that explores the intersection of moral principles and advanced technologies within the educational landscape. As AI continues to permeate various aspects of society, its integration into education raises significant ethical considerations. AI in education encompasses a broad range of applications, from personalized learning systems and intelligent tutoring to administrative tools and predictive analytics. These technologies have the potential to transform educational experiences, making learning more accessible, efficient, and tailored to individual needs. However, the ethical implications of AI in education must be carefully examined to ensure that these advancements promote fairness, equity, and the well-being of all stakeholders.

One major ethical concern is the potential for bias in AI algorithms, which can lead to discriminatory practices and reinforce existing inequalities in the education system. AI systems are often trained on historical data that may reflect societal biases, and without proper oversight, these biases can be perpetuated or even exacerbated. Additionally, the use of AI in education raises questions about data privacy and security. Educational institutions collect vast amounts of data on students, and the implementation of AI systems necessitates robust measures to protect this sensitive information from misuse or breaches.

Another crucial ethical consideration is the impact of AI on the teacher-student relationship. While AI can provide valuable support and insights, it should not replace the human elements of teaching that are essential for fostering critical thinking, empathy, and social skills. Teachers play a pivotal role in the educational process, and their professional judgment and interaction with students cannot be fully replicated by AI.

Moreover, the deployment of AI in education must be guided by principles of transparency and accountability. Stakeholders, including educators, students, and parents, should be informed about how AI systems are used, the data they collect, and the decisions they make. This transparency is vital to building trust and ensuring that AI is used responsibly and ethically.

THE ETHICAL DILEMMAS OF AI IN EDUCATION

The ethical dilemmas of AI in education encompass a range of complex issues that require careful consideration and ongoing dialogue. As AI technologies become increasingly integrated into educational systems, they bring with them the potential to enhance learning experiences and administrative efficiency. However, this integration also raises significant ethical questions. One major dilemma is the issue of bias in AI algorithms. These algorithms often rely on historical data, which may contain inherent biases reflecting societal inequalities. When these biases are not addressed, AI systems can perpetuate or even exacerbate existing disparities, leading to unfair treatment of certain groups of students.

Another ethical concern revolves around data privacy and security. The implementation of AI in education involves the collection and analysis of vast amounts of personal data from students. This raises questions about how this data is stored, who has access to it, and how it is used. Ensuring the privacy and security of student data is paramount to maintaining trust in AI systems. Additionally, there is the risk of data breaches, which can have serious consequences for the individuals involved.

The impact of AI on the teacher-student relationship also presents an ethical dilemma. While AI can offer personalized learning and support, it cannot replicate the human interaction and emotional intelligence that are crucial components of effective teaching. The use of AI should not diminish the role of teachers but rather support them in their efforts to provide a holistic education. There is a concern that over-reliance on AI could lead to a more impersonal learning environment, where the nuanced understanding and empathy of human teachers are undervalued.

Transparency and accountability in the use of AI in education are essential to addressing these ethical dilemmas. Stakeholders, including educators, students, and parents, need to be informed about how AI systems operate, the data they collect, and the decisions they make. This transparency is crucial for building trust and ensuring that AI is used in a manner that is ethical and aligned with educational values. Moreover, there must be clear mechanisms for accountability, where the consequences of AI-driven decisions can be reviewed and challenged if necessary.

PART I:

UNDERSTANDING AI IN EDUCATION

CHAPTER 1

AI AND MACHINE LEARNING IN EDUCATION

1.1 DEFINING ARTIFICIAL INTELLIGENCE AND MACHINE LEARNING

1.1.1 Artificial Intelligence

Artificial intelligence (AI), in its broadest sense, is intelligence exhibited by machines, particularly computer systems. It is a field of research in computer science that develops and studies methods and software that enable machines to perceive their environment and use learning and intelligence to take actions that maximize their chances of achieving defined goals. Such machines may be called AIs.

Some high-profile applications of AI include advanced web search engines (e.g., Google Search); recommendation systems (used by YouTube, Amazon, and Netflix); interacting via human speech (e.g., Google Assistant, Siri, and Alexa); autonomous vehicles (e.g., Waymo); generative and creative tools (e.g., ChatGPT, Apple Intelligence, and AI art); and superhuman play and analysis in strategy games (e.g., chess and Go). However, many AI applications are not perceived as AI: "A lot of cutting edge AI has filtered into general applications, often without being called AI because once something becomes useful enough and common enough it's not labeled AI anymore."

Alan Turing was the first person to conduct substantial research in the field that he called machine intelligence. Artificial intelligence was founded as an academic discipline in 1956, by those now considered the founding fathers of AI, John McCarthy, Marvin Minksy, Nathaniel Rochester, and Claude Shannon. The field went through multiple cycles of optimism, followed by periods of disappointment and loss of funding, known as AI winter.

Funding and interest vastly increased after 2012 when deep learning surpassed all previous AI techniques, and after 2017 with the transformer architecture. This led to the AI boom of the early 2020s, with companies, universities, and laboratories overwhelmingly based in the United States pioneering significant advances in artificial intelligence.

The growing use of artificial intelligence in the 21st century is influencing a societal and economic shift towards increased automation, data-driven decision-making, and the integration of AI systems into various economic sectors and areas of life, impacting job markets, healthcare, government, industry, education, propaganda, and disinformation. This raises questions about the long-term effects, ethical implications, and risks of AI, prompting discussions about regulatory policies to ensure the safety and benefits of the technology.

The various subfields of AI research are centered around particular goals and the use of particular tools. The traditional goals of AI research include reasoning, knowledge representation, planning, learning, natural language processing, perception, and support for robotics. General intelligence—the ability to complete any task performable by a human on an at least equal level—is among the field's long-term goals.

To reach these goals, AI researchers have adapted and integrated a wide range of techniques, including search and mathematical optimization, formal logic, artificial neural networks, and methods based on statistics, operations research, and economics. AI also draws upon psychology, linguistics, philosophy, neuroscience, and other fields.

History

The study of mechanical or "formal" reasoning began with philosophers and mathematicians in antiquity. The study of logic led directly to Alan Turing's theory of computation, which suggested that a machine, by shuffling symbols as simple as "0" and "1", could simulate any conceivable form of mathematical reasoning. This, along with concurrent discoveries in cybernetics, information theory and neurobiology, led researchers to consider the possibility of building an "electronic brain". They developed several areas of research that would become part of AI, such as McCullouch and Pitts design for "artificial neurons" in 1943, and Turing's influential 1950 paper 'Computing Machinery and Intelligence', which introduced the Turing test and showed that "machine intelligence" was plausible.

The field of AI research was founded at a workshop at Dartmouth College in 1956. The attendees became the leaders of AI research in the 1960s. They and their students produced programs that the press described as "astonishing": computers were learning checkers strategies, solving word problems in algebra, proving logical theorems and speaking English. Artificial intelligence laboratories were set up at a number of British and U.S. Universities in the latter 1950s and early 1960s.

Researchers in the 1960s and the 1970s were convinced that their methods would eventually succeed in creating a machine with general intelligence and considered this the goal of their field. Herbert Simon predicted, "machines will be capable, within twenty years, of doing any work a man can do". Marvin Minsky agreed, writing, "within a generation ... the problem of creating 'artificial intelligence' will substantially be solved". They had, however, underestimated the difficulty of the problem. In 1974, both the U.S. and British governments cut off exploratory research in response to the criticism of Sir James Lighthill and ongoing pressure from the U.S. Congress to fund more productive projects. Minsky's and Papert's book *Perceptrons* was understood as proving that artificial neural networks would never be useful for solving real-world tasks, thus discrediting the approach altogether. The "AI winter", a period when obtaining funding for AI projects was difficult, followed.

In the early 1980s, AI research was revived by the commercial success of expert systems, a form of AI program that simulated the knowledge and analytical skills of human experts. By 1985, the market for AI had reached over a billion dollars. At the same time, Japan's fifth generation computer project inspired the U.S. and British governments to restore funding for academic research. However, beginning with the collapse of the Lisp Machine market in 1987, AI once again fell into disrepute, and a second, longer-lasting winter began.

Up to this point, most of AI's funding had gone to projects that used high-level symbols to represent mental objects like plans, goals, beliefs, and known facts. In the 1980s, some researchers began to doubt that this approach would be able to imitate all the processes of human cognition, especially perception, robotics, learning and pattern recognition, and began to look into "sub-symbolic" approaches. Rodney Brooks rejected "representation" in general and focussed directly on engineering machines that move and survive. Judea Pearl, Lofti Zadeh and others developed methods that handled incomplete and uncertain information by making reasonable guesses rather than precise logic. But the most important development was the revival of "connectionism", including neural network research, by Geoffrey Hinton and others. In 1990, Yann LeCun successfully showed that convolutional neural networks can recognize handwritten digits, the first of many successful applications of neural networks.

AI gradually restored its reputation in the late 1990s and early 21st century by exploiting formal mathematical methods and by finding specific solutions to specific problems. This "narrow" and "formal" focus allowed researchers to produce verifiable results and collaborate with other fields (such as statistics, economics and mathematics).

By 2000, solutions developed by AI researchers were being widely used, although in the 1990s they were rarely described as "artificial intelligence". However, several academic researchers became concerned that AI was no longer pursuing its original goal of creating versatile, fully intelligent machines. Beginning around 2002, they founded the subfield of artificial general intelligence (or "AGI"), which had several well-funded institutions by the 2010s.

Deep learning began to dominate industry benchmarks in 2012 and was adopted throughout the field. For many specific tasks, other methods were abandoned. Deep learning's success was based on both hardware improvements (faster computers, graphics processing units, cloud computing) and access to large amounts of data (including curated datasets, such as ImageNet). Deep learning's success led to an enormous increase in interest and funding in AI. The amount of machine learning research (measured by total publications) increased by 50% in the years 2015–2019.

In 2016, issues of fairness and the misuse of technology were catapulted into center stage at machine learning conferences, publications vastly increased, funding became available, and many researchers re-focussed their careers on these issues. The alignment problem became a serious field of academic study.

In the late teens and early 2020s, AGI companies began to deliver programs that created enormous interest. In 2015, AlphaGo, developed by DeepMind, beat the world champion Go player. The program was taught only the rules of the game and developed strategy by itself. GPT-3 is a large language model that was released in 2020 by OpenAI and is capable of generating high-quality human-like text. These programs, and others, inspired an aggressive AI boom, where large companies began investing billions in AI research. According to AI Impacts, about $50 billion annually was invested in "AI" around 2022 in the U.S. alone and about 20% of the new U.S. Computer Science PhD graduates have specialized in "AI". About 800,000 "AI"-related U.S. job openings existed in 2022.

Philosophy

Defining Artificial Intelligence

Alan Turing wrote in 1950 "I propose to consider the question 'can machines think'?" He advised changing the question from whether a machine "thinks", to "whether or not it is possible for machinery to show intelligent behaviour". He devised the Turing test, which measures the ability of a machine to simulate human conversation. Since we can only observe the behavior of the machine, it does not matter if it is "actually" thinking or literally has a "mind". Turing notes that we can not determine these things about other people but "it is usual to have a polite convention that everyone thinks."

Russell and Norvig agree with Turing that intelligence must be defined in terms of external behavior, not internal structure. However, they are critical that the test requires the machine to imitate humans. "Aeronautical engineering texts," they wrote, "do not define the goal of their field as making 'machines that fly so exactly like pigeons that they can fool other pigeons.'" AI founder John McCarthy agreed, writing that "Artificial intelligence is not, by definition, simulation of human intelligence".

McCarthy defines intelligence as "the computational part of the ability to achieve goals in the world". Another AI founder, Marvin Minsky similarly describes it as "the ability to solve hard problems". The leading AI textbook defines it as the study of agents that perceive their environment and take actions that maximize their chances of achieving defined goals. These definitions view intelligence in terms of well-defined problems with well-defined solutions, where both the difficulty of the problem and the performance of the program are direct measures of the "intelligence" of the machine—and no other philosophical discussion is required, or may not even be possible.

Another definition has been adopted by Google, a major practitioner in the field of AI. This definition stipulates the ability of systems to synthesize information as the manifestation of intelligence, similar to the way it is defined in biological intelligence.

Evaluating Approaches to AI

No established unifying theory or paradigm has guided AI research for most of its history. The unprecedented success of statistical machine learning in the 2010s eclipsed all other approaches (so much so that some sources, especially in the business world, use the term "artificial intelligence" to mean "machine learning with neural networks"). This approach is mostly sub-symbolic, soft and narrow. Critics argue that these questions may have to be revisited by future generations of AI researchers.

Symbolic AI and its Limits

Symbolic AI (or "GOFAI") simulated the high-level conscious reasoning that people use when they solve puzzles, express legal reasoning and do mathematics. They were highly successful at "intelligent" tasks such as algebra or IQ tests. In the 1960s, Newell and Simon proposed the physical symbol systems hypothesis: "A physical symbol system has the necessary and sufficient means of general intelligent action."

However, the symbolic approach failed on many tasks that humans solve easily, such as learning, recognizing an object or commonsense reasoning. Moravec's paradox is the discovery that high-level "intelligent" tasks were easy for AI, but low level "instinctive" tasks were extremely difficult. Philosopher Hubert Dreyfus had argued since the 1960s that human expertise depends on unconscious instinct rather than conscious symbol manipulation, and on having a "feel" for the situation, rather than explicit symbolic knowledge. Although his arguments had been ridiculed and ignored when they were first presented, eventually, AI research came to agree with him.

The issue is not resolved: sub-symbolic reasoning can make many of the same inscrutable mistakes that human intuition does, such as algorithmic bias. Critics such as Noam Chomsky argue continuing research into symbolic AI will still be necessary to attain general intelligence, in part because sub-symbolic AI is a move away from explainable AI: it can be difficult or impossible to understand why a modern statistical AI program made a particular decision. The emerging field of neuro-symbolic artificial intelligence attempts to bridge the two approaches.

Neat vs. Scruffy

"Neats" hope that intelligent behavior is described using simple, elegant principles (such as logic, optimization, or neural networks). "Scruffies" expect that it necessarily requires solving a large number of unrelated problems. Neats defend their programs with theoretical rigor, scruffies rely mainly on incremental testing to see if they work. This issue was actively discussed in the 1970s and 1980s, but eventually was seen as irrelevant. Modern AI has elements of both.

Soft vs. Hard Computing

Finding a provably correct or optimal solution is intractable for many important problems. Soft computing is a set of techniques, including genetic algorithms, fuzzy logic and neural networks, that are tolerant of imprecision, uncertainty, partial truth and approximation. Soft computing was introduced in the late 1980s and most successful AI programs in the 21st century are examples of soft computing with neural networks.

Narrow vs. General AI

AI researchers are divided as to whether to pursue the goals of artificial general intelligence and superintelligence directly or to solve as many specific problems as possible (narrow AI) in hopes these solutions will lead indirectly to the field's long-term goals. General intelligence is difficult to define and difficult to measure, and modern AI has had more verifiable successes by focusing on specific problems with specific solutions. The experimental sub-field of artificial general intelligence studies this area exclusively.

Machine Consciousness, Sentience, and Mind

The philosophy of mind does not know whether a machine can have a mind, consciousness and mental states, in the same sense that human beings do. This issue considers the internal experiences of the machine, rather than its external behavior. Mainstream AI research considers this issue irrelevant because it does not affect the goals of the field: to build machines that can solve problems using intelligence. Russell and Norvig add that "[t]he additional project of making a machine conscious in exactly the way humans are is not one that we are equipped to take on." However, the question has become central to the philosophy of mind. It is also typically the central question at issue in artificial intelligence in fiction.

Consciousness

David Chalmers identified two problems in understanding the mind, which he named the "hard" and "easy" problems of consciousness. The easy problem is understanding how the brain processes signals, makes plans and controls behavior. The hard problem is explaining how this *feels* or why it should feel like anything at all, assuming we are right in thinking that it truly does feel like something (Dennett's consciousness illusionism says this is an illusion). While human information processing is easy to explain, human subjective experience is difficult to explain. For example, it is easy to imagine a color-blind person who has learned to identify which objects in their field of view are red, but it is not clear what would be required for the person to *know what red looks like.*

Computationalism and Functionalism

Computationalism is the position in the philosophy of mind that the human mind is an information processing system and that thinking is a form of computing. Computationalism argues that the relationship between mind and body is similar or identical to the relationship between software and hardware and thus may be a solution to the mind–body problem. This philosophical position was inspired by the work of AI researchers and cognitive scientists in the 1960s and was originally proposed by philosophers Jerry Fodor and Hilary Putnam.

Philosopher John Searle characterized this position as "strong AI": "The appropriately programmed computer with the right inputs and outputs would thereby have a mind in exactly the same sense human beings have minds." Searle counters this assertion with his Chinese room argument, which attempts to show that, even if a machine perfectly simulates human behavior, there is still no reason to suppose it also has a mind.

AI Welfare and Rights

It is difficult or impossible to reliably evaluate whether an advanced AI is sentient (has the ability to feel), and if so, to what degree. But if there is a significant chance that a given machine can feel and suffer, then it may be entitled to certain rights or welfare protection measures, similarly to animals. Sapience (a set of capacities related to high intelligence, such as discernment or self-awareness) may provide another moral basis for AI rights. Robot rights are also sometimes proposed as a practical way to integrate autonomous agents into society.

In 2017, the European Union considered granting "electronic personhood" to some of the most capable AI systems. Similarly to the legal status of companies, it would have conferred rights but also responsibilities. Critics argued in 2018 that granting rights to AI systems would downplay the importance of human rights, and that legislation should focus on user needs rather than speculative futuristic scenarios. They also noted that robots lacked the autonomy to take part to society on their own.

Progress in AI increased interest in the topic. Proponents of AI welfare and rights often argue that AI sentience, if it emerges, would be particularly easy to deny. They warn that this may be a moral blind spot analogous to slavery or factory farming, which could lead to large-scale suffering if sentient AI is created and carelessly exploited.

Goals

The general problem of simulating (or creating) intelligence has been broken into subproblems. These consist of particular traits or capabilities that researchers expect an intelligent system to display. The traits described below have received the most attention and cover the scope of AI research.

Reasoning and Problem-Solving

Early researchers developed algorithms that imitated step-by-step reasoning that humans use when they solve puzzles or make logical deductions. By the late 1980s and 1990s, methods were developed for dealing with uncertain or incomplete information, employing concepts from probability and economics. Many of these algorithms are insufficient for solving large reasoning problems because they experience a "combinatorial explosion": They become exponentially slower as the problems grow. Even humans rarely use the step-by-step deduction that early AI research could model. They solve most of their problems using fast, intuitive judgments. Accurate and efficient reasoning is an unsolved problem.

Knowledge Representation

Knowledge representation and knowledge engineering allow AI programs to answer questions intelligently and make deductions about real-world facts. Formal knowledge representations are used in content-based indexing and retrieval, scene interpretation, clinical decision support, knowledge discovery (mining "interesting" and actionable inferences from large databases), and other areas.

A knowledge base is a body of knowledge represented in a form that can be used by a program. An ontology is the set of objects, relations, concepts, and properties used by a particular domain of knowledge. Knowledge bases need to represent things such as objects, properties, categories, and relations between objects; situations, events, states, and time; causes and effects; knowledge about knowledge (what we know about what other people know); default reasoning (things that humans assume are true until they are told differently and will remain true even when other facts are changing); and many other aspects and domains of knowledge.

Among the most difficult problems in knowledge representation are the breadth of commonsense knowledge (the set of atomic facts that the average person knows is enormous); and the sub-symbolic form of most commonsense knowledge (much of what people know is not represented as "facts" or "statements" that they could express verbally). There is also the difficulty of knowledge acquisition, the problem of obtaining knowledge for AI applications.

Planning and Decision-Making

An "agent" is anything that perceives and takes actions in the world. A rational agent has goals or preferences and takes actions to make them happen. In automated planning, the agent has a specific goal. In automated decision-making, the agent has preferences—there are some situations it would prefer to be in, and some situations it is trying to avoid. The decision-making agent assigns a number to each situation (called the "utility") that measures how much the agent prefers it. For each possible action, it can calculate the "expected utility": the utility of all possible outcomes of the action, weighted by the probability that the outcome will occur. It can then choose the action with the maximum expected utility.

In classical planning, the agent knows exactly what the effect of any action will be. In most real-world problems, however, the agent may not be certain about the situation they are in (it is "unknown" or "unobservable") and it may not know for certain what will happen after each possible action (it is not "deterministic"). It must choose an action by making a probabilistic guess and then reassess the situation to see if the action worked.

In some problems, the agent's preferences may be uncertain, especially if there are other agents or humans involved. These can be learned (e.g., with inverse reinforcement learning), or the agent can seek information to improve its preferences. Information value theory can be used to weigh the value of exploratory or experimental actions. The space of possible future actions and situations is typically intractably large, so the agents must take actions and evaluate situations while being uncertain of what the outcome will be.

A Markov decision process has a transition model that describes the probability that a particular action will change the state in a particular way and a reward function that supplies the utility of each state and the cost of each action. A policy associates a decision with each possible state. The policy could be calculated (e.g., by iteration), be heuristic, or it can be learned. Game theory describes the rational behavior of multiple interacting agents and is used in AI programs that make decisions that involve other agents.

Learning

Machine learning is the study of programs that can improve their performance on a given task automatically. It has been a part of AI from the beginning. There are several kinds of machine learning. Unsupervised learning analyzes a stream of data and finds patterns and makes predictions without any other guidance. Supervised learning requires a human to label the input data first, and comes in two main varieties: classification (where the program must learn to predict what category the input belongs in) and regression (where the program must deduce a numeric function based on numeric input). In reinforcement learning, the agent is rewarded for good responses and punished for bad ones. The agent learns to choose responses that are classified as "good".

Transfer learning is when the knowledge gained from one problem is applied to a new problem. Deep learning is a type of machine learning that runs inputs through biologically inspired artificial neural networks for all of these types of learning. Computational learning theory can assess learners by computational complexity, by sample complexity (how much data is required), or by other notions of optimization.

Natural Language Processing

Natural language processing (NLP) allows programs to read, write and communicate in human languages such as English. Specific problems include speech recognition, speech synthesis, machine translation, information extraction, information retrieval and question answering.

Early work, based on Noam Chomsky's generative grammar and semantic networks, had difficulty with word-sense disambiguation unless restricted to small domains called "micro-worlds" (due to the common sense knowledge problem). Margaret Masterman believed that it was meaning and not grammar that was the key to understanding languages, and that thesauri and not dictionaries should be the basis of computational language structure.

Modern deep learning techniques for NLP include word embedding (representing words, typically as vectors encoding their meaning), transformers (a deep learning architecture using an attention mechanism), and others. In 2019, generative pre-trained transformer (or "GPT") language models began to generate coherent text, and by 2023 these models were able to get human-level scores on the bar exam, SAT test, GRE test, and many other real-world applications.

Perception

Machine perception is the ability to use input from sensors (such as cameras, microphones, wireless signals, active lidar, sonar, radar, and tactile sensors) to deduce aspects of the world. Computer vision is the ability to analyze visual input.

The field includes speech recognition, image classification, facial recognition, object recognition,object tracking, and robotic perception.

Social Intelligence

Affective computing is an interdisciplinary umbrella that comprises systems that recognize, interpret, process, or simulate human feeling, emotion, and mood. For example, some virtual assistants are programmed to speak conversationally or even to banter humorously; it makes them appear more sensitive to the emotional dynamics of human interaction, or to otherwise facilitate human–computer interaction.

However, this tends to give naïve users an unrealistic conception of the intelligence of existing computer agents. Moderate successes related to affective computing include textual sentiment analysis and, more recently, multimodal sentiment analysis, wherein AI classifies the affects displayed by a videotaped subject.

General Intelligence

A machine with artificial general intelligence should be able to solve a wide variety of problems with breadth and versatility similar to human intelligence.

Search and Optimization

AI can solve many problems by intelligently searching through many possible solutions. There are two very different kinds of search used in AI: state space search and local search.

State Space Search

- State space search searches through a tree of possible states to try to find a goal state. For example, planning algorithms search through trees of goals and subgoals, attempting to find a path to a target goal, a process called means-ends analysis.
- Simple exhaustive searches are rarely sufficient for most real-world problems: the search space (the number of places to search) quickly grows to astronomical numbers. The result is a search that is too slow or never completes. "Heuristics" or "rules of thumb" can help prioritize choices that are more likely to reach a goal.
- Adversarial search is used for game-playing programs, such as chess or Go. It searches through a tree of possible moves and counter-moves, looking for a winning position.

Local Search

- Local search uses mathematical optimization to find a solution to a problem. It begins with some form of guess and refines it incrementally.

- Gradient descent is a type of local search that optimizes a set of numerical parameters by incrementally adjusting them to minimize a loss function. Variants of gradient descent are commonly used to train neural networks.
- Another type of local search is evolutionary computation, which aims to iteratively improve a set of candidate solutions by "mutating" and "recombining" them, selecting only the fittest to survive each generation.
- Distributed search processes can coordinate via swarm intelligence algorithms. Two popular swarm algorithms used in search are particle swarm optimization (inspired by bird flocking) and ant colony optimization (inspired by ant trails).

Logic

Formal logic is used for reasoning and knowledge representation. Formal logic comes in two main forms: propositional logic (which operates on statements that are true or false and uses logical connectives such as "and", "or", "not" and "implies") and predicate logic (which also operates on objects, predicates and relations and uses quantifiers such as "*Every* X is a *Y*" and "There are *some* Xs that are *Y*s").

Deductive reasoning in logic is the process of proving a new statement (conclusion) from other statements that are given and assumed to be true (the premises). Proofs can be structured as proof trees, in which nodes are labelled by sentences, and children nodes are connected to parent nodes by inference rules.

Given a problem and a set of premises, problem-solving reduces to searching for a proof tree whose root node is labelled by a solution of the problem and whose leaf nodes are labelled by premises or axioms. In the case of Horn clauses, problem-solving search can be performed by reasoning forwards from the premises or backwards from the problem. In the more general case of the clausal form of first-order logic, resolution is a single, axiom-free rule of inference, in which a problem is solved by proving a contradiction from premises that include the negation of the problem to be solved.

Inference in both Horn clause logic and first-order logic is undecidable, and therefore intractable. However, backward reasoning with Horn clauses, which underpins computation in the logic programming language Prolog, is Turing complete. Moreover, its efficiency is competitive with computation in other symbolic programming languages.

Fuzzy logic assigns a "degree of truth" between 0 and 1. It can therefore handle propositions that are vague and partially true. Non-monotonic logics, including logic programming with negation as failure, are designed to handle default reasoning. Other specialized versions of logic have been developed to describe many complex domains.

Probabilistic Methods for Uncertain Reasoning

Many problems in AI (including in reasoning, planning, learning, perception, and robotics) require the agent to operate with incomplete or uncertain information. AI researchers have devised a number of tools to solve these problems using methods from probability theory and economics. Precise mathematical tools have been developed that analyze how an agent can make choices and plan, using decision theory, decision analysis, and information value theory. These tools include models such as Markov decision processes, dynamic decision networks, game theory and mechanism design.

Bayesian networks are a tool that can be used for reasoning (using the Bayesian inference algorithm), learning (using the expectation-maximization algorithm), planning (using decision networks) and perception (using dynamic Bayesian networks).

Probabilistic algorithms can also be used for filtering, prediction, smoothing, and finding explanations for streams of data, thus helping perception systems analyze processes that occur over time (e.g., hidden Markov models or Kalman filters).

Classifiers and Statistical Learning Methods

The simplest AI applications can be divided into two types: classifiers (e.g., "if shiny then diamond"), on one hand, and controllers (e.g., "if diamond then pick up"), on the other hand. Classifiers are functions that use pattern matching to determine the closest match. They can be fine-tuned based on chosen examples using supervised learning. Each pattern (also called an "observation") is labeled with a certain predefined class. All the observations combined with their class labels are known as a data set. When a new observation is received, that observation is classified based on previous experience.

There are many kinds of classifiers in use. The decision tree is the simplest and most widely used symbolic machine learning algorithm. K-nearest neighbor algorithm was the most widely used analogical AI until the mid-1990s, and Kernel methods such as the support vector machine (SVM) displaced k-nearest neighbor in the 1990s. The naive Bayes classifier is reportedly the "most widely used learner" at Google, due in part to its scalability. Neural networks are also used as classifiers.

Artificial Neural Networks

An artificial neural network is based on a collection of nodes also known as artificial neurons, which loosely model the neurons in a biological brain. It is trained to recognise patterns; once trained, it can recognise those patterns in fresh data. There is an input, at least one hidden layer of nodes and an output. Each node applies a function and once the weight crosses its specified threshold, the data is transmitted to the next layer. A network is typically called a deep neural network if it has at least 2 hidden layers.

Learning algorithms for neural networks use local search to choose the weights that will get the right output for each input during training. The most common training technique is the backpropagation algorithm. Neural networks learn to model complex relationships between inputs and outputs and find patterns in data. In theory, a neural network can learn any function.

In feedforward neural networks the signal passes in only one direction. Recurrent neural networks feed the output signal back into the input, which allows short-term memories of previous input events. Long short term memory is the most successful network architecture for recurrent networks. Perceptrons use only a single layer of neurons, deep learning uses multiple layers. Convolutional neural networks strengthen the connection between neurons that are "close" to each other—this is especially important in image processing, where a local set of neurons must identify an "edge" before the network can identify an object.

Deep Learning

Deep learning uses several layers of neurons between the network's inputs and outputs. The multiple layers can progressively extract higher-level features from the raw input. For example, in image processing, lower layers may identify edges, while higher layers may identify the concepts relevant to a human such as digits, letters, or faces.

Deep learning has profoundly improved the performance of programs in many important subfields of artificial intelligence, including computer vision, speech recognition, natural language processing, image classification, and others. The reason that deep learning performs so well in so many applications is not known as of 2023. The sudden success of deep learning in 2012–2015 did not occur because of some new discovery or theoretical breakthrough (deep neural networks and backpropagation had been described by many people, as far back as the 1950s) but because of two factors: the incredible increase in computer power (including the hundred-fold increase in speed by switching to GPUs) and the availability of vast amounts of training data, especially the giant curated datasets used for benchmark testing, such as ImageNet.

GPT

Generative pre-trained transformers (GPT) are large language models that are based on the semantic relationships between words in sentences (natural language processing). Text-based GPT models are pre-trained on a large corpus of text which can be from the internet. The pre-training consists in predicting the next token (a token being usually a word, subword, or punctuation). Throughout this pre-training, GPT models accumulate knowledge about the world, and can then generate human-like text by repeatedly predicting the next token.

Typically, a subsequent training phase makes the model more truthful, useful and harmless, usually with a technique called reinforcement learning from human feedback (RLHF). Current GPT models are still prone to generating falsehoods called "hallucinations", although this can be reduced with RLHF and quality data. They are used in chatbots, which allow you to ask a question or request a task in simple text.

Current models and services include: Gemini (formerly Bard), ChatGPT, Grok, Claude, Copilot and LLaMA. Multimodal GPT models can process different types of data (modalities) such as images, videos, sound, and text.

Specialized Hardware and Software

In the late 2010s, graphics processing units (GPUs) that were increasingly designed with AI-specific enhancements and used with specialized TensorFlow software had replaced previously used central processing unit (CPUs) as the dominant means for large-scale (commercial and academic) machine learning models' training. Specialized programming languages such as Prolog were used in early AI research, but general-purpose programming languages like Python have become predominant.

1.1.2 Machine Learning

Machine learning (ML) is a field of study in artificial intelligence concerned with the development and study of statistical algorithms that can learn from data and generalize to unseen data and thus perform tasks without explicit instructions. Recently, artificial neural networks have been able to surpass many previous approaches in performance.

ML finds application in many fields, including natural language processing, computer vision, speech recognition, email filtering, agriculture, and medicine. When applied to business problems, it is known under the name predictive analytics. Although not all machine learning is statistically based, computational statistics is an important source of the field's methods.

The mathematical foundations of ML are provided by mathematical optimization (mathematical programming) methods. Data mining is a related (parallel) field of study, focusing on exploratory data analysis (EDA) through unsupervised learning. From a theoretical viewpoint, probably approximately correct (PAC) learning provides a framework for describing machine learning.

History

The term *machine learning* was coined in 1959 by Arthur Samuel, an IBM employee and pioneer in the field of computer gaming and artificial intelligence. The synonym *self-teaching computers* was also used in this time period.

Although the earliest machine learning model was introduced in the 1950s when Arthur Samuel invented a program that calculated the winning chance in checkers for each side, the history of machine learning roots back to decades of human desire and effort to study human cognitive processes. In 1949, Canadian psychologist Donald Hebb published the book *The Organization of Behavior*, in which he introduced a theoretical neural structure formed by certain interactions among nerve cells. Hebb's model of neurons interacting with one another set a groundwork for how AIs and machine learning algorithms work under nodes, or artificial neurons used by computers to communicate data. Other researchers who have studied human cognitive systems contributed to the modern machine learning technologies as well, including logician Walter Pitts and Warren McCulloch, who proposed the early mathematical models of neural networks to come up with algorithms that mirror human thought processes.

By the early 1960s an experimental "learning machine" with punched tape memory, called Cybertron, had been developed by Raytheon Company to analyze sonar signals, electrocardiograms, and speech patterns using rudimentary reinforcement learning. It was repetitively "trained" by a human operator/teacher to recognize patterns and equipped with a "goof" button to cause it to reevaluate incorrect decisions.

A representative book on research into machine learning during the 1960s was Nilsson's book on Learning Machines, dealing mostly with machine learning for pattern classification. Interest related to pattern recognition continued into the 1970s, as described by Duda and Hart in 1973. In 1981 a report was given on using teaching strategies so that an artificial neural network learns to recognize 40 characters (26 letters, 10 digits, and 4 special symbols) from a computer terminal.

Tom M. Mitchell provided a widely quoted, more formal definition of the algorithms studied in the machine learning field: "A computer program is said to learn from experience *E* with respect to some class of tasks *T* and performance measure *P* if its performance at tasks in *T*, as measured by *P*, improves with experience *E*." This definition of the tasks in which machine learning is concerned offers a fundamentally operational definition rather than defining the field in cognitive terms.

This follows Alan Turing's proposal in his paper "Computing Machinery and Intelligence", in which the question "Can machines think?" is replaced with the question "Can machines do what we (as thinking entities) can do?".

Modern-day machine learning has two objectives. One is to classify data based on models which have been developed; the other purpose is to make predictions for future outcomes based on these models. A hypothetical algorithm specific to classifying data may use computer vision of moles coupled with supervised learning in order to train it to classify the cancerous moles. A machine learning algorithm for stock trading may inform the trader of future potential predictions.

Relationships with Artificial intelligence

As a scientific endeavor, machine learning grew out of the quest for artificial intelligence (AI). In the early days of AI as an academic discipline, some researchers were interested in having machines learn from data. They attempted to approach the problem with various symbolic methods, as well as what were then termed "neural networks"; these were mostly perceptrons and other models that were later found to be reinventions of the generalized linear models of statistics. Probabilistic reasoning was also employed, especially in automated medical diagnosis.

However, an increasing emphasis on the logical, knowledge-based approach caused a rift between AI and machine learning. Probabilistic systems were plagued by theoretical and practical problems of data acquisition and representation. By 1980, expert systems had come to dominate AI, and statistics was out of favor. Work on symbolic/knowledge-based learning did continue within AI, leading to inductive logic programming(ILP), but the more statistical line of research was now outside the field of AI proper, in pattern recognition and information retrieval. Neural networks research had been abandoned by AI and computer science around the same time. This line, too, was continued outside the AI/CS field, as "connectionism", by researchers from other disciplines including Hopfield, Rumelhart, and Hinton. Their main success came in the mid-1980s with the reinvention of backpropagation.

Machine learning (ML), reorganized and recognized as its own field, started to flourish in the 1990s. The field changed its goal from achieving artificial intelligence to tackling solvable problems of a practical nature. It shifted focus away from the symbolic approaches it had inherited from AI, and toward methods and models borrowed from statistics, fuzzy logic, and probability theory.

Relationships with Data Compression

There is a close connection between machine learning and compression. A system that predicts the posterior probabilities of a sequence given its entire history can be used for optimal data compression (by using arithmetic coding on the output distribution). Conversely, an optimal compressor can be used for prediction (by finding the symbol that compresses best, given the previous history). This equivalence has been used as a justification for using data compression as a benchmark for "general intelligence".

An alternative view can show compression algorithms implicitly map strings into implicit feature space vectors, and compression-based similarity measures compute similarity within these feature spaces. For each compressor C(.) we define an associated vector space ℵ, such that C(.) maps an input string x, corresponding to the vector norm ||~x||. An exhaustive examination of the feature spaces underlying all compression algorithms is precluded by space; instead, feature vectors chooses to examine three representative lossless compression methods, LZW, LZ77, and PPM.

According to AIXI theory, a connection more directly explained in Hutter Prize, the best possible compression of x is the smallest possible software that generates x. For example, in that model, a zip file's compressed size includes both the zip file and the unzipping software, since you can not unzip it without both, but there may be an even smaller combined form.

Examples of AI-powered audio/video compression software include NVIDIA Maxine, AIVC. Examples of software that can perform AI-powered image compression include OpenCV, TensorFlow, MATLAB's Image Processing Toolbox (IPT) and High-Fidelity Generative Image Compression.

In unsupervised machine learning, k-means clustering can be utilized to compress data by grouping similar data points into clusters. This technique simplifies handling extensive datasets that lack predefined labels and finds widespread use in fields such as image compression.

Data compression aims to reduce the size of data files, enhancing storage efficiency and speeding up data transmission. K-means clustering, an unsupervised machine learning algorithm, is employed to partition a dataset into a specified number of clusters, k, each represented by the centroid of its points. This process condenses extensive datasets into a more compact set of representative points. Particularly beneficial in image and signal processing, k-means clustering aids in data reduction by replacing groups of data points with their centroids, thereby preserving the core information of the original data while significantly decreasing the required storage space.

Large language models (LLMs) are also capable of lossless data compression, as demonstrated by DeepMind's research with the Chinchilla 70B model. Developed by DeepMind, Chinchilla 70B effectively compressed data, outperforming conventional methods such as Portable Network Graphics (PNG) for images and Free Lossless Audio Codec (FLAC) for audio. It achieved compression of image and audio data to 43.4% and 16.4% of their original sizes, respectively.

Relationships with Data Mining

Machine learning and data mining often employ the same methods and overlap significantly, but while machine learning focuses on prediction, based on *known* properties learned from the training data, data mining focuses on the discovery of (previously) *unknown* properties in the data (this is the analysis step of knowledge discovery in databases). Data mining uses many machine learning methods, but with different goals; on the other hand, machine learning also employs data mining methods as "unsupervised learning" or as a preprocessing step to improve learner accuracy. Much of the confusion between these two research communities (which do often have separate conferences and separate journals, ECML PKDD being a major exception) comes from the basic assumptions they work with: in machine learning, performance is usually evaluated with respect to the ability to *reproduce known* knowledge, while in knowledge discovery and data mining (KDD) the key task is the discovery of previously *unknown* knowledge. Evaluated with respect to known knowledge, an uninformed (unsupervised) method will easily be outperformed by other supervised methods, while in a typical KDD task, supervised methods cannot be used due to the unavailability of training data.

Machine learning also has intimate ties to optimization: Many learning problems are formulated as minimization of some loss function on a training set of examples. Loss functions express the discrepancy between the predictions of the model being trained and the actual problem instances (for example, in classification, one wants to assign a label to instances, and models are trained to correctly predict the preassigned labels of a set of examples).

Relationships with Generalization

The difference between optimization and machine learning arises from the goal of generalization: While optimization algorithms can minimize the loss on a training set, machine learning is concerned with minimizing the loss on unseen samples. Characterizing the generalization of various learning algorithms is an active topic of current research, especially for deep learning algorithms.

Relationships with Statistics

Machine learning and statistics are closely related fields in terms of methods, but distinct in their principal goal: statistics draws population inferences from a sample, while machine learning finds generalizable predictive patterns. According to Michael I. Jordan, the ideas of machine learning, from methodological principles to theoretical tools, have had a long pre-history in statistics. He also suggested the term data science as a placeholder to call the overall field.

Conventional statistical analyses require the a priori selection of a model most suitable for the study data set. In addition, only significant or theoretically relevant variables based on previous experience are included for analysis. In contrast, machine learning is not built on a pre-structured model; rather, the data shape the model by detecting underlying patterns. The more variables (input) used to train the model, the more accurate the ultimate model will be.

Leo Breiman distinguished two statistical modeling paradigms: data model and algorithmic model, wherein "algorithmic model" means more or less the machine learning algorithms like Random Forest. Some statisticians have adopted methods from machine learning, leading to a combined field that they call *statistical learning*.

Relationships with Statistical Physics

Analytical and computational techniques derived from deep-rooted physics of disordered systems can be extended to large-scale problems, including machine learning, e.g., to analyze the weight space of deep neural networks. Statistical physics is thus finding applications in the area of medical diagnostics.

Theory

A core objective of a learner is to generalize from its experience. Generalization in this context is the ability of a learning machine to perform accurately on new, unseen examples/tasks after having experienced a learning data set. The training examples come from some generally unknown probability distribution (considered representative of the space of occurrences) and the learner has to build a general model about this space that enables it to produce sufficiently accurate predictions in new cases.

The computational analysis of machine learning algorithms and their performance is a branch of theoretical computer science known as computational learning theory via the Probably Approximately Correct Learning (PAC) model. Because training sets are finite and the future is uncertain, learning theory usually does not yield guarantees of the performance of algorithms. Instead, probabilistic bounds on the performance are quite common. The bias–variance decomposition is one way to quantify generalization error.

For the best performance in the context of generalization, the complexity of the hypothesis should match the complexity of the function underlying the data. If the hypothesis is less complex than the function, then the model has under fitted the data. If the complexity of the model is increased in response, then the training error decreases. But if the hypothesis is too complex, then the model is subject to overfitting and generalization will be poorer.

In addition to performance bounds, learning theorists study the time complexity and feasibility of learning. In computational learning theory, a computation is considered feasible if it can be done in polynomial time. There are two kinds of time complexity results: Positive results show that a certain class of functions can be learned in polynomial time. Negative results show that certain classes cannot be learned in polynomial time.

1.2 THE EVOLUTION OF AI IN EDUCATION

The integration of artificial intelligence (AI) into education has been a gradual yet transformative process, reshaping traditional learning paradigms and offering new possibilities for personalized education, administrative efficiency, and educational equity. The evolution of AI in education has been marked by significant advancements and transformative changes. From early computer-assisted instruction to sophisticated intelligent tutoring systems and adaptive learning technologies, AI has continually pushed the boundaries of what is possible in education. By enhancing personalized learning, streamlining administrative tasks, and promoting accessibility and inclusion, AI has the potential to make education more effective and equitable.

However, the integration of AI in education also presents ethical challenges that must be addressed to ensure that its benefits are realized without compromising fairness, privacy, and accountability. As AI continues to evolve, it is essential for educators, technologists, policymakers, and other stakeholders to work together to navigate these challenges and harness the full potential of AI in creating a brighter future for education.

1.2.1 Early Beginnings: Computer-Assisted Instruction

The roots of AI in education can be traced back to the 1960s and 1970s, with the advent of computer-assisted instruction (CAI). During this period, computers were primarily used to support basic instructional tasks. Early CAI systems, such as IBM's PLATO and Stanford's TUTOR, aimed to provide students with automated feedback on their performance. These systems utilized rudimentary algorithms to offer drill-and-practice exercises and simple tutorials, laying the groundwork for more sophisticated AI applications in education.

Despite their limitations, these early systems demonstrated the potential of technology to augment traditional teaching methods. They provided a glimpse into how computers could offer individualized instruction and immediate feedback, which are core tenets of modern AI-driven educational tools.

1.2.2 The Rise of Intelligent Tutoring Systems

The 1980s and 1990s saw significant advancements in AI research, leading to the development of intelligent tutoring systems (ITS). These systems represented a leap forward from the basic CAI models, incorporating more complex algorithms to simulate human tutoring. ITS aimed to provide personalized instruction by adapting to the individual needs and learning pace of each student.

Notable examples of ITS include the SCHOLAR system, which used natural language processing to engage students in dialogue, and the Geometry Tutor, which provided step-by-step guidance in solving geometric problems. These systems utilized expert models to represent the knowledge of a subject and student models to track the learner's understanding and misconceptions. By dynamically adjusting the instructional content and feedback, ITS could offer a more tailored learning experience.

1.2.3 The Advent of Adaptive Learning Technologies

The early 2000s marked the emergence of adaptive learning technologies, which leveraged advancements in data analytics and machine learning to provide even more personalized educational experiences. Unlike traditional one-size-fits-all approaches, adaptive learning systems continuously assessed a student's performance and adjusted the instructional content accordingly.

One prominent example is the Knewton platform, which used sophisticated algorithms to analyze vast amounts of data on student interactions and performance. By identifying patterns and predicting future performance, Knewton could tailor the learning path for each student, ensuring that they received the right content at the right time. This approach not only improved learning outcomes but also highlighted the potential of AI to address diverse learning needs.

1.2.4 The Integration of AI in Administrative Tasks

While the primary focus of AI in education has been on enhancing the learning experience, AI has also made significant inroads into administrative tasks. From automating routine tasks such as grading and attendance tracking to providing insights into student performance and resource allocation, AI has the potential to streamline administrative processes and improve institutional efficiency.

Automated grading systems, for instance, can evaluate multiple-choice questions and even short-answer responses with high accuracy. This reduces the burden on educators, allowing them to focus more on teaching and student engagement. Predictive analytics, another application of AI, can help institutions identify students at risk of dropping out or falling behind, enabling timely interventions to support student success.

1.2.5 The Role of AI in Enhancing Accessibility and Inclusion

AI has also played a crucial role in enhancing accessibility and inclusion in education. By providing tools and resources tailored to the needs of diverse learners, AI has the potential to bridge gaps and ensure that education is more equitable.

For students with disabilities, AI-powered assistive technologies such as speech recognition, text-to-speech, and predictive text input can provide significant support. These tools enable students to engage with educational content more effectively and participate in classroom activities. Additionally, AI can help create more inclusive learning environments by offering real-time translation services for non-native speakers, making education more accessible to students from different linguistic backgrounds.

1.2.6 Ethical Considerations and Challenges

Despite the numerous benefits of AI in education, its integration also raises several ethical considerations and challenges that must be addressed. One of the primary concerns is the potential for bias in AI algorithms. AI systems are trained on historical data, which may contain inherent biases that can lead to discriminatory practices. Ensuring that AI systems are fair and unbiased is crucial to maintaining equity in education.

Data privacy and security are also significant concerns. The use of AI in education involves the collection and analysis of vast amounts of personal data from students. Protecting this data from breaches and misuse is paramount to maintaining trust in AI systems. Additionally, there is a need for transparency and accountability in how AI systems operate and make decisions, ensuring that stakeholders are informed and can challenge or review AI-driven outcomes.

1.3 AI APPLICATIONS IN EDUCATIONAL SETTINGS

Artificial intelligence (AI) has emerged as a powerful tool in education, transforming the way students learn, teachers teach, and institutions operate. AI applications in educational settings span a wide range of functionalities, from personalized learning and intelligent tutoring to administrative efficiencies and support for diverse learners.

AI applications in educational settings are transforming the way education is delivered and experienced. From personalized learning and intelligent tutoring to automated grading and predictive analytics, AI offers powerful tools to enhance teaching, learning, and administration. These advancements have the potential to make education more effective, efficient, and inclusive.

1.3.1 Personalized Learning

Personalized learning is one of the most significant advancements brought about by AI in education. Traditional educational models often adopt a one-size-fits-all approach, which can be ineffective for addressing the diverse needs of individual students. AI-driven personalized learning systems analyze a student's performance, learning pace, and preferences to tailor educational content accordingly.

For example, platforms like DreamBox and Knewton use adaptive learning technologies to continuously assess a student's understanding and adjust instructional materials to suit their needs. These systems provide targeted exercises and resources, ensuring that each student receives the appropriate level of challenge and support. This personalized approach can lead to improved learning outcomes, greater student engagement, and increased motivation.

1.3.2 Intelligent Tutoring Systems

Intelligent Tutoring Systems (ITS) represent another major application of AI in education. ITS are designed to mimic the one-on-one interaction between a student and a human tutor, providing personalized instruction and feedback. These systems utilize natural language processing, machine learning, and cognitive modeling to understand and respond to students' needs.

One notable example is the Cognitive Tutor, developed by Carnegie Learning, which offers personalized support in subjects like mathematics. The Cognitive Tutor continuously monitors a student's progress, identifies misconceptions, and provides targeted hints and explanations. By adapting to the individual learner's needs, ITS can enhance understanding and mastery of complex subjects.

1.3.3 Automated Grading and Assessment

Automated grading systems are revolutionizing the way educators evaluate student performance. These AI-driven systems can efficiently grade multiple-choice tests, short-answer responses, and even essays, reducing the workload on teachers and providing immediate feedback to students.

Tools like Gradescope and Turnitin use AI to assess student work, providing detailed feedback on grammar, style, and content. These systems can also detect patterns of plagiarism, ensuring academic integrity. Automated grading allows educators to allocate more time to interactive and meaningful teaching activities, while students benefit from timely feedback that can guide their learning process.

1.3.4 Predictive Analytics for Student Success

Predictive analytics is another powerful AI application in education, helping institutions identify students at risk of academic failure or dropout. By analyzing historical data on student performance, attendance, and engagement, predictive analytics can identify patterns and predict future outcomes.

For instance, platforms like IBM's Watson Education use predictive analytics to monitor student progress and flag those who may need additional support. Educators can then intervene early, providing targeted assistance to help at-risk students succeed. This proactive approach can improve retention rates and ensure that more students achieve their academic goals.

1.3.5 Virtual Classrooms and AI Teaching Assistants

The rise of online education and virtual classrooms has been accelerated by AI technologies. AI-powered teaching assistants, such as Georgia Tech's Jill Watson, are now being used to support instructors in managing large online courses. These AI assistants can answer frequently asked questions, provide resources, and facilitate discussions, freeing up instructors to focus on more complex tasks.

Virtual classrooms, enhanced by AI, offer interactive and immersive learning experiences. Tools like ClassIn and Blackboard Collaborate use AI to support real-time collaboration, automatic attendance tracking, and personalized feedback. These platforms create dynamic and engaging learning environments that can accommodate a wide range of learning styles and preferences.

1.3.6 Enhancing Accessibility and Inclusion

AI applications in education are also playing a crucial role in enhancing accessibility and inclusion. For students with disabilities, AI-powered assistive technologies provide essential support, enabling them to engage with educational content more effectively. Speech recognition tools, like Google's Live Transcribe, convert spoken words into text in real-time, assisting students with hearing impairments. Text-to-speech software, such as Microsoft's Immersive Reader, helps students with visual impairments or dyslexia by reading text aloud. Additionally, AI-driven language translation services, like Google Translate, facilitate communication for non-native speakers, promoting a more inclusive learning environment.

1.3.7 Streamlining Administrative Tasks

AI is streamlining various administrative tasks in educational institutions, improving efficiency and freeing up valuable resources. Automated systems for enrollment, scheduling, and resource management reduce the administrative burden on staff, allowing them to focus on more strategic initiatives.

For example, AI-powered chatbots, like AdmitHub, assist prospective students with the admissions process by answering questions, providing information, and guiding them through application procedures. Similarly, AI-driven systems for scheduling optimize the allocation of classrooms and resources, ensuring that institutions operate smoothly and efficiently.

1.3.8 Supporting Teacher Professional Development

AI applications are also supporting the professional development of teachers, providing tools and resources to enhance their instructional practices. AI-driven platforms, like Coursera and Udacity, offer personalized learning pathways for educators, helping them acquire new skills and knowledge.

Moreover, AI-powered analytics can provide insights into teaching effectiveness, identifying areas where instructors may need additional support or training. By offering targeted professional development opportunities, AI helps educators stay current with best practices and emerging trends in education.

1.3.9 Ethical Considerations and Challenges

While AI offers numerous benefits in educational settings, it also raises important ethical considerations and challenges that must be addressed. One major concern is the potential for bias in AI algorithms. If not carefully monitored, AI systems can perpetuate or exacerbate existing inequalities, leading to unfair treatment of certain groups of students.

Data privacy and security are also critical issues. The use of AI involves the collection and analysis of vast amounts of personal data, raising concerns about how this data is stored, used, and protected. Ensuring the privacy and security of student information is essential to maintaining trust in AI systems.

Additionally, there is a need for transparency and accountability in AI applications. Stakeholders, including educators, students, and parents, should be informed about how AI systems operate, the data they collect, and the decisions they make. Clear mechanisms for accountability are necessary to ensure that AI-driven outcomes can be reviewed and challenged if needed.

1.3.10 The Future of AI in Education

The future of AI in education holds exciting possibilities for further innovation and transformation. As AI technologies continue to advance, they are likely to become even more integrated into educational systems, offering new ways to enhance learning and teaching.

One potential area of growth is the use of AI for real-time feedback and assessment. AI-powered tools could provide immediate insights into student performance, allowing educators to adjust their teaching strategies on the fly. This real-time feedback could also empower students to take greater control of their learning, fostering a more active and engaged learning experience.

Another promising development is the use of AI to support lifelong learning. As the nature of work and skills required by the job market continue to evolve, there is a growing need for continuous education and upskilling. AI can help create personalized learning pathways that adapt to an individual's career goals and learning preferences, making lifelong learning more accessible and effective.

CHAPTER 2

THE PROMISE AND POTENTIAL OF AI

2.1 ADVANTAGES AND OPPORTUNITIES OF AI IN EDUCATION

The advent of artificial intelligence (AI) in education has ushered in a new era of learning and teaching, offering numerous advantages and opportunities that have the potential to transform educational experiences. From personalized learning and intelligent tutoring to administrative efficiencies and enhanced accessibility, AI technologies are reshaping the educational landscape in profound ways.

AI in education offers numerous advantages and opportunities that have the potential to transform the way we teach and learn. From personalized learning and intelligent tutoring to automated grading and predictive analytics, AI technologies are enhancing educational experiences, improving efficiency, and promoting accessibility and inclusion. These advancements can lead to better learning outcomes, more effective teaching practices, and more equitable educational environments.

However, the integration of AI in education also presents challenges that must be addressed to ensure that its benefits are realized without compromising fairness, privacy, and accountability. As AI continues to evolve, it is essential for educators, technologists, policymakers, and other stakeholders to work together to harness the full potential of AI in education, creating a brighter and more inclusive future for learners worldwide.

2.1.1 Personalized Learning Experiences

One of the most significant advantages of AI in education is its ability to provide personalized learning experiences tailored to the unique needs and preferences of each student. Traditional educational models often follow a one-size-fits-all approach, which can be ineffective for addressing the diverse learning styles and paces of individual students. AI-powered adaptive learning systems overcome this limitation by continuously analyzing a student's performance, behavior, and preferences to customize instructional content.

For example, platforms like DreamBox and Knewton use adaptive learning algorithms to adjust the difficulty level of exercises and recommend resources based on a student's progress. This personalized approach ensures that students receive the appropriate level of challenge and support, leading to improved engagement and better learning outcomes. By catering to individual needs, AI-powered personalized learning can help students achieve their full potential.

2.1.2 Intelligent Tutoring Systems

Intelligent Tutoring Systems (ITS) are another powerful application of AI in education, offering personalized instruction and feedback that mimic the one-on-one interaction between a student and a human tutor. ITS utilize natural language processing, machine learning, and cognitive modeling to understand and respond to students' needs in real-time. One notable example is Carnegie Learning's Cognitive Tutor, which provides step-by-step guidance in subjects like mathematics. The Cognitive Tutor continuously monitors a student's problem-solving process, identifies misconceptions, and offers targeted hints and explanations. By adapting to the individual learner's needs, ITS can enhance understanding and mastery of complex subjects, providing a more effective and personalized learning experience.

2.1.3 Automated Grading and Immediate Feedback

Automated grading systems are revolutionizing the way educators evaluate student performance, offering significant advantages in terms of efficiency and immediacy. These AI-driven systems can quickly and accurately grade multiple-choice tests, short-answer responses, and even essays, reducing the administrative burden on teachers and providing immediate feedback to students.

Tools like Gradescope and Turnitin use AI to assess student work, offering detailed feedback on grammar, style, and content. Automated grading not only saves time for educators but also ensures consistency and objectivity in assessment. Immediate feedback allows students to understand their mistakes and learn from them more quickly, enhancing the overall learning process.

2.1.4 Predictive Analytics for Student Success

Predictive analytics is a powerful tool that leverages AI to analyze historical and real-time data to predict future outcomes. In education, predictive analytics can identify students at risk of academic failure or dropout, enabling timely interventions to support student success.

For instance, platforms like IBM's Watson Education use predictive analytics to monitor student progress and flag those who may need additional support. By analyzing data on attendance, participation, and performance, predictive analytics can identify patterns that indicate potential challenges. Educators can then provide targeted assistance, such as tutoring or counseling, to help at-risk students stay on track and achieve their academic goals.

2.1.5 Enhanced Accessibility and Inclusion

AI applications are playing a crucial role in enhancing accessibility and inclusion in education. For students with disabilities, AI-powered assistive technologies provide essential support, enabling them to engage with educational content more effectively and participate in classroom activities.

Speech recognition tools, like Google's Live Transcribe, convert spoken words into text in real-time, assisting students with hearing impairments. Text-to-speech software, such as Microsoft's Immersive Reader, helps students with visual impairments or dyslexia by reading text aloud. Additionally, AI-driven language translation services, like Google Translate, facilitate communication for non-native speakers, promoting a more inclusive learning environment. By addressing the diverse needs of learners, AI can help create more equitable educational experiences.

2.1.6 Streamlined Administrative Processes

AI is streamlining various administrative tasks in educational institutions, improving efficiency and freeing up valuable resources for more strategic initiatives. Automated systems for enrollment, scheduling, and resource management reduce the administrative burden on staff, allowing them to focus on enhancing the educational experience.

For example, AI-powered chatbots, like AdmitHub, assist prospective students with the admissions process by answering questions, providing information, and guiding them through application procedures. Similarly, AI-driven systems for scheduling optimize the allocation of classrooms and resources, ensuring that institutions operate smoothly and efficiently. By automating routine tasks, AI allows educators and administrators to devote more time and energy to supporting student learning and success.

2.1.7 Professional Development for Educators

AI is also supporting the professional development of educators by providing tools and resources that enhance their instructional practices. AI-driven platforms, such as Coursera and Udacity, offer personalized learning pathways for teachers, helping them acquire new skills and knowledge in various subjects.

Moreover, AI-powered analytics can provide insights into teaching effectiveness, identifying areas where instructors may need additional support or training. For example, platforms like Edthena use AI to analyze classroom videos and provide feedback on teaching practices. By offering targeted professional development opportunities, AI helps educators stay current with best practices and emerging trends in education, ultimately improving the quality of instruction.

2.1.8 Real-Time Feedback and Assessment

The use of AI for real-time feedback and assessment represents a significant opportunity to enhance the learning experience. AI-powered tools can provide immediate insights into student performance, allowing educators to adjust their teaching strategies on the fly. This real-time feedback can also empower students to take greater control of their learning, fostering a more active and engaged learning experience.

For instance, platforms like Nearpod use AI to deliver interactive lessons and real-time assessments, providing instant feedback to both students and teachers. This immediate feedback loop helps students understand their strengths and areas for improvement, while teachers can make data-driven decisions to support student learning more effectively.

2.1.9 Supporting Lifelong Learning

As the nature of work and the skills required by the job market continue to evolve, there is a growing need for continuous education and upskilling. AI can support lifelong learning by creating personalized learning pathways that adapt to an individual's career goals and learning preferences.

Platforms like LinkedIn Learning and Coursera use AI to recommend courses and learning resources based on a user's profile, interests, and previous learning history. By offering tailored learning experiences, AI makes it easier for individuals to acquire new skills and stay competitive in the job market. This focus on lifelong learning is essential for personal and professional growth in an ever-changing world.

2.2 IMPROVING LEARNING OUTCOMES WITH AI

Artificial Intelligence (AI) has rapidly evolved from a niche field of computer science into a transformative force reshaping numerous sectors, including education. The integration of AI into educational systems has opened new avenues for enhancing learning outcomes, personalizing education, and making learning more accessible.

AI has the potential to revolutionize education by personalizing learning, providing intelligent tutoring, offering data-driven insights, enhancing accessibility, and streamlining administrative tasks. However, the successful integration of AI in education requires careful consideration of data privacy, equity, and the adaptation of teachers and students to new technologies. By addressing these challenges, AI can significantly improve learning outcomes and create more inclusive and effective educational experiences for all students.

2.2.1 Personalized Learning

Personalized learning, individualized instruction, personal learning environment and direct instruction all refer to efforts to tailor education to meet the different needs of students. The use of the term "personalized learning" dates back to at least the early 1960s, but there is no widespread agreement on the definition and components of a personal learning environment. Even enthusiasts for the concept admit that personal learning is an evolving term and doesn't have any widely accepted definition.

In 2005, Dan Buckley defined two ends of the personalized learning spectrum: "personalization for the learner", in which the teacher tailors the learning, and "personalization by the learner", in which the learner develops skills to tailor his own learning. This spectrum was adopted by the (2006) Microsoft's Practical Guide to Envisioning and Transforming Education.

Definitions

The United States National Education Technology Plan 2017 defines personalized learning as follows:

- Personalized learning refers to instruction in which the pace of learning and the instructional approach are optimized for the needs of each learner. Learning objectives, instructional approaches, and instructional content (and its sequencing) may all vary based on learner needs. In addition, learning activities are meaningful and relevant to learners, driven by their interests, and often self-initiated.

Typically technology is used to try to facilitate personalized learning environments. According to researcher Eduard Pogorskiy:

- ICT can be a powerful tool for personalized learning as it allows learners access to research and information, and provides a mechanism for communication, debate, and recording learning achievements. However, personalized learning is not exclusive to digital technologies or environments. In the rhetoric around 21st Century Skills, personalized learning is often equated with 'customization' (as found in the business world), with digital personalization used to frame the learning experience as highly efficient. Problematic in this is the discounting of the highly relational and socially constructed space well defined in the research on learning. Narrowing personalized learning to its digital form also raises the concern of the echo chamber effect emerging in (hyper)personalized online experiences.

Instructional Design

Proponents of personalized learning say that many elements of curriculum, assessment, and instructional design must be present in classrooms for students to succeed and often use software systems to manage and facilitate student-led instruction. Proponents argue that classroom learning activities must build upon students' prior knowledge and teachers need to allocate time for practice. Advocates argue that teachers must continuously assess student learning against clearly defined standards and goals, and student input into the assessment process is integral.

Conferring

As stated above by the 2017 United States National Education Technology Plan, "Personalized learning refers to instruction in which the pace of learning and the instructional approach are optimized the needs for each learner." Conferring is a process in which this can be accomplished. Conferring, as defined by Julie Kallio, is a "regular, goal-oriented meeting between the teacher and student(s) where they talk about learning progress, process, and/or products." Conferring, more simply, is a way to provide more personalized feedback.

Learning, in any context, requires some form of feedback. In schools, this feedback is almost entirely thought of as the teacher providing feedback to the student. The idea of providing feedback to advance student learning is best understood in the framework of the "zone of proximal development" or ZPD. Psychologist Lev Vygotski has defined the ZPD as "the distance between the actual developmental level as determined by independent problem solving and the level of potential development as determined through problem solving under adult guidance or in collaboration with more capable peers". More plainly, a student has a certain level they can achieve by themselves and with support they are able to achieve a higher level of learning. However, there is still some level in which the student is incapable of reaching, no matter what support is provided. For example, a student may be working on double digit addition. Their current knowledge may already provide them with the skills to move on to triple digit addition without any help. If the student is introduced to multiplication, however, they will need help to understand that multiplication is a quicker way to represent the same number being added onto itself a defined number of times. Where this help occurs is the student's ZPD. Even with help though, it is not reasonable to expect the student to learn how to solve a calculus problem. The struggle for teachers is how to provide the right amount of help to each student. If a teacher provides information to the whole class too quickly, some students are left behind trying to figure out the first step. Conversely, if a teacher provides information to the whole class too slowly, some students will finish rapidly and be left with nothing to do. Conferring is a tool that teachers have used to help mitigate that issue.

Conferring first gained prominence in the book *One to one: the art of conferring with young writers* by Lucy Calkins, Amanda Hartman, and Zoe Ryder White. In the work,

Calkins and her co-writers describe how effective writing workshops for students included individual writing conferences (conferring), where teachers would sit and talk with their students about their writing. Per the book, "Conferring can give us the force that makes our mini-lessons and curriculum development and assessment and everything else more powerful. It gives us an endless resource of teaching wisdom, an endless source of accountability, a system of checks and balances. And, it gives us laughter and human connection -the understanding of our children that gives spirit to our teaching." Calkins believed that there were three main components to every conferring session: Research, Decide, and Teach. Research focused on where the student was in their current writing, Decide would help the teacher choose what to teach the student, and Teach would use modeling and guiding practice to further advance student learning. In their book *The Writing Workshop*, Katie Wood Ray and Lester L. Laminack added a fourth component in where after the teaching portion, the student and/or the teacher would "Make a Record". This modified model can be thought in the terms of: research, decide, teach, record. The benefits of using conferring have been documented in a couple of studies.

Using a mix method case study approach in observing a group of 4th grade students, Javaye Devette Stubbs posed the question: "How does the implementation of one-on-one conferring promote higher order thinking skills in students with difficulties in reading?" The results from her pre and post-test found that "even those with reading difficulties did show a significant gain in higher order thinking skills". In a separate study, the educator Antony Smith examined the effectiveness of using teacher-student writing conference for English language learners (ELLs). Observing two students who were ELLs in a second-grade classroom working on a book project, Smith found that the work produced "looks similar to what is produced by native English speakers".

Smith later suggests that the success of the two students were largely tied to the writing conferences, and goes on to state that writing conferences are the "heart of the writing process, and with this in mind, the potential of the teacher-student writing conference becomes clear".

The information can be summarized into three main takeaways. First, building student knowledge is dependent on the current level of knowledge the student has and what kind of support they are provided. Second, conferring is a model that can provide student support through a structured four-part process. Third, conferring has been shown to increase student learning in both reading and writing.

Debate

Andy Hargreaves and Dennis Shirley write that while there are advantages in students being able to access information instantly on-line, one should not mistake such processes for "something deeper, more challenging, and more connected to compelling issues in their world and their lives".

Alfie Kohn wrote that while personalized learning may sound like a useful strategy for education, in practice it is mostly just about selling technology products. Personalized learning promises a strategy to specifically adjust education to the unique needs and skills of individual children, he argued, but really it means merely "adjusting the difficulty level of prefabricated skills-based exercises based on students' test scores... [and] requires the purchase of software from one of those companies that can afford full-page ads in *Education Week*". While "certain forms of technology can be used to support progressive education", Kohn wrote, "...meaningful (and truly personal) learning never *requires* technology. Therefore, if an idea like personalization is presented from the start as entailing software or a screen, we ought to be extremely skeptical about who really benefits."

Next Steps for Research

Dr. Ces'Ari Garcia-Delmuro advocated in her research on personalized learning for other researchers to continue including teacher voice in their studies of personalized learning programs as a way to improve these programs for teachers and students. She said more studies should be conducted that focus on other low SES schools implementing personalized learning. Furthermore, donors that are giving to the advancement of personalized learning need to consult new research to ensure that they are donating to programs that benefit all students including those who belong to vulnerable populations (students in special education, bilingual emergent students, and students of low socioeconomic status), not just those students who are able to self-direct. In future research, it is important to continue to study these schools who are piloting personalized learning to see how their needs change over time. Because these programs are still relatively new, it would be helpful to understand the perceptions of teachers who are using these programs for five years or longer to continue assisting teacher and school sites as they mature in their personalized learning use. Additionally, research which compares teacher perception of personalized learning compared to student academic outcomes will be helpful once schools new to personalized learning overcome their fifth year of implementation.

2.2.2 Intelligent Tutoring Systems

An intelligent tutoring system (ITS) is a computer system that imitates human tutors and aims to provide immediate and customized instruction or feedback to learners, usually without requiring intervention from a human teacher. ITSs have the common goal of enabling learning in a meaningful and effective manner by using a variety of computing technologies. There are many examples of ITSs being used in both formal education and professional settings in which they have demonstrated their capabilities and limitations. There is a close relationship between intelligent tutoring, cognitive learning theories and design; and there is ongoing research to improve the effectiveness of ITS. An ITS typically aims to replicate the demonstrated benefits of one-to-one, personalized tutoring, in contexts where students would otherwise have access to one-to-many instruction from a single teacher (e.g., classroom lectures), or no teacher at all (e.g., online homework). ITSs are often designed with the goal of providing access to high quality education to each and every student.

Early Mechanical Systems

The possibility of intelligent machines has been discussed for centuries. Blaise Pascal created the first calculating machine capable of mathematical functions in the 17th century simply called Pascal's Calculator. At this time the mathematician and philosopher Gottfried Wilhelm Leibniz envisioned machines capable of reasoning and applying rules of logic to settle disputes. These early works inspired later developments.

The concept of intelligent machines for instructional use date back as early as 1924, when Sidney Pressey of Ohio State University created a mechanical teaching machine to instruct students without a human teacher. His machine resembled closely a typewriter with several keys and a window that provided the learner with questions. The Pressey Machine allowed user input and provided immediate feedback by recording their score on a counter.

Pressey was influenced by Edward L. Thorndike, a learning theorist and educational psychologist at the Columbia University Teachers' College of the late 19th and early 20th centuries. Thorndike posited laws for maximizing learning. Thorndike's laws included the law of effect, the law of exercise, and the law of recency. By later standards, Pressey's teaching and testing machine would not be considered intelligent as it was mechanically run and was based on one question and answer at a time, but it set an early precedent for future projects.

By the 1950s and 1960s, new perspectives on learning were emerging. Burrhus Frederic "B.F." Skinner at Harvard University did not agree with Thorndike's learning theory of connectionism or Pressey's teaching machine. Rather, Skinner was a behaviorist who believed that learners should construct their answers and not rely on recognition. He too, constructed a teaching machine with an incremental mechanical system that would reward students for correct responses to questions.

Early Electronic Systems

In the period following the second world war, mechanical binary systems gave way to binary based electronic machines. These machines were considered intelligent when compared to their mechanical counterparts as they had the capacity to make logical decisions. However, the study of defining and recognizing a machine intelligence was still in its infancy.

Alan Turing, a mathematician, logician and computer scientist, linked computing systems to thinking. One of his most notable papers outlined a hypothetical test to assess the intelligence of a machine which came to be known as the Turing test. Essentially, the test would have a person communicate with two other agents, a human and a computer asking questions to both recipients. The computer passes the test if it can respond in such a way that the human posing the questions cannot differentiate between the other human and the computer. The Turing test has been used in its essence for more than two decades as a model for current ITS development. The main ideal for ITS systems is to effectively communicate. As early as the 1950s programs were emerging displaying intelligent features. Turing's work as well as later projects by researchers such as Allen Newell, Clifford Shaw, and Herb Simon showed programs capable of creating logical proofs and theorems. Their program, The Logic Theorist exhibited complex symbol manipulation and even generation of new information without direct human control and is considered by some to be the first AI program. Such breakthroughs would inspire the new field of Artificial Intelligence officially named in 1956 by John McCarthy at the Dartmouth Conference. This conference was the first of its kind that was devoted to scientists and research in the field of AI.

The latter part of the 1960s and 1970s saw many new CAI (Computer-Assisted instruction) projects that built on advances in computer science. The creation of the ALGOL programming language in 1958 enabled many schools and universities to begin developing Computer Assisted Instruction (CAI) programs. Major computer vendors and federal agencies in the US such as IBM, HP, and the National Science Foundation funded the development of these projects. Early implementations in education focused on programmed instruction (PI), a structure based on a computerized input-output system. Although many supported this form of instruction, there was limited evidence supporting its effectiveness. The programming language LOGO was created in 1967 by Wally Feurzeig, Cynthia Solomon, and Seymour Papert as a language streamlined for education. PLATO, an educational terminal featuring displays, animations, and touch controls that could store and deliver large amounts of course material, was developed by Donald Bitzer in the University of Illinois in the early 1970s. Along with these, many other CAI projects were initiated in many countries including the US, the UK, and Canada.

At the same time that CAI was gaining interest, Jaime Carbonell suggested that computers could act as a teacher rather than just a tool (Carbonell, 1970). A new perspective would emerge that focused on the use of computers to intelligently coach students called Intelligent Computer Assisted Instruction or Intelligent Tutoring Systems (ITS). Where CAI used a behaviourist perspective on learning based on Skinner's theories (Dede & Swigger, 1988), ITS drew from work in cognitive psychology, computer science, and especially artificial intelligence. There was a shift in AI research at this time as systems moved from the logic focus of the previous decade to knowledge based systems—systems could make intelligent decisions based on prior knowledge (Buchanan, 2006). Such a program was created by Seymour Papert and Ira Goldstein who created Dendral, a system that predicted possible chemical structures from existing data. Further work began to showcase analogical reasoning and language processing. These changes with a focus on knowledge had big implications for how computers could be used in instruction. The technical requirements of ITS, however, proved to be higher and more complex than CAI systems and ITS systems would find limited success at this time.

Towards the latter part of the 1970s interest in CAI technologies began to wane. Computers were still expensive and not as available as expected. Developers and instructors were reacting negatively to the high cost of developing CAI programs, the inadequate provision for instructor training, and the lack of resources.

Microcomputers and Intelligent Systems

The microcomputer revolution in the late 1970s and early 1980s helped to revive CAI development and jumpstart development of ITS systems. Personal computers such as the Apple 2, Commodore PET, and TRS-80 reduced the resources required to own computers and by 1981, 50% of US schools were using computers (Chambers & Sprecher, 1983). Several CAI projects utilized the Apple 2 as a system to deliver CAI programs in high schools and universities including the British Columbia Project and California State University Project in 1981.

The early 1980s would also see Intelligent Computer-Assisted Instruction (ICAI) and ITS goals diverge from their roots in CAI. As CAI became increasingly focused on deeper interactions with content created for a specific area of interest, ITS sought to create systems that focused on knowledge of the task and the ability to generalize that knowledge in non-specific ways (Larkin & Chabay, 1992). The key goals set out for ITS were to be able to teach a task as well as perform it, adapting dynamically to its situation. In the transition from CAI to ICAI systems, the computer would have to distinguish not only between the correct and incorrect response but the type of incorrect response to adjust the type of instruction. Research in Artificial Intelligence and Cognitive Psychology fueled the new principles of ITS. Psychologists considered how a computer could solve problems and perform 'intelligent' activities. An ITS programme would have to be able to represent, store and retrieve knowledge and even search its own database to derive its own new knowledge to respond to learner's questions. Basically, early specifications for ITS or (ICAI) require it to "diagnose errors and tailor remediation based on the diagnosis". The idea of diagnosis and remediation is still in use today when programming ITS.

A key breakthrough in ITS research was the creation of The LISP Tutor, a program that implemented ITS principles in a practical way and showed promising effects increasing student performance. The LISP Tutor was developed and researched in 1983 as an ITS system for teaching students the LISP programming language.

The LISP Tutor could identify mistakes and provide constructive feedback to students while they were performing the exercise. The system was found to decrease the time required to complete the exercises while improving student test scores.

Other ITS systems beginning to develop around this time include TUTOR created by Logica in 1984 as a general instructional tool and PARNASSUS created in Carnegie Mellon University in 1989 for language instruction.

Modern ITS

After the implementation of initial ITS, more researchers created a number of ITS for different students. In the late 20th century, Intelligent Tutoring Tools (ITTs) was developed by the Byzantium project, which involved six universities. The ITTs were general purpose tutoring system builders and many institutions had positive feedback while using them.

This builder, ITT, would produce an Intelligent Tutoring Applet (ITA) for different subject areas. Different teachers created the ITAs and built up a large inventory of knowledge that was accessible by others through the Internet. Once an ITS was created, teachers could copy it and modify it for future use.

This system was efficient and flexible. However, Kinshuk and Patel believed that the ITS was not designed from an educational point of view and was not developed based on the actual needs of students and teachers. Recent work has employed ethnographic and design research methods to examine the ways ITSs are actually used by students and teachers across a range of contexts, often revealing unanticipated needs that they meet, fail to meet, or in some cases, even create.

Modern day ITSs typically try to replicate the role of a teacher or a teaching assistant, and increasingly automate pedagogical functions such as problem generation, problem selection, and feedback generation.

However, given a current shift towards blended learning models, recent work on ITSs has begun focusing on ways these systems can effectively leverage the complementary strengths of human-led instruction from a teacher or peer, when used in co-located classrooms or other social contexts.

There were three ITS projects that functioned based on conversational dialogue: AutoTutor, Atlas and Why2. The idea behind these projects was that since students learn best by constructing knowledge themselves, the programs would begin with leading questions for the students and would give out answers as a last resort. AutoTutor's students focused on answering questions about computer technology, Atlas's students focused on solving quantitative problems, and Why2's students focused on explaining physical systems qualitatively. Other similar tutoring systems such as Andes tend to provide hints and immediate feedback for students when students have trouble answering the questions. They could guess their answers and have correct answers without deep understanding of the concepts. Research was done with a small group of students using Atlas and Andes respectively. The results showed that students using Atlas made significant improvements compared with students who used Andes. However, since the above systems require analysis of students' dialogues, improvement is yet to be made so that more complicated dialogues can be managed.

Structure

Intelligent tutoring systems (ITSs) consist of four basic components based on a general consensus amongst researchers:

- The Domain model,
- The Student model,
- The Tutoring model, and
- The User interface model.

The *domain model* (also known as the cognitive model or expert knowledge model) is built on a theory of learning, such as the ACT-R theory which tries to take into account all the possible steps required to solve a problem. More specifically, this model "contains the concepts, rules, and problem-solving strategies of the domain to be learned. It can fulfill several roles: as a source of expert knowledge, a standard for evaluating the student's performance or for detecting errors, etc." Another approach for developing domain models is based on Stellan Ohlsson's Theory of Learning from performance errors, known as constraint-based modelling (CBM). In this case, the domain model is presented as a set of constraints on correct solutions.

The *student model* can be thought of as an overlay on the domain model. It is considered as the core component of an ITS paying special attention to student's cognitive and affective states and their evolution as the learning process advances. As the student works step-by-step through their problem solving process, an ITS engages in a process called *model tracing*. Anytime the student model deviates from the domain model, the system identifies, or *flags*, that an error has occurred. On the other hand, in constraint-based tutors the student model is represented as an overlay on the constraint set. Constraint-based tutors evaluate the student's solution against the constraint set, and identify satisfied and violated constraints. If there are any violated constraints, the student's solution is incorrect, and the ITS provides feedback on those constraints. Constraint-based tutors provide negative feedback (i.e. feedback on errors) and also positive feedback.

The *tutor model* accepts information from the domain and student models and makes choices about tutoring strategies and actions. At any point in the problem-solving process the learner may request guidance on what to do next, relative to their current location in the model. In addition, the system recognizes when the learner has deviated from the production rules of the model and provides timely feedback for the learner, resulting in a shorter period of time to reach proficiency with the targeted skills. The tutor model may contain several hundred production rules that can be said to exist in one of two states, *learned* or *unlearned*. Every time a student successfully applies a rule to a problem, the system updates a probability estimate that the student has learned the rule. The system continues to drill students on exercises that require effective application of a rule until the probability that the rule has been learned reaches at least 95% probability.

Knowledge tracing tracks the learner's progress from problem to problem and builds a profile of strengths and weaknesses relative to the production rules. The cognitive tutoring system developed by John Anderson at Carnegie Mellon University presents information from knowledge tracing as a *skillometer*, a visual graph of the learner's success in each of the monitored skills related to solving algebra problems. When a learner requests a hint, or an error is flagged, the knowledge tracing data and the skillometer are updated in real-time.

The *user interface* component "integrates three types of information that are needed in carrying out a dialogue: knowledge about patterns of interpretation (to understand a speaker) and action (to generate utterances) within dialogues; domain knowledge needed for communicating content; and knowledge needed for communicating intent".

Nkambou et al., make mention of Nwana's review of different architectures underlining a strong link between architecture and paradigm (or philosophy). Nwana declares, "[I]t is almost a rarity to find two ITSs based on the same architecture [which] results from the experimental nature of the work in the area". He further explains that differing tutoring philosophies emphasize different components of the learning process (i.e., domain, student or tutor).

The architectural design of an ITS reflects this emphasis, and this leads to a variety of architectures, none of which, individually, can support all tutoring strategies. Moreover, ITS projects may vary according to the relative level of intelligence of the components. As an example, a project highlighting intelligence in the domain model may generate solutions to complex and novel problems so that students can always have new problems to work on, but it might only have simple methods for teaching those problems, while a system that concentrates on multiple or novel ways of teaching a particular topic might find a less sophisticated representation of that content sufficient.

Design and Development Methods

Apart from the discrepancy amongst ITS architectures each emphasizing different elements, the development of an ITS is much the same as any instructional design process. Corbett et al., summarized ITS design and development as consisting of four iterative stages:

- Needs assessment,
- Cognitive task analysis,
- Initial tutor implementation and
- Evaluation.

The first stage known as needs assessment is common to any instructional design process, especially software development. This involves a *learner analysis*, consultation with subject matter experts and/or the instructor(s). This first step is part of the development of the expert/knowledge and student domain.

The goal is to specify learning goals and to outline a general plan for the curriculum; it is imperative not to computerize traditional concepts but develop a new curriculum structure by defining the task in general and understanding learners' possible behaviours dealing with the task and to a lesser degree the tutor's behavior. In doing so, three crucial dimensions need to be dealt with:

- The probability a student is able to solve problems;
- The time it takes to reach this performance level; and
- The probability the student will actively use this knowledge in the future.

Another important aspect that requires analysis is cost effectiveness of the interface. Moreover, teachers and student entry characteristics such as prior knowledge must be assessed since both groups are going to be system users. The second stage, cognitive task analysis, is a detailed approach to expert systems programming with the goal of developing a valid computational model of the required problem solving knowledge. Chief methods for developing a domain model include:

- Interviewing domain experts,
- Conducting "think aloud" protocol studies with domain experts,

- Conducting "think aloud" studies with novices, and
- Observation of teaching and learning behavior.

Although the first method is most commonly used, experts are usually incapable of reporting cognitive components. The "think aloud" methods, in which the experts is asked to report aloud what s/he is thinking when solving typical problems, can avoid this problem. Observation of actual online interactions between tutors and students provides information related to the processes used in problem-solving, which is useful for building dialogue or interactivity into tutoring systems.

The third stage, initial tutor implementation, involves setting up a problem solving environment to enable and support an authentic learning process. This stage is followed by a series of evaluation activities as the final stage which is again similar to any software development project.

The fourth stage, evaluation includes:

- Pilot studies to confirm basic usability and educational impact;
- Formative evaluations of the system under development;
- Parametric studies that examine the effectiveness of system features; and
- Summative evaluations of the final tutor's effect: learning rate and asymptotic achievement levels.

A variety of authoring tools have been developed to support this process and create intelligent tutors, including ASPIRE, the Cognitive Tutor Authoring Tools (CTAT), GIFT, ASSISTments Builder and AutoTutor tools. The goal of most of these authoring tools is to simplify the tutor development process, making it possible for people with less expertise than professional AI programmers to develop Intelligent Tutoring Systems.

Eight Principles of ITS Design and Development

Anderson et al., outlined eight principles for intelligent tutor design and Corbett et al., later elaborated on those principles highlighting an all-embracing principle which they believed governed intelligent tutor design, they referred to this principle as:

- **Principle 0:** An intelligent tutor system should enable the student to work to the successful conclusion of problem solving.
- Represent student competence as a production set.
- Communicate the goal structure underlying the problem solving.
- Provide instruction in the problem solving context.

- Promote an abstract understanding of the problem-solving knowledge.
- Minimize working memory load.
- Provide immediate feedback on errors.
- Adjust the grain size of instruction with learning.
- Facilitate successive approximations to the target skill.

Use in Practice

All this is a substantial amount of work, even if authoring tools have become available to ease the task. This means that building an ITS is an option only in situations in which they, in spite of their relatively high development costs, still reduce the overall costs through reducing the need for human instructors or sufficiently boosting overall productivity. Such situations occur when large groups need to be tutored simultaneously or many replicated tutoring efforts are needed. Cases in point are technical training situations such as training of military recruits and high school mathematics. One specific type of intelligent tutoring system, the Cognitive Tutor, has been incorporated into mathematics curricula in a substantial number of United States high schools, producing improved student learning outcomes on final exams and standardized tests. Intelligent tutoring systems have been constructed to help students learn geography, circuits, medical diagnosis, computer programming, mathematics, physics, genetics, chemistry, etc. Intelligent Language Tutoring Systems (ILTS), e.g. this one, teach natural language to first or second language learners. ILTS requires specialized natural language processing tools such as large dictionaries and morphological and grammatical analyzers with acceptable coverage.

Applications

During the rapid expansion of the web boom, new computer-aided instruction paradigms, such as e-learning and distributed learning, provided an excellent platform for ITS ideas. Areas that have used ITS include natural language processing, machine learning, planning, multi-agent systems, ontologies, Semantic Web, and social and emotional computing. In addition, other technologies such as multimedia, object-oriented systems, modeling, simulation, and statistics have also been connected to or combined with ITS. Historically non-technological areas such as the educational sciences and psychology have also been influenced by the success of ITS.

In recent years, ITS has begun to move away from the search-based to include a range of practical applications. ITS have expanded across many critical and complex cognitive domains, and the results have been far reaching. ITS systems have cemented a place within formal education and these systems have found homes in the sphere of corporate training and organizational learning. ITS offers learners several affordances such as individualized learning, just in time feedback, and flexibility in time and space.

While Intelligent tutoring systems evolved from research in cognitive psychology and artificial intelligence, there are now many applications found in education and in organizations. Intelligent tutoring systems can be found in online environments or in a traditional classroom computer lab, and are used in K-12 classrooms as well as in universities. There are a number of programs that target mathematics but applications can be found in health sciences, language acquisition, and other areas of formalized learning. Reports of improvement in student comprehension, engagement, attitude, motivation, and academic results have all contributed to the ongoing interest in the investment in and research of theses systems. The personalized nature of the intelligent tutoring systems affords educators the opportunity to create individualized programs. Within education there are a plethora of intelligent tutoring systems, an exhaustive list does not exist but several of the more influential programs are listed below.

Education

As of May 2024, AI tutors make up five of the top 20 education apps in Apple's App Store, and two of the leaders are from Chinese developers.

- **Algebra Tutor:** PAT (PUMP Algebra Tutor or Practical Algebra Tutor) developed by the Pittsburgh Advanced Cognitive Tutor Center at Carnegie Mellon University, engages students in anchored learning problems and uses modern algebraic tools to engage students in problem solving and sharing of their results. The aim of PAT is to tap into a student's prior knowledge and everyday experiences with mathematics to promote growth. The success of PAT is well documented (ex. Miami-Dade County Public Schools Office of Evaluation and Research) from both a statistical (student results) and emotional (student and instructor feedback) perspective.
- **SQL-Tutor:** SQL-Tutor is the first ever constraint-based tutor developed by the Intelligent Computer Tutoring Group (ICTG) at the University of Canterbury, New Zealand. SQL-Tutor teaches students how to retrieve data from databases using the SQL SELECT statement.
- **EER-Tutor:** EER-Tutor is a constraint-based tutor (developed by ICTG) that teaches conceptual database design using the Entity Relationship model. An earlier version of EER-Tutor was KERMIT, a stand-alone tutor for ER modelling, which resulted in significant improvement of student's knowledge after one hour of learning (with the effect size of 0.6).

- **COLLECT-UML:** COLLECT-UML is a constraint-based tutor that supports pairs of students working collaboratively on UML class diagrams. The tutor provides feedback on the domain level as well as on collaboration.
- **StoichTutor:** StoichTutor is a web-based intelligent tutor that helps high school students learn chemistry, specifically the sub-area of chemistry known as stoichiometry. It has been used to explore a variety of learning science principles and techniques, such as worked examples and politeness.
- **Mathematics Tutor:** The Mathematics Tutor helps students solve word problems using fractions, decimals and percentages. The tutor records the success rates while a student is working on problems while providing subsequent, lever-appropriate problems for the student to work on. The subsequent problems that are selected are based on student ability and a desirable time in is estimated in which the student is to solve the problem.
- **eTeacher:** eTeacher is an intelligent agent or pedagogical agent, that supports personalized e-learning assistance. It builds student profiles while observing student performance in online courses. eTeacher then uses the information from the student's performance to suggest a personalized courses of action designed to assist their learning process.
- **ZOSMAT:** ZOSMAT was designed to address all the needs of a real classroom. It follows and guides a student in different stages of their learning process. This is a student-centered ITS does this by recording the progress in a student's learning and the student program changes based on the student's effort. ZOSMAT can be used for either individual learning or in a real classroom environment alongside the guidance of a human tutor.
- **REALP:** REALP was designed to help students enhance their reading comprehension by providing reader-specific lexical practice and offering personalized practice with useful, authentic reading materials gathered from the Web. The system automatically build a user model according to student's performance. After reading, the student is given a series of exercises based on the target vocabulary found in reading.
- **CIRCSlM-Tutor:** CIRCSIM_Tutor is an intelligent tutoring system that is used with first year medical students at the Illinois Institute of Technology. It uses natural dialogue based, Socratic language to help students learn about regulating blood pressure.

- **Why2-Atlas:** Why2-Atlas is an ITS that analyses students explanations of physics principles. The students input their work in paragraph form and the program converts their words into a proof by making assumptions of student beliefs that are based on their explanations. In doing this, misconceptions and incomplete explanations are highlighted. The system then addresses these issues through a dialogue with the student and asks the student to correct their essay. A number of iterations may take place before the process is complete.
- **SmartTutor:** The University of Hong Kong (HKU) developed a SmartTutor to support the needs of continuing education students. Personalized learning was identified as a key need within adult education at HKU and SmartTutor aims to fill that need. SmartTutor provides support for students by combining Internet technology, educational research and artificial intelligence.
- **AutoTutor:** AutoTutor assists college students in learning about computer hardware, operating systems and the Internet in an introductory computer literacy course by simulating the discourse patterns and pedagogical strategies of a human tutor. AutoTutor attempts to understand learner's input from the keyboard and then formulate dialog moves with feedback, prompts, correction and hints.
- **ActiveMath:** ActiveMath is a web-based, adaptive learning environment for mathematics. This system strives for improving long-distance learning, for complementing traditional classroom teaching, and for supporting individual and lifelong learning.
- **ESC101-ITS:** The Indian Institute of Technology, Kanpur, India developed the ESC101-ITS, an intelligent tutoring system for introductory programming problems.
- **AdaptErrEx:** is an adaptive intelligent tutor that uses interactive erroneous examples to help students learn decimal arithmetic.

Corporate Training and Industry

- **Generalized Intelligent Framework for Tutoring (GIFT):** An educational software designed for creation of computer-based tutoring systems. Developed by the U.S. Army Research Laboratory from 2009 to 2011, GIFT was released for commercial use in May 2012. GIFT is open-source and domain independent, and can be downloaded online for free. The software allows an instructor to design a tutoring program that can cover various disciplines through adjustments to existing courses. It includes coursework tools intended for use by researchers, instructional designers, instructors, and students. GIFT is compatible with other teaching materials, such as PowerPoint presentations, which can be integrated into the program.

- **SHERLOCK:** "SHERLOCK" is used to train Air Force technicians to diagnose problems in the electrical systems of F-15 jets. The ITS creates faulty schematic diagrams of systems for the trainee to locate and diagnose. The ITS provides diagnostic readings allowing the trainee to decide whether the fault lies in the circuit being tested or if it lies elsewhere in the system. Feedback and guidance are provided by the system and help is available if requested.
- **Cardiac Tutor:** The Cardiac Tutor's aim is to support advanced cardiac support techniques to medical personnel. The tutor presents cardiac problems and, using a variety of steps, students must select various interventions. Cardiac Tutor provides clues, verbal advice, and feedback in order to personalize and optimize the learning. Each simulation, regardless of whether the students were successfully able to help their patients, results in a detailed report which students then review.
- **CODES:** Cooperative Music Prototype Design is a Web-based environment for cooperative music prototyping. It was designed to support users, especially those who are not specialists in music, in creating musical pieces in a prototyping manner. The musical examples (prototypes) can be repeatedly tested, played and modified. One of the main aspects of CODES is interaction and cooperation between the music creators and their partners.

Effectiveness

Assessing the effectiveness of ITS programs is problematic. ITS vary greatly in design, implementation, and educational focus. When ITS are used in a classroom, the system is not only used by students, but by teachers as well. This usage can create barriers to effective evaluation for a number of reasons; most notably due to teacher intervention in student learning.

Teachers often have the ability to enter new problems into the system or adjust the curriculum. In addition, teachers and peers often interact with students while they learn with ITSs (e.g., during an individual computer lab session or during classroom lectures falling in between lab sessions) in ways that may influence their learning with the software. Prior work suggests that the vast majority of students' help-seeking behavior in classrooms using ITSs may occur entirely outside of the software - meaning that the nature and quality of peer and teacher feedback in a given class may be an important mediator of student learning in these contexts. In addition, aspects of classroom climate, such as students' overall level of comfort in publicly asking for help, or the degree to which a teacher is physically active in monitoring individual students may add additional sources of variation across evaluation contexts. All of these variables make evaluation of an ITS complex, and may help explain variation in results across evaluation studies.

Despite the inherent complexities, numerous studies have attempted to measure the overall effectiveness of ITS, often by comparisons of ITS to human tutors. Reviews of early ITS systems showed an effect size of $d = 1.0$ in comparison to no tutoring, where as human tutors were given an effect size of $d = 2.0$. Kurt VanLehn's much more recent overview of modern ITS found that there was no statistical difference in effect size between expert one-on-one human tutors and step-based ITS. Some individual ITS have been evaluated more positively than others. Studies of the Algebra Cognitive Tutor found that the ITS students outperformed students taught by a classroom teacher on standardized test problems and real-world problem solving tasks. Subsequent studies found that these results were particularly pronounced in students from special education, non-native English, and low-income backgrounds.

A more recent meta-analysis suggests that ITSs can exceed the effectiveness of both CAI and human tutors, especially when measured by local (specific) tests as opposed to standardized tests. "Students who received intelligent tutoring outperformed students from conventional classes in 46 (or 92%) of the 50 controlled evaluations, and the improvement in performance was great enough to be considered of substantive importance in 39 (or 78%) of the 50 studies. The median ES in the 50 studies was 0.66, which is considered a moderate-to-large effect for studies in the social sciences. It is roughly equivalent to an improvement in test performance from the 50th to the 75th percentile.

This is stronger than typical effects from other forms of tutoring. C.-L. C. Kulik and Kulik's (1991) meta-analysis, for example, found an average ES of 0.31 in 165 studies of CAI tutoring. ITS gains are about twice as high. The ITS effect is also greater than typical effects from human tutoring. As we have seen, programs of human tutoring typically raise student test scores about 0.4 standard deviations over control levels. Developers of ITSs long ago set out to improve on the success of CAI tutoring and to match the success of human tutoring. Our results suggest that ITS developers have already met both of these goals.... Although effects were moderate to strong in evaluations that measured outcomes on locally developed tests, they were much smaller in evaluations that measured outcomes on standardized tests. Average ES on studies with local tests was 0.73; average ES on studies with standardized tests was 0.13. This discrepancy is not unusual for meta-analyses that include both local and standardized tests... local tests are likely to align well with the objectives of specific instructional programs. Off-the-shelf standardized tests provide a looser fit. ... Our own belief is that both local and standardized tests provide important information about instructional effectiveness, and when possible, both types of tests should be included in evaluation studies." Some recognized strengths of ITS are their ability to provide immediate yes/no feedback, individual task selection, on-demand hints, and support mastery learning.

Limitations

Intelligent tutoring systems are expensive both to develop and implement. The research phase paves the way for the development of systems that are commercially viable. However, the research phase is often expensive; it requires the cooperation and input of subject matter experts, the cooperation and support of individuals across both organizations and organizational levels. Another limitation in the development phase is the conceptualization and the development of software within both budget and time constraints. There are also factors that limit the incorporation of intelligent tutors into the real world, including the long timeframe required for development and the high cost of the creation of the system components. A high portion of that cost is a result of content component building. For instance, surveys revealed that encoding an hour of online instruction time took 300 hours of development time for tutoring content. Similarly, building the Cognitive Tutor took a ratio of development time to instruction time of at least 200:1 hours. The high cost of development often eclipses replicating the efforts for real world application. Intelligent tutoring systems are not, in general, commercially feasible for real-world applications.

A criticism of Intelligent Tutoring Systems currently in use, is the pedagogy of immediate feedback and hint sequences that are built in to make the system "intelligent". This pedagogy is criticized for its failure to develop deep learning in students. When students are given control over the ability to receive hints, the learning response created is negative. Some students immediately turn to the hints before attempting to solve the problem or complete the task. When it is possible to do so, some students bottom out the hints – receiving as many hints as possible as fast as possible – in order to complete the task faster. If students fail to reflect on the tutoring system's feedback or hints, and instead increase guessing until positive feedback is garnered, the student is, in effect, learning to do the right thing for the wrong reasons. Most tutoring systems are currently unable to detect shallow learning, or to distinguish between productive versus unproductive struggle. For these and many other reasons (e.g., overfitting of underlying models to particular user populations), the effectiveness of these systems may differ significantly across users.

Another criticism of intelligent tutoring systems is the failure of the system to ask questions of the students to explain their actions. If the student is not learning the domain language than it becomes more difficult to gain a deeper understanding, to work collaboratively in groups, and to transfer the domain language to writing. For example, if the student is not "talking science" than it is argued that they are not being immersed in the culture of science, making it difficult to undertake scientific writing or participate in collaborative team efforts. Intelligent tutoring systems have been criticized for being too "instructivist" and removing intrinsic motivation, social learning contexts, and context realism from learning.

Practical concerns, in terms of the inclination of the sponsors/authorities and the users to adapt intelligent tutoring systems, should be taken into account. First, someone must have a willingness to implement the ITS. Additionally an authority must recognize the necessity to integrate an intelligent tutoring software into current curriculum and finally, the sponsor or authority must offer the needed support through the stages of the system development until it is completed and implemented.

Evaluation of an intelligent tutoring system is an important phase; however, it is often difficult, costly, and time-consuming. Even though there are various evaluation techniques presented in the literature, there are no guiding principles for the selection of appropriate evaluation method(s) to be used in a particular context. Careful inspection should be undertaken to ensure that a complex system does what it claims to do. This assessment may occur during the design and early development of the system to identify problems and to guide modifications (i.e. formative evaluation). In contrast, the evaluation may occur after the completion of the system to support formal claims about the construction, behaviour of, or outcomes associated with a completed system (i.e. summative evaluation). The great challenge introduced by the lack of evaluation standards resulted in neglecting the evaluation stage in several existing ITS'.

Improvements

Intelligent tutoring systems are less capable than human tutors in the areas of dialogue and feedback. For example, human tutors are able to interpret the affective state of the student, and potentially adapt instruction in response to these perceptions. Recent work is exploring potential strategies for overcoming these limitations of ITSs, to make them more effective.

Dialogue

Human tutors have the ability to understand a person's tone and inflection within a dialogue and interpret this to provide continual feedback through an ongoing dialogue. Intelligent tutoring systems are now being developed to attempt to simulate natural conversations. To get the full experience of dialogue there are many different areas in which a computer must be programmed; including being able to understand tone, inflection, body language, and facial expression and then to respond to these. Dialogue in an ITS can be used to ask specific questions to help guide students and elicit information while allowing students to construct their own knowledge. The development of more sophisticated dialogue within an ITS has been a focus in some current research partially to address the limitations and create a more constructivist approach to ITS. In addition, some current research has focused on modeling the nature and effects of various social cues commonly employed within a dialogue by human tutors and tutees, in order to build trust and rapport (which have been shown to have positive impacts on student learning).

Emotional Affect

A growing body of work is considering the role of affect on learning, with the objective of developing intelligent tutoring systems that can interpret and adapt to the different emotional states. Humans do not just use cognitive processes in learning but the affective processes they go through also plays an important role. For example, learners learn better when they have a certain level of disequilibrium (frustration), but not enough to make the learner feel completely overwhelmed. This has motivated affective computing to begin to produce and research creating intelligent tutoring systems that can interpret the affective process of an individual. An ITS can be developed to read an individual's expressions and other signs of affect in an attempt to find and tutor to the optimal affective state for learning. There are many complications in doing this since affect is not expressed in just one way but in multiple ways so that for an ITS to be effective in interpreting affective states it may require a multimodal approach (tone, facial expression, etc...). These ideas have created a new field within ITS, that of Affective Tutoring Systems (ATS). One example of an ITS that addresses affect is Gaze Tutor which was developed to track students eye movements and determine whether they are bored or distracted and then the system attempts to reengage the student.

Rapport Building

To date, most ITSs have focused purely on the cognitive aspects of tutoring and not on the social relationship between the tutoring system and the student. As demonstrated by the Computers are social actors paradigm humans often project social heuristics onto computers. For example, in observations of young children interacting with *Sam the CastleMate,* a collaborative story telling agent, children interacted with this simulated child in much the same manner as they would a human child. It has been suggested that to effectively design an ITS that builds rapport with students, the ITS should mimic strategies of instructional immediacy, behaviors which bridge the apparent social distance between students and teachers such as smiling and addressing students by name. With regard to teenagers, Ogan et al. draw from observations of close friends tutoring each other to argue that in order for an ITS to build rapport as a peer to a student, a more involved process of trust building is likely necessary which may ultimately require that the tutoring system possess the capability to effectively respond to and even produce seemingly rude behavior in order to mediate motivational and affective student factors through playful joking and taunting.

Teachable Agents

Traditionally ITSs take on the role of autonomous tutors, however they can also take on the role of tutees for the purpose of learning by teaching exercises. Evidence suggests that learning by teaching can be an effective strategy for mediating self-explanation, improving feelings of self-efficacy, and boosting educational outcomes and retention. In order to replicate this effect the roles of the student and ITS can be switched. This can be achieved by designing the ITS to have the appearance of being taught as is the case in the Teachable Agent Arithmetic Game and Betty's Brain. Another approach is to have students teach a machine learning agent which can learn to solve problems by demonstration and correctness feedback as is the case in the APLUS system built with SimStudent. In order to replicate the educational effects of learning by teaching teachable agents generally have a social agent built on top of them which poses questions or conveys confusion. For example, Betty from Betty's Brain will prompt the student to ask her questions to make sure that she understands the material, and Stacy from APLUS will prompt the user for explanations of the feedback provided by the student.

2.2.3 Data-Driven Insights

Data-driven models are a class of computational models that primarily rely on historical data collected throughout a system's or process' lifetime to establish relationships between input, internal, and output variables. Commonly found in numerous articles and publications, data-driven models have evolved from earlier statistical models, overcoming limitations posed by strict assumptions about probability distributions. These models have gained prominence across various fields, particularly in the era of big data, artificial intelligence, and machine learning, where they offer valuable insights and predictions based on the available data.

Background

These models have evolved from earlier statistical models, which were based on certain assumptions about probability distributions that often proved to be overly restrictive. The emergence of data-driven models in the 1950s and 1960s coincided with the development of digital computers, advancements in artificial intelligence research, and the introduction of new approaches in non-behavioural modelling, such as pattern recognition and automatic classification.

Key Concepts

Data-driven models encompass a wide range of techniques and methodologies that aim to intelligently process and analyse large datasets. Examples include fuzzy logic, fuzzy and rough sets for handling uncertainty, neural networks for approximating functions, global optimization and evolutionary computing, statistical learning theory, and Bayesian methods. These models have found applications in various fields, including economics, customer relations management, financial services, medicine, and the military, among others.

Machine learning, a subfield of artificial intelligence, is closely related to data-driven modelling as it also focuses on using historical data to create models that can make predictions and identify patterns. In fact, many data-driven models incorporate machine learning techniques, such as regression, classification, and clustering algorithms, to process and analyse data.

In recent years, the concept of data-driven models has gained considerable attention in the field of water resources, with numerous applications, academic courses, and scientific publications using the term as a generalization for models that rely on data rather than physics. This classification has been featured in various publications and has even spurred the development of hybrid models in the past decade. Hybrid models attempt to quantify the degree of physically based information used in hydrological models and determine whether the process of building the model is primarily driven by physics or purely data-based. As a result, data-driven models have become an essential topic of discussion and exploration within water resources management and research.

The term "data-driven modelling" (DDM) refers to the overarching paradigm of using historical data in conjunction with advanced computational techniques, including machine learning and artificial intelligence, to create models that can reveal underlying trends, patterns, and, in some cases, make predictions Data-driven models can be built with or without detailed knowledge of the underlying processes governing the system behavior, which makes them particularly useful when such knowledge is missing or fragmented.

2.2.4 Enhancing Accessibility

AI has the potential to make education more accessible to diverse populations, including students with disabilities and those in remote or underserved areas.

Assistive Technologies

AI-powered assistive technologies can support students with disabilities by providing tools such as speech-to-text, text-to-speech, and predictive text applications. These tools help students with visual, auditory, or motor impairments access educational content and participate in learning activities more effectively. Additionally, AI can create personalized learning environments that accommodate various needs, ensuring that all students have equal opportunities to succeed.

Remote and Online Learning

AI-driven platforms facilitate remote and online learning, making education accessible to students regardless of their geographical location. Intelligent systems can offer interactive and engaging learning experiences, simulate classroom environments, and provide virtual tutoring.

This flexibility is particularly beneficial for students in rural or conflict-affected regions who may not have access to quality education otherwise.

2.2.5 Administrative Efficiencies

AI also streamlines administrative tasks, allowing educators to focus more on teaching and student engagement.

Automated Grading

Automated grading systems use AI to evaluate assignments, quizzes, and exams. These systems can handle large volumes of work quickly and accurately, reducing the burden on teachers and providing students with timely feedback.

While some skepticism exists regarding the assessment of creative or subjective work, AI grading systems are continually improving in their ability to evaluate a broader range of tasks.

Resource Allocation

AI can optimize resource allocation within educational institutions. By analyzing data on student performance and needs, AI systems can suggest the most effective deployment of resources such as teaching staff, classroom materials, and technology. This optimization ensures that resources are used efficiently to support student learning and institutional goals.

2.2.6 Challenges and Considerations

While AI holds great promise for improving learning outcomes, it also presents several challenges and ethical considerations.

Data Privacy and Security

The use of AI in education involves the collection and analysis of vast amounts of personal data.

Ensuring the privacy and security of this data is paramount. Educational institutions must implement robust data protection measures and adhere to privacy regulations to safeguard student information.

Equity and Bias

AI systems are only as good as the data they are trained on. If the data contains biases, the AI can perpetuate and even amplify these biases, leading to unequal educational opportunities. It is crucial to ensure that AI systems are developed and trained using diverse and representative data sets to promote equity in education.

Teacher and Student Adaptation

The integration of AI into education requires teachers and students to adapt to new technologies and methods. Professional development and training for educators are essential to ensure they can effectively use AI tools and incorporate them into their teaching practices. Similarly, students need support and guidance to navigate AI-driven learning environments.

2.3 PERSONALIZATION AND ADAPTIVELY IN EDUCATION

The evolution of educational technology has ushered in an era where learning can be highly personalized and adaptive. This paradigm shift, driven by the integration of artificial intelligence (AI) and data analytics, promises to cater to individual learning needs, enhance student engagement, and ultimately improve educational outcomes.

Personalization and adaptivity represent a transformative shift in education, offering tailored and responsive learning experiences that cater to individual needs. By harnessing the power of AI and data analytics, educators can enhance student engagement, improve learning outcomes, and create a more inclusive and effective educational environment. While challenges such as data privacy, equity, and teacher training must be addressed, the potential benefits of personalized and adaptive learning make it a compelling approach for the future of education.

2.3.1 The Concept of Personalization in Education

Definition and Importance

Personalization in education refers to tailoring learning experiences to meet the unique needs, preferences, and abilities of each student. Unlike the traditional one-size-fits-all approach, personalized education acknowledges that students learn at different paces, have diverse interests, and require various levels of support. By customizing learning paths, resources, and assessments, educators can foster a more engaging and effective learning environment.

Learning Management Systems (LMS)

A learning management system (LMS) or virtual learning environment (VLE) is a software application for the administration, documentation, tracking, reporting, automation, and delivery of educational courses, training programs, materials or learning and development programs. The learning management system concept emerged directly from e-Learning. Learning management systems make up the largest segment of the learning system market.

The first introduction of the LMS was in the late 1990s. LMSs have been adopted by almost all higher education institutions in the English-speaking world. Learning management systems have faced a massive growth in usage due to the emphasis on remote learning during the COVID-19 pandemic.

Learning management systems were designed to identify training and learning gaps, using analytical data and reporting. LMSs are focused on online learning delivery but support a range of uses, acting as a platform for online content, including courses, both asynchronous based and synchronous based.

In the higher education space, an LMS may offer classroom management for instructor-led training or a flipped classroom. Modern LMSs include intelligent algorithms to make automated recommendations for courses based on a user's skill profile as well as extract metadata from learning materials to make such recommendations even more accurate.

Purpose

An LMS delivers and manages all types of content, including videos, courses, workshops, and documents. In the education and higher education markets, an LMS will include a variety of functionality that is similar to corporate but will have features such as rubrics, teacher and instructor-facilitated learning, a discussion board, and often the use of a syllabus.

A syllabus is rarely a feature in the corporate LMS, although courses may start with a heading-level index to give learners an overview of topics covered.

Correspondence Teaching

The first known document of correspondence teaching dates back to 1723, through the advertisement in the *Boston Gazette* of Caleb Phillips, professor of shorthand, offering teaching materials and tutorials.

The first testimony of a bi-directional communication organized correspondence course comes from England, in 1840, when Isaac Pitman initiated a shorthand course, wherein he sent a passage of the Bible to students, who would send it back in full transcription.

The success of the course resulted in the foundation of the phonographic correspondence society in 1843. The pioneering milestone in distance language teaching was in 1856 by Charles Toussaint and Gustav Langenscheidt, who began the first European institution of distance learning. This is the first known instance of the use of materials for independent language study.

Multimedia Teaching: The Emergence and Development of the Distance Learning Idea

The concept of e-learning began developing in the early 20th century, marked by the appearance of audio-video communication systems used for remote teaching. In 1909, E.M. Forster published his story 'The Machine Stops' and explained the benefits of using audio communication to deliver lectures to remote audiences.

In 1924, Sidney L. Pressey developed the first teaching machine which offered multiple types of practical exercises and question formats. Nine years later, University of Alberta's Professor M.E. Zerte transformed this machine into a problem cylinder able to compare problems and solutions.

This, in a sense, was "multimedia", because it made use of several media formats to reach students and provide instruction. Later, printed materials would be joined by telephone, radio broadcasts, TV broadcasts, audio, and videotapes. The earliest networked learning system was the Plato Learning Management system (PLM) developed in the 1970s by Control Data Corporation.

Telematic Teaching

In the 1980s, modern telecommunications started to be used in education. Computers became prominent in the daily use of higher education institutions, as well as instruments to student learning. Computer-aided teaching aimed to integrate technical and educational means. The trend then shifted to video communication, as a result of which Houston University decided to hold telecast classes to their students for approximately 13–15 hours a week. The classes took place in 1953, while in 1956, Robin McKinnon Wood and Gordon Pask released the first adaptive teaching system for corporate environments SAKI. The idea of automating teaching operations also inspired the University of Illinois experts to develop their Programmed Logic for Automated Teaching Operations (PLATO) which enabled users to exchange content regardless of their location. In the period between 1970 and 1980, educational venues were rapidly considering the idea of computerizing courses, including the Western Behavioral Sciences Institute from California which introduced the first accredited online-taught degree.

Teaching through the Internet: The Appearance of the First LMS

The history of the application of computers to education is filled with broadly descriptive terms such as computer-managed instruction (CMI), and integrated learning systems (ILS), computer-based instruction (CBI), computer-assisted instruction (CAI), and computer-assisted learning (CAL). These terms describe drill-and-practice programs, more sophisticated tutorials, and more individualized instruction, respectively. The term is currently used to describe a number of different educational computer applications. FirstClass by SoftArc, used by the United Kingdom's Open University in the 1990s and 2000s to deliver online learning across Europe, was one of the earliest internet-based LMSs.

The first fully-featured Learning Management System (LMS) was called *EKKO*, developed and released by Norway's NKI Distance Education Network in 1991. Three years later, New Brunswick's NB Learning Network presented a similar system designed for DOS-based teaching, and devoted exclusively to business learners.

Technical Aspects

An LMS can be either hosted locally or by a vendor. A vendor-hosted cloud system tends to follow a SaaS (software as a service) model. All data in a vendor-hosted system is housed by the supplier and accessed by users through the internet, on a computer or mobile device. Vendor-hosted systems are typically easier to use and require less technical expertise. An LMS that is locally hosted sees all data pertaining to the LMS hosted internally on the users' internal servers. Locally hosted LMS software will often be open-source, meaning users will acquire (either through payment or free of charge) the LMS software and its code. With this, the user is able to modify and maintain the software through an internal team. Individuals and smaller organizations tend to stick with cloud-based systems due to the cost of internal hosting and maintenance.

There are a variety of integration strategies for embedding content into LMSs, including AICC, xAPI (also called 'Tin Can'), SCORM (Sharable Content Object Reference Model) and LTI (Learning Tools Interoperability).

Through an LMS, teachers may create and integrate course materials, articulate learning goals, align content and assessments, track studying progress, and create customized tests for students. An LMS allows the communication of learning objectives, and organize learning timelines. An LMS perk is that it delivers learning content and tools straight to learners, and assessment can be automated. It can also reach marginalized groups through special settings. Such systems have built-in customizable features including assessment and tracking. Thus, learners can see in real time their progress and instructors can monitor and communicate the effectiveness of learning. One of the most important features of LMS is trying to create a streamline communication between learners and instructors. Such systems, besides facilitating online learning, tracking learning progress, providing digital learning tools, managing communication, and maybe selling content, may be used to provide different communication features.

Managing Courses, Users and Roles

Learning management systems may be used to create professionally structured course content. The teacher can add text, images, videos, pdfs, tables, links and text formatting, interactive tests, slideshows, etc. Moreover, they can create different types of users, such as teachers, students, parents, visitors and editors (hierarchies). It helps control which content students can access, track studying progress and engage students with contact tools. Teachers can manage courses and modules, enroll students or set up self-enrollment.

Online Assessment

An LMS can enable instructors to create automated assessments and assignments for learners, which are accessible and submitted online. Most platforms allow a variety of different question types such as: one/multi-line answer; multiple choice answer; ordering; free text; matching; essay; true or false/yes or no; fill in the gaps; agreement scale and offline tasks.

User Feedback

Students' exchange of feedback both with teachers and their peers is possible through LMS. Teachers may create discussion groups to allow students feedback, share their knowledge on topics and increase the interaction in course. Students' feedback is an instrument which help teachers to improve their work, helps identify what to add or remove from a course, and ensures students feel comfortable and included.

Synchronous and Asynchronous Learning

Students can either learn asynchronously (on demand, self-paced) through course content such as pre-recorded videos, PDF, SCORM (Sharable Content Object Reference Model), discussion forums or they can undertake synchronous learning utilizing video conference communication, live discussions and chats.

Learning Analytics

Learning management systems will often incorporate dashboards to track student or user progress. They can then report on key items such as completion rates, attendance data and success likelihood. Utilising these metrics can help facilitators better understand gaps in user knowledge.

Learning Management Industry

In the relatively new LMS market, commercial providers for corporate applications and education range from new entrants to those that entered the market in 1990. In addition to commercial packages, many open-source solutions are available.

In the U.S. higher education market as of spring 2021, the top three LMSs by a number of institutions were Canvas (38%), Blackboard (25%), and Moodle (15%). Worldwide, the picture was different, with Moodle having over 50% of the market share in Europe, Latin America, and Oceania. Many users of LMSs use an authoring tool to create content, which is then hosted on an LMS. In some cases, LMSs that do use a standard include a primitive authoring tool for basic content manipulation. More modern systems, in particular SaaS solutions have decided not to adopt a standard and have rich course authoring tools. There are several standards for creating and integrating complex content into an LMS, including AICC, SCORM, xAPI, and Learning Tools Interoperability. However, using SCORM or an alternative standardized course protocol is not always required and can be restrictive when used unnecessarily. Evaluation of LMSs is a complex task and significant research supports different forms of evaluation, including iterative processes where students' experiences and approaches to learning are evaluated.

Advantages

There are six major advantages of LMS which in themselves constitute the concept of LMS.

- **Interoperability:** Data standards on LMS allow information to be exchanged from one system to another
- **Accessibility:** The consistent layout using on LMS provides students with disabilities better opportunity to access web content.
- **Reusability:** Reusability refers to the LMS system's ability to be reused for educational content. A critical aspect in lowering the high expenses of developing educational experiences in e-learning settings.
- **Durability:** Due to the rising adoption of technology into academics, the growth of LMS market is expected to reach a CAGR of 17.1% by 2028.
- **Maintenance Ability:** LMS allows developers to continually enhance their software and better adapt them to their user base.
- **Adaptability:** LMS is always improving, updating, and learning new behaviours quickly. LMS has been active since 1990s and keeps adjusting to the changing society today.

Disadvantages

- Teachers have to be willing to adapt their curricula from face-to-face lectures to online lectures.
- There is the potential for instructors to try to directly translate existing support materials into courses which can result in very low interactivity and engagement for learners if not done well.

COVID-19 and Learning Management Systems

The suspension of in-school learning caused by the COVID-19 pandemic started a dramatic shift in the way teachers and students at all levels interact with each other and learning materials. UNESCO estimated that as of May 25, 2020, approximately 990,324,537 learners, or 56.6% of the total enrolled students have been affected by COVID-19 related school closures. In many countries, online education through the use of Learning Management Systems became the focal point of teaching and learning. For example, statistics taken from a university's LMS during the initial school closure period (March to June 2020) indicate that student submissions and activity nearly doubled from pre-pandemic usage levels.

Student satisfaction with LMS usage during this period is closely tied to the information quality contained within LMS modules and maintaining student self-efficacy. From the teacher perspective, a study of K-12 teachers in Finland reported high levels of acceptance for LMS technology, however, training support and developing methods for maintaining student engagement are key to long-term success. In developing nations, the transition to LMS usage faced many challenges, which included a lower number of colleges and universities using LMSs before the pandemic, technological infrastructure limitations, and negative attitudes toward technology amongst users.

Personalized Learning Plans (PLPs): Implementation Strategy

Personalized Learning Plans (PLPs) are tailored educational roadmaps designed to address individual student goals, strengths, and areas for improvement. Educators, often in collaboration with students and parents, develop these plans to outline specific learning objectives, strategies, and timelines. PLPs help students stay motivated and focused by providing clear, achievable targets.

Benefits of Personalization

Enhanced Engagement and Motivation

Personalized learning keeps students engaged by aligning educational content with their interests and needs. When students feel that their learning experiences are relevant and meaningful, their motivation to learn increases. This engagement is crucial for maintaining their interest and commitment to their studies.

Improved Learning Outcomes

By addressing individual learning needs, personalized education helps students grasp concepts more effectively. Tailored support and resources enable students to overcome challenges and achieve mastery in their subjects. This individualized approach leads to better academic performance and deeper understanding.

2.3.2 The Role of Adaptivity in Education

Definition and Significance

Adaptivity in education involves the continuous adjustment of instructional strategies and content based on real-time data about student performance. Adaptive learning technologies respond dynamically to student interactions, providing immediate feedback and modifying learning paths to suit individual progress. This approach ensures that students receive the appropriate level of challenge and support throughout their learning journey.

Implementation Strategies

Adaptive Learning Platforms

Adaptive learning platforms use sophisticated algorithms to analyze student data and adjust instructional content accordingly. These platforms can identify patterns in student behavior, such as areas of struggle or proficiency, and adapt lessons to address these patterns. By continuously monitoring and responding to student performance, adaptive learning platforms create a personalized and responsive learning environment.

Intelligent Tutoring Systems

Intelligent Tutoring Systems (ITS) simulate one-on-one tutoring by adapting to the learner's needs in real-time. These systems provide personalized feedback, hints, and guidance, helping students navigate complex problems and concepts. ITS can engage students in interactive dialogues, encouraging critical thinking and deeper understanding.

Benefits of Adaptivity

Real-time Feedback and Support

One of the key advantages of adaptive learning is the provision of real-time feedback and support. Immediate feedback allows students to recognize and correct mistakes promptly, reinforcing correct understanding and preventing misconceptions from becoming ingrained. This timely intervention accelerates the learning process and enhances student confidence.

Efficient Use of Instructional Time

Adaptive learning optimizes instructional time by focusing on areas where students need the most support. Educators can allocate their time and resources more effectively, addressing individual needs without compromising the progress of the entire class. This efficiency ensures that all students receive the attention they require to succeed.

2.3.3 Synergy between Personalization and Adaptivity

Complementary Approaches

Personalization and adaptivity are complementary approaches that, when integrated, create a powerful educational framework. Personalization sets the stage by tailoring learning experiences to individual needs and preferences, while adaptivity ensures that these experiences are continuously refined based on real-time data. Together, they provide a holistic and dynamic learning environment that fosters student growth and achievement.

Case Studies and Examples

Knewton

Knewton is an example of an adaptive learning platform that uses AI to personalize education. The platform analyzes student performance data to adjust the difficulty of tasks and recommend targeted resources. By personalizing content delivery and continuously adapting to student needs, Knewton enhances learning efficiency and outcomes.

DreamBox Learning

DreamBox Learning is an adaptive math program for K-8 students. The platform adjusts lessons in real-time based on student interactions, providing personalized feedback and support. DreamBox's adaptive technology ensures that students are challenged appropriately and receive the help they need to master mathematical concepts.

2.3.4 Challenges and Considerations

Data Privacy and Security

The implementation of personalized and adaptive learning technologies involves the collection and analysis of vast amounts of student data. Ensuring the privacy and security of this data is paramount. Educational institutions must adhere to strict data protection regulations and employ robust security measures to safeguard student information.

Equity and Access

While personalized and adaptive learning technologies offer significant benefits, ensuring equitable access is a challenge. Students from underserved communities may lack access to the necessary technology and resources. Addressing this digital divide is crucial to ensure that all students can benefit from personalized and adaptive learning.

Teacher Training and Support

The successful implementation of personalized and adaptive learning requires educators to be proficient in using these technologies. Professional development and ongoing support are essential to help teachers integrate these tools into their teaching practices effectively. Educators must be equipped with the skills and knowledge to leverage personalized and adaptive learning to its fullest potential.

CHAPTER 3
ETHICAL FOUNDATIONS

3.1 ETHICAL THEORIES AND FRAMEWORKS

Ethical theories and frameworks provide structured approaches to understanding, evaluating, and guiding human behavior and decision-making. These theories offer various lenses through which moral dilemmas and ethical questions can be examined, helping individuals and organizations navigate complex moral landscapes.

Ethical theories and frameworks provide valuable tools for navigating moral complexities in various aspects of life. Deontological ethics emphasizes duty and principles, utilitarianism focuses on outcomes, virtue ethics highlights character development, and care ethics prioritizes relationships and compassion. Each framework has its strengths and limitations, and effective ethical decision-making often involves integrating multiple perspectives.

By understanding and applying these theories, individuals and organizations can better address ethical challenges and promote moral integrity in their actions.

3.1.1 Deontological Ethics

In moral philosophy, deontological ethics or deontology is the normative ethical theory that the morality of an action should be based on whether that action itself is right or wrong under a series of rules and principles, rather than based on the consequences of the action. It is sometimes described as duty-, obligation-, or rule-based ethics. Deontological ethics is commonly contrasted to consequentialism, utilitarianism, virtue ethics, and pragmatic ethics. In this terminology, action is more important than the consequences.

The term *deontological* was first used to describe the current, specialised definition by C. D. Broad in his 1930 book, *Five Types of Ethical Theory*. Older usage of the term goes back to Jeremy Bentham, who coined it prior to 1816 as a synonym of *dicastic* or *censorial ethics* (i.e., ethics based on judgement). The more general sense of the word is retained in French, especially in the term *code de déontologie* (ethical code), in the context of professional ethics.

Depending on the system of deontological ethics under consideration, a *moral obligation* may arise from an external or internal source, such as a set of rules inherent to the universe (ethical naturalism), religious law, or a set of personal or cultural values (any of which may be in conflict with personal desires).

Deontological Philosophies

There are numerous formulations of deontological ethics.

Kantianism

Immanuel Kant's theory of ethics is considered deontological for several different reasons. First, Kant argues that in order to act in the morally right way, people must act from duty (*Pflicht*). Second, Kant argued that it was not the consequences of actions that make them right or wrong, but the motives of the person who carries out the action.

Kant's first argument begins with the premise that the highest good must be both good in itself and good without qualification. Something is "good in itself" when it is intrinsically good; and is "good without qualification" when the addition of that thing never makes a situation ethically worse.

Kant then argues that those things that are usually thought to be good, such as intelligence, perseverance, and pleasure, fail to be either intrinsically good or good without qualification. Pleasure, for example, appears not to be good without qualification, because when people take pleasure in watching someone suffer, this seems to make the situation ethically worse. He concludes that there is only one thing that is truly good:

- **Nothing in the World:** Indeed nothing even beyond the world—can possibly be conceived which could be called good without qualification except a *good will.*

Kant then argues that the consequences of an act of willing cannot be used to determine that the person has a good will; good consequences could arise by accident from an action that was motivated by a desire to cause harm to an innocent person, and bad consequences could arise from an action that was well-motivated. Instead, he claims, a person has a good will when he "acts out of respect for the moral law." People "act out of respect for the moral law" when they act in some way *because* they have a duty to do so. Thus, the only thing that is truly good in itself is a good will, and a good will is only good when the willer chooses to do something because it is that person's duty; i.e., out of respect for the law. He defines *respect* as "the concept of a worth which thwarts my self-love."

Kant's three significant formulations of the categorical imperative are:

- Act only according to that maxim by which you can also will that it would become a universal law;

- Act in such a way that you always treat humanity, whether in your own person or in the person of any other, never simply as a means, but always at the same time as an end; and
- Every rational being must so act as if he were through his maxim always a legislating member in a universal kingdom of ends.

Kant argued that the only absolutely good thing is a good will, and so the single determining factor of whether an action is morally right is the will, or motive of the person doing it. If they are acting on a bad maxim — e.g., 'I will lie' — then their action is wrong, even if some good consequences come of it.

In his essay, "On a Supposed Right to Lie Because of Philanthropic Concerns", arguing against the position of Benjamin Constant, *Des réactions politiques*, Kant states that:

- Hence a lie defined merely as an intentionally untruthful declaration to another man does not require the additional condition that it must do harm to another, as jurists require in their definition (*mendacium est falsiloquium in praeiudicium alterius*). For a lie always harms another; if not some human being, then it nevertheless does harm to humanity in general, inasmuch as it vitiates the very source of right [*Rechtsquelle*].... All practical principles of right must contain rigorous truth.... This is because such exceptions would destroy the universality on account of which alone they bear the name of principles.

Divine Command Theory

Although not all deontologists are religious, some believe in the *divine command theory*, which is actually a cluster of related theories that essentially state that an action is right if God has decreed that it is right. According to English philosopher Ralph Cudworth, William of Ockham, René Descartes, and 18th-century Calvinists all accepted various versions of this moral theory, as they all held that moral obligations arise from God's commands.

The *divine command theory* is a form of deontology because, according to it, the rightness of any action depends upon that action being performed because it is a duty, not because of any good consequences arising from that action. If God commands people not to work on Sabbath, then people act rightly if they do not work on Sabbath *because God has commanded that they do not do so.* If they do not work on Sabbath because they are lazy, then their action is not, truly speaking, "right" even though the actual physical action performed is the same. If God commands not to covet a neighbour's goods, this theory holds that it would be immoral to do so, even if coveting provides the beneficial outcome of a drive to succeed or do well.

One thing that clearly distinguishes Kantian deontologism from divine command deontology is that Kantianism maintains that man, as a rational being, makes the moral law universal, whereas divine command maintains that God makes the moral law universal.

Ross's Deontological Pluralism

W. D. Ross objects to Kant's monistic deontology, which bases ethics in only one foundational principle, the categorical imperative. He contends that there is a plurality of prima facie duties determining what is right. Some duties originate from our own previous actions, like the *duty of fidelity* (to keep promises and to tell the truth), and the *duty of reparation* (to make amends for wrongful acts). The *duty of gratitude* (to return kindnesses received) arises from the actions of others. Other duties include the *duty of non-injury* (not to hurt others), the *duty of beneficence* (to promote the maximum of aggregate good), the *duty of self-improvement* (to improve one's own condition) and the *duty of justice* (to distribute benefits and burdens equably). One problem the deontological pluralist has to face is that cases can arise where the demands of one duty violate another duty, so-called moral dilemmas. For example, there are cases where it is necessary to break a promise in order to relieve someone's distress. Ross makes use of the distinction between *prima facie duties* and *absolute duty* to solve this problem. The duties listed above are *prima facie duties*; they are general principles whose validity is self-evident to morally mature persons. They are factors that do not take all considerations into account. *Absolute duty*, on the other hand, is particular to one specific situation, taking everything into account, and has to be judged on a case-by-case basis. It is *absolute duty* that determines which acts are right or wrong.

Contemporary Deontology

Contemporary deontologists (i.e., scholars born in the first half of the 20th century) include Józef Maria Bocheński, Thomas Nagel, T. M. Scanlon, and Roger Scruton.

Bocheński (1965) makes a distinction between *deontic* and *epistemic* authority:

- A typical example of epistemic authority in Bocheński's usage would be "the relation of a teacher to her students." A teacher has epistemic authority when making declarative sentences that the student presumes is reliable knowledge and appropriate but feels no obligation to accept or obey.
- An example of deontic authority would be "the relation between an employer and her employee." An employer has deontic authority in the act of issuing an order that the employee is obliged to accept and obey regardless of its reliability or appropriateness.

Scruton (2017), in his book *On Human Nature*, is critical of consequentialism and similar ethical theories, such as hedonism and utilitarianism, instead proposing a deontological ethical approach. He implies that proportional duty and obligation are essential components of the ways in which we decide to act, and he defends natural law against opposing theories. He also expresses admiration for virtue ethics, and believes that the two ethical theories are not, as is frequently portrayed, mutually exclusive.

Principle of Permissible Harm

Frances Kamm's "Principle of Permissible Harm" (1996) is an effort to derive a deontological constraint that coheres with our considered case judgments while also relying heavily on Kant's categorical imperative. The principle states that one may harm in order to save more if and only if the harm is an effect or an aspect of the greater good itself. This principle is meant to address what Kamm feels are most people's considered case judgments, many of which involve deontological intuitions. For instance, Kamm argues that we believe it would be impermissible to kill one person to harvest his organs in order to save the lives of five others. Yet, we think it is morally permissible to divert a runaway trolley that would otherwise kill five innocent, immobile people, onto a sidetrack where only one innocent and immobile person will be killed. Kamm believes the Principle of Permissible Harm explains the moral difference between these and other cases, and more importantly expresses a constraint telling us exactly when we may not act to bring about good ends—such as in the organ harvesting case.

In 2007, Kamm published *Intricate Ethics*, a book that presents a new theory, the "Doctrine of Productive Purity", that incorporates aspects of her "Principle of Permissible Harm". Like the "Principle", the "Doctrine of Productive Purity" is an attempt to provide a deontological prescription for determining the circumstances in which people are permitted to act in a way that harms others.

Reconciling Deontology with Consequentialism

Various attempts have been made to reconcile deontology with consequentialism. Threshold deontology holds that rules ought to govern up to a point despite adverse consequences; but when the consequences become so dire that they cross a stipulated threshold, consequentialism takes over. Theories put forth by Thomas Nagel and Michael S. Moore attempt to reconcile deontology with consequentialism by assigning each a jurisdiction. Iain King's 2008 book *How to Make Good Decisions and Be Right All the Time* uses quasi-realism and a modified form of utilitarianism to develop deontological principles that are compatible with ethics based on virtues and consequences. King develops a hierarchy of principles to link his meta-ethics, which is more inclined towards consequentialism, with the deontological conclusions he presents in his book.

Secular Deontology

Intuition-based deontology is a concept within secular ethics. A classical example of literature on secular ethics is the Kural text, authored by the ancient Tamil Indian philosopher Valluvar. It can be argued that some concepts from deontological ethics date back to this text. Concerning ethical intuitionism, 20th century philosopher C.D. Broad coined the term "deontological ethics" to refer to the normative doctrines associated with intuitionism, leaving the phrase "ethical intuitionism" free to refer to the epistemological doctrines.

3.1.2 Utilitarianism

In ethical philosophy, utilitarianism is a family of normative ethical theories that prescribe actions that maximize happiness and well-being for the affected individuals. In other words, utilitarian ideas encourage actions that ensure the greatest good for the greatest number. Although different varieties of utilitarianism admit different characterizations, the basic idea behind all of them is, in some sense, to maximize utility, which is often defined in terms of well-being or related concepts. For instance, Jeremy Bentham, the founder of utilitarianism, described *utility* thus:

- That property in any object, whereby it tends to produce benefit, advantage, pleasure, good, or happiness ... [or] to prevent the happening of mischief, pain, evil, or unhappiness to the party whose interest is considered.

Utilitarianism is a version of consequentialism, which states that the consequences of any action are the only standard of right and wrong. Unlike other forms of consequentialism, such as egoism and altruism, utilitarianism considers either the interests of all humanity and/or all sentient beings equally.

Proponents of utilitarianism have disagreed on a number of issues, such as whether actions should be chosen based on their likely results (*act utilitarianism*), or whether agents should conform to rules that maximize utility (*rule utilitarianism*). There is also disagreement as to whether total utility (*total utilitarianism*) or average utility (*average utilitarianism*) should be maximized.

The seeds of the theory can be found in the hedonists Aristippus and Epicurus who viewed happiness as the only good, the consequentialism of the ancient Chinese philosopher Mozi who developed a theory to maximize benefit and minimize harm, and in the work of the medieval Indian philosopher Śāntideva.

The tradition of modern utilitarianism began with Jeremy Bentham, and continued with such philosophers as John Stuart Mill, Henry Sidgwick, R. M. Hare, and Peter Singer.

The concept has been applied towards social welfare economics, questions of justice, the crisis of global poverty, the ethics of raising animals for food, and the importance of avoiding existential risks to humanity.

Pre-Modern Formulations

The importance of happiness as an end for humans has long been recognized. Forms of hedonism were put forward by the ancient Greek philosophers Aristippus and Epicurus. Aristotle argued that *eudaimonia* is the highest human good. Augustine wrote that "all men agree in desiring the last end, which is happiness". The idea that conduct should to be judged by its consequences also existed within the ancient world. Consequentialist theories were first developed by the ancient Chinese philosopher Mozi, who proposed a system that sought to maximize benefit and eliminate harm. Mohist consequentialism advocated communitarian moral goods, including political stability, population growth, and wealth, but did not support the utilitarian notion of maximizing individual happiness.

Utilitarian ideas can also be found in the work of medieval philosophers. In medieval India, the 8th-century Indian philosopher Śāntideva wrote that we ought "to stop all the present and future pain and suffering of all sentient beings, and to bring about all present and future pleasure and happiness." In medieval Europe, happiness was explored in depth by Thomas Aquinas, in his *Summa Theologica.* During the Renaissance, consequentialist ideas are present in the work of political philosophy of Niccolò Machiavelli.

18th Century

Utilitarianism as a distinct ethical position only emerged in the 18th century, and although it is usually thought to have begun with Jeremy Bentham, there were earlier writers who presented theories that were strikingly similar.

Hutcheson

Francis Hutcheson first introduced a key utilitarian phrase in *An Inquiry into the Original of Our Ideas of Beauty and Virtue* (1725): when choosing the most moral action, the amount of virtue in a particular action is proportionate to the number of people it brings happiness to. In the same way, moral evil, or *vice*, is proportionate to the number of people made to suffer. The best action is the one that procures the greatest happiness of the greatest numbers, and the worst is the one that causes the most misery. In the first three editions of the book, Hutcheson included various mathematical algorithms "to compute the Morality of any Actions." In doing so, he pre-figured the hedonic calculus of Bentham.

John Gay

Some claim that John Gay developed the first systematic theory of utilitarian ethics. In *Concerning the Fundamental Principle of Virtue or Morality* (1731), Gay argues that:

- Happiness, private happiness, is the proper or ultimate end of all our actions... each particular action may be said to have its proper and peculiar end...(but)...they still tend or ought to tend to something farther; as is evident from hence, viz. that a man may ask and expect a reason why either of them are pursued: now to ask the reason of any action or pursuit, is only to enquire into the end of it: but to expect a reason, i.e. an end, to be assigned for an ultimate end, is absurd. To ask why I pursue happiness, will admit of no other answer than an explanation of the terms.

This pursuit of happiness is given a theological basis:

- Now it is evident from the nature of God, viz. his being infinitely happy in himself from all eternity, and from his goodness manifested in his works, that he could have no other design in creating mankind than their happiness; and therefore he wills their happiness; therefore the means of their happiness: therefore that my behaviour, as far as it may be a means of the happiness of mankind, should be such...thus the will of God is the immediate criterion of Virtue, and the happiness of mankind the criterion of the will of God; and therefore the happiness of mankind may be said to be the criterion of virtue, but once removed... (and)...I am to do whatever lies in my power towards promoting the happiness of mankind.

Hume

In *An Enquiry Concerning the Principles of Morals* (1751), David Hume writes:

- In all determinations of morality, this circumstance of public utility is ever principally in view; and wherever disputes arise, either in philosophy or common life, concerning the bounds of duty, the question cannot, by any means, be decided with greater certainty, than by ascertaining, on any side, the true interests of mankind. If any false opinion, embraced from appearances, has been found to prevail; as soon as farther experience and sounder reasoning have given us juster notions of human affairs, we retract our first sentiment, and adjust anew the boundaries of moral good and evil.

Paley

Gay's theological utilitarianism was developed and popularized by William Paley. It has been claimed that Paley was not a very original thinker and that the philosophies in his treatise on ethics is "an assemblage of ideas developed by others and is presented to be learned by students rather than debated by colleagues." Nevertheless, his book *The Principles of Moral and Political Philosophy* (1785) was a required text at Cambridge and Smith (1954) says that Paley's writings were "once as well known in American colleges as were the readers and spellers of William McGuffey and Noah Webster in the elementary schools." Schneewind (1977) writes that "utilitarianism first became widely known in England through the work of William Paley."

The now-forgotten significance of Paley can be judged from the title of Thomas Rawson Birks's 1874 work *Modern Utilitarianism or the Systems of Paley, Bentham and Mill Examined and Compared.* Apart from restating that happiness as an end is grounded in the nature of God, Paley also discusses the place of rules, writing:

- [A]ctions are to be estimated by their tendency. Whatever is expedient, is right. It is the utility of any moral rule alone, which constitutes the obligation of it.
- But to all this there seems a plain objection, viz. that many actions are useful, which no man in his senses will allow to be right. There are occasions, in which the hand of the assassin would be very useful.... The true answer is this; that these actions, after all, are not useful, and for that reason, and that alone, are not right.
- To see this point perfectly, it must be observed that the bad consequences of actions are twofold, particular and general. The particular bad consequence of an action, is the mischief which that single action directly and immediately occasions. The general bad consequence is, the violation of some necessary or useful general rule....
- You cannot permit one action and forbid another, without showing a difference between them. Consequently, the same sort of actions must be generally permitted or generally forbidden. Where, therefore, the general permission of them would be pernicious, it becomes necessary to lay down and support the rule which generally forbids them.

Classical Utilitarianism

Jeremy Bentham

Bentham's book An Introduction to the Principles of Morals and Legislation was printed in 1780 but not published until 1789. It is possible that Bentham was spurred on to publish after he saw the success of Paley's Principles of Moral and Political Philosophy. Though Bentham's book was not an immediate success, his ideas were spread further when Pierre Étienne Louis Dumont translated edited selections from a variety of Bentham's manuscripts into French. Traité de législation civile et pénale was published in 1802 and then later retranslated back into English by Hildreth as The Theory of Legislation, although by this time significant portions of Dumont's work had already been retranslated and incorporated into Sir John

Bowring's edition of Bentham's works, which was issued in parts between 1838 and 1843.

Perhaps aware that Francis Hutcheson eventually removed his algorithms for calculating the greatest happiness because they "appear'd useless, and were disagreeable to some readers," Bentham contends that there is nothing novel or unwarranted about his method, for "in all this there is nothing but what the practice of mankind, wheresoever they have a clear view of their own interest, is perfectly conformable to."

Rosen (2003) warns that descriptions of utilitarianism can bear "little resemblance historically to utilitarians like Bentham and J. S. Mill" and can be more "a crude version of act utilitarianism conceived in the twentieth century as a straw man to be attacked and rejected." It is a mistake to think that Bentham is not concerned with rules. His seminal work is concerned with the principles of legislation and the hedonic calculus is introduced with the words "Pleasures then, and the avoidance of pains, are the ends that the legislator has in view." In Chapter VII, Bentham says: "The business of government is to promote the happiness of the society, by punishing and rewarding.... In proportion as an act tends to disturb that happiness, in proportion as the tendency of it is pernicious, will be the demand it creates for punishment."

Bentham's work opens with a statement of the principle of utility:

- Nature has placed mankind under the governance of two sovereign masters, pain and pleasure. It is for them alone to point out what we ought to do.... By the principle of utility is meant that principle which approves or disapproves of every action whatsoever according to the tendency it appears to have to augment or diminish the happiness of the party whose interest is in question: or, what is the same thing in other words to promote or to oppose that happiness. I say of every action whatsoever, and therefore not only of every action of a private individual, but of every measure of government.

In Chapter IV, Bentham introduces a method of calculating the value of pleasures and pains, which has come to be known as the hedonic calculus. Bentham says that the value of a pleasure or pain, considered by itself, can be measured according to its intensity, duration, certainty/uncertainty and propinquity/remoteness. In addition, it is necessary to consider "the tendency of any act by which it is produced" and, therefore, to take account of the act's fecundity, or the chance it has of being followed by sensations of the same kind and its purity, or the chance it has of not being followed by sensations of the opposite kind. Finally, it is necessary to consider the extent, or the number of people affected by the action.

The question then arises as to when, if at all, it might be legitimate to break the law. This is considered in *The Theory of Legislation*, where Bentham distinguishes between evils of the first and second order. Those of the first order are the more immediate consequences; those of the second are when the consequences spread through the community causing "alarm" and "danger".

- It is true there are cases in which, if we confine ourselves to the effects of the first order, the good will have an incontestable preponderance over the evil. Were the offence considered only under this point of view, it would not be easy to assign any good reasons to justify the rigour of the laws. Every thing depends upon the evil of the second order; it is this which gives to such actions the character of crime, and which makes punishment necessary. Let us take, for example, the physical desire of satisfying hunger. Let a beggar, pressed by hunger, steal from a rich man's house a loaf, which perhaps saves him from starving, can it be possible to compare the good which the thief acquires for himself, with the evil which the rich man suffers?... It is not on account of the evil of the first order that it is necessary to erect these actions into offences, but on account of the evil of the second order.

John Stuart Mill

Mill was brought up as a Benthamite with the explicit intention that he would carry on the cause of utilitarianism. Mill's book *Utilitarianism* first appeared as a series of three articles published in *Fraser's Magazine* in 1861 and was reprinted as a single book in 1863.

Mill rejects a purely quantitative measurement of utility and says:

- It is quite compatible with the principle of utility to recognize the fact, that some kinds of pleasure are more desirable and more valuable than others. It would be absurd that while, in estimating all other things, quality is considered as well as quantity, the estimation of pleasures should be supposed to depend on quantity alone.

The word *utility* is used to mean general well-being or happiness, and Mill's view is that utility is the consequence of a good action. Utility, within the context of utilitarianism, refers to people performing actions for social utility. With social utility, he means the well-being of many people. Mill's explanation of the concept of utility in his work, Utilitarianism, is that people really do desire happiness, and since each individual desires their own happiness, it must follow that all of us desire the happiness of everyone, contributing to a larger social utility. Thus, an action that results in the greatest pleasure for the utility of society is the best action, or as Jeremy Bentham, the founder of early Utilitarianism put it, as the greatest happiness of the greatest number.

Mill not only viewed actions as a core part of utility, but as the directive rule of moral human conduct. The rule being that we should only be committing actions that provide pleasure to society. This view of pleasure was hedonistic, as it pursued the thought that pleasure is the highest good in life. This concept was adopted by Bentham and can be seen in his works. According to Mill, good actions result in pleasure, and that there is no higher end than pleasure. Mill says that good actions lead to pleasure and define good character. Better put, the justification of character, and whether an action is good or not, is based on how the person contributes to the concept of social utility. In the long run the best proof of a good character is good actions; and resolutely refuse to consider any mental disposition as good, of which the predominant tendency is to produce bad conduct. In the last chapter of Utilitarianism, Mill concludes that justice, as a classifying factor of our actions (being just or unjust) is one of the certain moral requirements, and when the requirements are all regarded collectively, they are viewed as greater according to this scale of "social utility" as Mill puts it.

He also notes that, contrary to what its critics might say, there is "no known Epicurean theory of life which does not assign to the pleasures of the intellect ... a much higher value as pleasures than to those of mere sensation." However, he accepts that this is usually because the intellectual pleasures are thought to have circumstantial advantages, i.e. "greater permanency, safety, uncostliness, &c." Instead, Mill will argue that some pleasures are intrinsically better than others.

The accusation that hedonism is a "doctrine worthy only of swine" has a long history. In *Nicomachean Ethics* (Book 1 Chapter 5), Aristotle says that identifying the good with pleasure is to prefer a life suitable for beasts. The theological utilitarians had the option of grounding their pursuit of happiness in the will of God; the hedonistic utilitarians needed a different defence. Mill's approach is to argue that the pleasures of the intellect are intrinsically superior to physical pleasures.

- Few human creatures would consent to be changed into any of the lower animals, for a promise of the fullest allowance of a beast's pleasures; no intelligent human being would consent to be a fool, no instructed person would be an ignoramus, no person of feeling and conscience would be selfish and base, even though they should be persuaded that the fool, the dunce, or the rascal is better satisfied with his lot than they are with theirs. ... A being of higher faculties requires more to make him happy, is capable probably of more acute suffering, and certainly accessible to it at more points, than one of an inferior type; but in spite of these liabilities, he can never really wish to sink into what he feels to be a lower grade of existence. ... It is better to be a human being dissatisfied than a pig satisfied; better to be Socrates dissatisfied than a

> fool satisfied. And if the fool, or the pig, are of a different opinion, it is because they only know their own side of the question...

Mill argues that if people who are "competently acquainted" with two pleasures show a decided preference for one even if it be accompanied by more discontent and "would not resign it for any quantity of the other," then it is legitimate to regard that pleasure as being superior in quality. Mill recognizes that these "competent judges" will not always agree, and states that, in cases of disagreement, the judgment of the majority is to be accepted as final. Mill also acknowledges that "many who are capable of the higher pleasures, occasionally, under the influence of temptation, postpone them to the lower. But this is quite compatible with a full appreciation of the intrinsic superiority of the higher." Mill says that this appeal to those who have experienced the relevant pleasures is no different from what must happen when assessing the quantity of pleasure, for there is no other way of measuring "the acutest of two pains, or the intensest of two pleasurable sensations." "It is indisputable that the being whose capacities of enjoyment are low, has the greatest chance of having them fully satisfied; and a highly-endowed being will always feel that any happiness which he can look for, as the world is constitute, is imperfect."

Mill also thinks that "intellectual pursuits have value out of proportion to the amount of contentment or pleasure (the mental state) that they produce." Mill also says that people should pursue these grand ideals, because if they choose to have gratification from petty pleasures, "some displeasure will eventually creep in. We will become bored and depressed." Mill claims that gratification from petty pleasures only gives short-term happiness and, subsequently, worsens the individual who may feel that his life lacks happiness, since the happiness is transient. Whereas, intellectual pursuits give long-term happiness because they provide the individual with constant opportunities throughout the years to improve his life, by benefiting from accruing knowledge. Mill views intellectual pursuits as "capable of incorporating the 'finer things' in life" while petty pursuits do not achieve this goal. Mill is saying that intellectual pursuits give the individual the opportunity to escape the constant depression cycle since these pursuits allow them to achieve their ideals, while petty pleasures do not offer this. Although debate persists about the nature of Mill's view of gratification, this suggests bifurcation in his position.

In Chapter Four of *Utilitarianism*, Mill considers what proof can be given for the principle of utility:

- The only proof capable of being given that an object is visible, is that people actually see it. The only proof that a sound is audible, is that people hear it.... In like manner, I apprehend, the sole evidence it is possible to produce that anything is desirable, is that people do actually desire it....

> No reason can be given why the general happiness is desirable, except that each person, so far as he believes it to be attainable, desires his own happiness...we have not only all the proof which the case admits of, but all which it is possible to require, that happiness is a good: that each person's happiness is a good to that person, and the general happiness, therefore, a good to the aggregate of all persons.

It is usual to say that Mill is committing a number of fallacies:

- **Naturalistic Fallacy:** Mill is trying to deduce what people ought to do from what they in fact do;
- **Equivocation Fallacy:** Mill moves from the fact that (1) something is desirable, i.e. is capable of being desired, to the claim that (2) it is desirable, i.e. that it ought to be desired; and
- **The Fallacy of Composition:** The fact that people desire their own happiness does not imply that the aggregate of all persons will desire the general happiness.

Such allegations began to emerge in Mill's lifetime, shortly after the publication of *Utilitarianism*, and persisted for well over a century, though the tide has been turning in recent discussions. Nonetheless, a defence of Mill against all three charges, with a chapter devoted to each, can be found in Necip Fikri Alican's *Mill's Principle of Utility: A Defense of John Stuart Mill's Notorious Proof* (1994). This is the first, and remains the only, book-length treatment of the subject matter. Yet the alleged fallacies in the proof continue to attract scholarly attention in journal articles and book chapters.

Hall (1949) and Popkin (1950) defend Mill against this accusation pointing out that he begins Chapter Four by asserting that "questions of ultimate ends do not admit of proof, in the ordinary acceptation of the term" and that this is "common to all first principles". Therefore, according to Hall and Popkin, Mill does not attempt to "establish that what people do desire is desirable but merely attempts to make the principles acceptable." The type of "proof" Mill is offering "consists only of some considerations which, Mill thought, might induce an honest and reasonable man to accept utilitarianism."

Having claimed that people do, in fact, desire happiness, Mill now has to show that it is the *only* thing they desire. Mill anticipates the objection that people desire other things such as virtue. He argues that whilst people might start desiring virtue as a *means* to happiness, eventually, it becomes part of someone's happiness and is then desired as an end in itself.

- The principle of utility does not mean that any given pleasure, as music, for instance, or any given exemption from pain, as for example health, are to be looked upon as means to a collective something termed happiness, and to be desired on that account. They are desired and desirable in and for themselves; besides being means, they are a part of the end. Virtue, according to the utilitarian doctrine, is not naturally and originally part of the end, but it is capable of becoming so; and in those who love it disinterestedly it has become so, and is desired and cherished, not as a means to happiness, but as a part of their happiness.

- We may give what explanation we please of this unwillingness; we may attribute it to pride, a name which is given indiscriminately to some of the most and to some of the least estimable feelings of which is mankind are capable; we may refer it to the love of liberty and personal independence, an appeal to which was with the Stoics one of the most effective means for the inculcation of it; to the love of power, or the love of excitement, both of which do really enter into and contribute to it: but its most appropriate appellation is a sense of dignity, which all humans beings possess in one form or other, and in some, though by no means in exact, proportion to their higher faculties, and which is so essential a part of the happiness of those in whom it is strong, that nothing which conflicts with it could be, otherwise than momentarily, an object of desire to them.

Henry Sidgwick

Sidgwick's book *The Methods of Ethics* has been referred to as the peak or culmination of classical utilitarianism. His main goal in this book is to ground utilitarianism in the principles of *common-sense morality* and thereby dispense with the doubts of his predecessors that these two are at odds with each other. For Sidgwick, ethics is about which actions are objectively right. Our knowledge of right and wrong arises from common-sense morality, which lacks a coherent principle at its core. The task of philosophy in general and ethics in particular is not so much to create new knowledge but to systematize existing knowledge. Sidgwick tries to achieve this by formulating *methods of ethics*, which he defines as rational procedures "for determining right conduct in any particular case". He identifies three methods: intuitionism, which involves various independently valid moral principles to determine what ought to be done, and two forms of *hedonism*, in which rightness only depends on the pleasure and pain following from the action. Hedonism is subdivided into *egoistic hedonism*, which only takes the agent's own well-being into account, and *universal hedonism* or *utilitarianism*, which is concerned with everyone's well-being.

Intuitionism holds that we have intuitive, i.e. non-inferential, knowledge of moral principles, which are self-evident to the knower. The criteria for this type of knowledge include that they are expressed in clear terms, that the different principles are mutually consistent with each other and that there is expert consensus on them. According to Sidgwick, commonsense moral principles fail to pass this test, but there are some more abstract principles that pass it, like that "what is right for me must be right for all persons in precisely similar circumstances" or that "one should be equally concerned with all temporal parts of one's life". The most general principles arrived at this way are all compatible with *utilitarianism*, which is why Sidgwick sees a harmony between *intuitionism* and *utilitarianism*. There are also less general intuitive principles, like the duty to keep one's promises or to be just, but these principles are not universal and there are cases where different duties stand in conflict with each other. Sidgwick suggests that we resolve such conflicts in a utilitarian fashion by considering the consequences of the conflicting actions.

The harmony between intuitionism and utilitarianism is a partial success in Sidgwick's overall project, but he sees full success impossible since egoism, which he considers as equally rational, cannot be reconciled with utilitarianism unless *religious assumptions* are introduced. Such assumptions, for example, the existence of a personal God who rewards and punishes the agent in the afterlife, could reconcile egoism and utilitarianism. But without them, we have to admit a "dualism of practical reason" that constitutes a "fundamental contradiction" in our moral consciousness.

Developments in the 20th Century

Ideal Utilitarianism

The description of ideal utilitarianism was first used by Hastings Rashdall in *The Theory of Good and Evil* (1907), but it is more often associated with G. E. Moore. In *Ethics* (1912), Moore rejects a purely hedonistic utilitarianism and argues that there is a range of values that might be maximized. Moore's strategy was to show that it is intuitively implausible that pleasure is the sole measure of what is good. He says that such an assumption:

- Involves our saying, for instance, that a world in which absolutely nothing except pleasure existed—no knowledge, no love, no enjoyment of beauty, no moral qualities—must yet be intrinsically better—better worth creating—provided only the total quantity of pleasure in it were the least bit greater, than one in which all these things existed as well as pleasure. It involves our saying that, even if the total quantity of pleasure in each was exactly equal, yet the fact that all the beings in the one possessed, in addition knowledge of many different kinds and a full appreciation of all that was beautiful or worthy of love in their world, whereas none of the beings in the other possessed any of these

> things, would give us no reason whatever for preferring the former to the latter.

Moore admits that it is impossible to prove the case either way, but he believed that it was intuitively obvious that even if the amount of pleasure stayed the same a world that contained such things as beauty and love would be a better world. He adds that, if a person was to take the contrary view, then "I think it is self-evident that he would be wrong."

Act and Rule Utilitarianism

In the mid-20th century, a number of philosophers focused on the place of rules in utilitarian thought. It was already considered necessary to use rules to help choose the right action, because estimating the consequences every time seemed error-prone and unlikely to bring the best outcome. Paley had justified the use of rules and Mill says:

- It is truly a whimsical supposition that, if mankind were agreed in considering utility to be the test of morality, they would remain without any agreement as to what is useful, and would take no measures for having their notions on the subject taught to the young, and enforced by law and opinion... to consider the rules of morality as improvable, is one thing; to pass over the intermediate generalisations entirely, and endeavour to test each individual action directly by the first principle, is another.... The proposition that happiness is the end and aim of morality, does not mean that no road ought to be laid down to that goal.... Nobody argues that the art of navigation is not founded on astronomy, because sailors cannot wait to calculate the Nautical Almanack. Being rational creatures, they go to sea with it ready calculated; and all rational creatures go out upon the sea of life with their minds made up on the common questions of right and wrong.

However, rule utilitarianism proposes a more central role for rules that was thought to rescue the theory from some of its more devastating criticisms, particularly problems to do with justice and promise keeping. Smart (1956) and McCloskey (1957) initially use the terms *extreme* and *restricted* utilitarianism but eventually settled on the prefixes *act* and *rule* instead. Likewise, throughout the 1950s and 1960s, articles were published both for and against the new form of utilitarianism, and through this debate the theory we now call *rule utilitarianism* was created. In an introduction to an anthology of these articles, the editor was able to say: "The development of this theory was a dialectical process of formulation, criticism, reply and reformulation; the record of this process well illustrates the co-operative development of a philosophical theory."

The essential difference is in what determines whether or not an action is the right action. *Act utilitarianism* maintains that an action is right if it maximizes utility; *rule utilitarianism* maintains that an action is right if it conforms to a rule that maximizes utility.

In 1956, Urmson published an influential article arguing that Mill justified rules on utilitarian principles. From then on, articles have debated this interpretation of Mill. In all probability, it was not a distinction that Mill was particularly trying to make and so the evidence in his writing is inevitably mixed. A collection of Mill's writing published in 1977 includes a letter that seems to tip the balance in favour of the notion that Mill is best classified as an *act utilitarian*. In the letter, Mill says:

- I agree with you that the right way of testing actions by their consequences, is to test them by the natural consequences of the particular action, and not by those which would follow if everyone did the same. But, for the most part, the consideration of what would happen if everyone did the same, is the only means we have of discovering the tendency of the act in the particular case.

Some school level textbooks and at least one British examination board make a further distinction between strong and weak rule utilitarianism. However, it is not clear that this distinction is made in the academic literature. It has been argued that rule utilitarianism collapses into act utilitarianism, because for any given rule, in the case where breaking the rule produces more utility, the rule can be refined by the addition of a sub-rule that handles cases like the exception. This process holds for all cases of exceptions, and so the "rules" have as many "sub-rules" as there are exceptional cases, which, in the end, makes an agent seek out whatever outcome produces the maximum utility.

Two-Level Utilitarianism

In *Principles* (1973), R. M. Hare accepts that rule utilitarianism collapses into act utilitarianism but claims that this is a result of allowing the rules to be "as specific and un-general as we please." He argues that one of the main reasons for introducing rule utilitarianism was to do justice to the general rules that people need for moral education and character development and he proposes that "a difference between act-utilitarianism and rule-utilitarianism can be introduced by limiting the specificity of the rules, i.e., by increasing their generality." This distinction between a "specific rule utilitarianism" (which collapses into act utilitarianism) and "general rule utilitarianism" forms the basis of Hare's *two-level utilitarianism.*

When we are "playing God or the ideal observer", we use the specific form, and we will need to do this when we are deciding what general principles to teach and follow. When we are "inculcating" or in situations where the biases of our human nature are likely to prevent us doing the calculations properly, then we should use the more general rule utilitarianism.

Hare argues that in practice, most of the time, we should be following the general principles:

- One ought to abide by the general principles whose general inculcation is for the best; harm is more likely to come, in actual moral situations, from questioning these rules than from sticking to them, unless the situations are very extra-ordinary; the results of sophisticated felicific calculations are not likely, human nature and human ignorance being what they are, to lead to the greatest utility.

In *Moral Thinking*, Hare illustrated the two extremes. The "archangel" is the hypothetical person who has perfect knowledge of the situation and no personal biases or weaknesses and always uses critical moral thinking to decide the right thing to do.

In contrast, the "prole" is the hypothetical person who is completely incapable of critical thinking and uses nothing but intuitive moral thinking and, of necessity, has to follow the general moral rules they have been taught or learned through imitation. It is not that some people are archangels and others proles, but rather that "we all share the characteristics of both to limited and varying degrees and at different times."

Hare does not specify when we should think more like an "archangel" and more like a "prole" as this will, in any case, vary from person to person. However, the critical moral thinking underpins and informs the more intuitive moral thinking. It is responsible for formulating and, if necessary, reformulating the general moral rules. We also switch to critical thinking when trying to deal with unusual situations or in cases where the intuitive moral rules give conflicting advice.

Preference Utilitarianism

Preference utilitarianism entails promoting actions that fulfil the preferences of those beings involved. The concept of preference utilitarianism was first proposed in 1977 by John Harsanyi in *Morality and the Theory of Rational Behaviour*, however the concept is more commonly associated with R. M. Hare, Peter Singer, and Richard Brandt.

Harsanyi claims that his theory is indebted to:

- Adam Smith, who equated the moral point of view with that of an impartial but sympathetic observer;
- Immanuel Kant, who insisted on the criterion of universality, which may also be described as a criterion of reciprocity;

- The classical utilitarians who made maximizing social utility the basic criterion of morality; and
- "The modern theory of rational behaviour under risk and uncertainty, usually described as Bayesian decision theory."

Harsanyi rejects hedonistic utilitarianism as being dependent on an outdated psychology saying that it is far from obvious that everything we do is motivated by a desire to maximize pleasure and minimize pain. He also rejects ideal utilitarianism because "it is certainly not true as an empirical observation that people's only purpose in life is to have 'mental states of intrinsic worth'."

According to Harsanyi, "preference utilitarianism is the only form of utilitarianism consistent with the important philosophical principle of preference autonomy. By this I mean the principle that, in deciding what is good and what is bad for a given individual, the ultimate criterion can only be his own wants and his own preferences."

Harsanyi adds two caveats. Firstly, people sometimes have irrational preferences. To deal with this, Harsanyi distinguishes between "manifest" preferences and "true" preferences. The former are those "manifested by his observed behaviour, including preferences possibly based on erroneous factual beliefs, or on careless logical analysis, or on strong emotions that at the moment greatly hinder rational choice"; whereas the latter are "the preferences he would have if he had all the relevant factual information, always reasoned with the greatest possible care, and were in a state of mind most conducive to rational choice." It is the latter that preference utilitarianism tries to satisfy.

The second caveat is that antisocial preferences, such as sadism, envy, and resentment, have to be excluded. Harsanyi achieves this by claiming that such preferences partially exclude those people from the moral community:

- Utilitarian ethics makes all of us members of the same moral community. A person displaying ill will toward others does remain a member of this community, but not with his whole personality. That part of his personality that harbours these hostile antisocial feelings must be excluded from membership, and has no claim for a hearing when it comes to defining our concept of social utility.

Negative Utilitarianism

In *The Open Society and its Enemies* (1945), Karl Popper argues that the principle "maximize pleasure" should be replaced by "minimize pain". He believes that "it is not only impossible but very dangerous to attempt to maximize the pleasure or the happiness of the people, since such an attempt must lead to totalitarianism." He claims that:

- There is, from the ethical point of view, no symmetry between suffering and happiness, or between pain and pleasure... In my opinion human suffering makes a direct moral appeal, namely, the appeal for help, while there is no similar call to increase the happiness of a man who is doing well anyway. A further criticism of the Utilitarian formula "Maximize pleasure" is that it assumes a continuous pleasure-pain scale that lets us treat degrees of pain as negative degrees of pleasure. But, from the moral point of view, pain cannot be outweighed by pleasure, and especially not one man's pain by another man's pleasure. Instead of the greatest happiness for the greatest number, one should demand, more modestly, the least amount of avoidable suffering for all...

The actual term *negative utilitarianism* itself was introduced by R. N. Smart as the title to his 1958 reply to Popper in which he argues that the principle would entail seeking the quickest and least painful method of killing the entirety of humanity.

In response to Smart's argument, Simon Knutsson has argued that classical utilitarianism and similar consequentialist views are roughly equally likely to entail killing the entirety of humanity, as they would seem to imply that one should kill existing beings and replace them with happier beings if possible. Consequently, Knutsson argues:

- The world destruction argument is not a reason to reject negative utilitarianism in favour of these other forms of consequentialism, because there are similar arguments against such theories that are at least as persuasive as the world destruction argument is against negative utilitarianism.

Furthermore, Knutsson notes that one could argue that other forms of consequentialism, such as classical utilitarianism, in some cases have less plausible implications than negative utilitarianism, such as in scenarios where classical utilitarianism implies it would be right to kill everyone and replace them in a manner that creates more suffering, but also more well-being such that the sum, on the classical utilitarian calculus, is net positive. Negative utilitarianism, in contrast, would not allow such killing.

Some versions of negative utilitarianism include:

- **Negative Total Utilitarianism:** Tolerates suffering that can be compensated within the same person.
- **Negative Preference Utilitarianism:** Avoids the problem of moral killing with reference to existing preferences that such killing would violate, while it still demands a justification for the creation of new

lives. A possible justification is the reduction of the average level of preference-frustration.

- Pessimistic Representatives of negative utilitarianism, which can be found in the environment of Buddhism.

Some see negative utilitarianism as a branch within modern hedonistic utilitarianism, which assigns a higher weight to the avoidance of suffering than to the promotion of happiness. The moral weight of suffering can be increased by using a "compassionate" utilitarian metric, so that the result is the same as in prioritarianism.

Motive Utilitarianism

Motive utilitarianism was first proposed by Robert Merrihew Adams in 1976. Whereas act utilitarianism requires us to choose our actions by calculating which action will maximize utility and rule utilitarianism requires us to implement rules that will, on the whole, maximize utility, *motive utilitarianism* "has the utility calculus being used to select motives and dispositions according to their general felicific effects, and those motives and dispositions then dictate our choices of actions."

The arguments for moving to some form of motive utilitarianism at the personal level can be seen as mirroring the arguments for moving to some form of rule utilitarianism at the social level. Adams (1976) refers to Sidgwick's observation that "Happiness (general as well as individual) is likely to be better attained if the extent to which we set ourselves consciously to aim at it be carefully restricted." Trying to apply the utility calculation on each and every occasion is likely to lead to a sub-optimal outcome.

It is argued that applying carefully selected rules at the social level and encouraging appropriate motives at the personal level are likely to lead to better overall outcomes; even though on some individual occasions it leads to the wrong action when assessed according to act utilitarian standards.

Adams concludes that "right action, by act-utilitarian standards, and right motivation, by motive-utilitarian standards, are incompatible in some cases." The necessity of this conclusion is rejected by Fred Feldman who argues that "the conflict in question results from an inadequate formulation of the utilitarian doctrines; motives play no essential role in it ... [and that] ... [p]recisely the same sort of conflict arises even when MU is left out of consideration and AU is applied by itself." Instead, Feldman proposes a variant of act utilitarianism that results in there being no conflict between it and motive utilitarianism.

Criticisms and Responses

Because utilitarianism is not a single theory, but rather a cluster of related theories that have been developed over two hundred years, criticisms can be made for different reasons and have different targets.

Quantifying Utility

A common objection to utilitarianism is the inability to quantify, compare, or measure happiness or well-being. Rachael Briggs writes in the *Stanford Encyclopedia of Philosophy*:

- One objection to this interpretation of utility is that there may not be a single good (or indeed any good) which rationality requires us to seek. But if we understand "utility" broadly enough to include all potentially desirable ends—pleasure, knowledge, friendship, health and so on—it's not clear that there is a unique correct way to make the tradeoffs between different goods so that each outcome receives a utility. There may be no good answer to the question of whether the life of an ascetic monk contains more or less good than the life of a happy libertine—but assigning utilities to these options forces us to compare them.

Utility Ignores Justice

As Rosen (2003) has pointed out, claiming that act utilitarians are not concerned about having rules is to set up a "straw man". Similarly, R.M. Hare refers to "the crude caricature of act utilitarianism which is the only version of it that many philosophers seem to be acquainted with." Given what Bentham says about second order evils, it would be a serious misrepresentation to say that he and similar act utilitarians would be prepared to punish an innocent person for the greater good. Nevertheless, whether they would agree or not, this is what critics of utilitarianism claim is entailed by the theory.

Sheriff Scenario

A classic version of this criticism was given by H. J. McCloskey in his 1957 "sheriff scenario":

- Suppose that a sheriff were faced with the choice either of framing a Negro for a rape that had aroused hostility to the Negroes (a particular Negro generally being believed to be guilty but whom the sheriff knows not to be guilty)—and thus preventing serious anti-Negro riots which would probably lead to some loss of life and increased hatred of each other by whites and Negroes—or of hunting for the guilty person and thereby allowing the anti-Negro riots to occur, while doing the best he can to combat them. In such a case the sheriff, if he were an extreme utilitarian, would appear to be committed to framing the Negro.

By "extreme" utilitarian, McCloskey is referring to what later came to be called act utilitarianism. He suggests one response might be that the sheriff would not frame the innocent negro because of another rule: "do not punish an innocent person". Another response might be that the riots the sheriff is trying to avoid might have positive utility in the long run by drawing attention to questions of race and resources to help address tensions between the communities. In a later article, McCloskey says:

- Surely the utilitarian must admit that whatever the facts of the matter may be, it is logically possible that an 'unjust' system of punishment—e.g. a system involving collective punishments, retroactive laws and punishments, or punishments of parents and relations of the offender—may be more useful than a 'just' system of punishment?

The Brothers Karamazov

An older form of this argument was presented by Fyodor Dostoyevsky in his book *The Brothers Karamazov*, in which Ivan challenges his brother Alyosha to answer his question:

- Tell me straight out, I call on you—answer me: imagine that you yourself are building the edifice of human destiny with the object of making people happy in the finale, of giving them peace and rest at last, but for that you must inevitably and unavoidably torture just one tiny creature, [one child], and raise your edifice on the foundation of her unrequited tears—would you agree to be the architect on such conditions? ... And can you admit the idea that the people for whom you are building would agree to accept their happiness on the unjustified blood of a tortured child, and having accepted it, to remain forever happy?

This scenario was illustrated in more depth in 1973 by Ursula K. Le Guin in the celebrated short story *The Ones Who Walk Away from Omelas.*

Predicting Consequences

Some argue that it is impossible to do the calculation that utilitarianism requires because consequences are inherently unknowable. Daniel Dennett describes this as the "Three Mile Island effect". Dennett points out that not only is it impossible to assign a precise utility value to the incident, it is impossible to know whether, ultimately, the near-meltdown that occurred was a good or bad thing. He suggests that it would have been a good thing if plant operators learned lessons that prevented future serious incidents.

Russell Hardin (1990) rejects such arguments. He argues that it is possible to distinguish the moral impulse of utilitarianism (which is "to define the right as good consequences and to motivate people to achieve these") from our ability to correctly apply rational principles that, among other things, "depend on the perceived facts of the case and on the particular moral actor's mental equipment."

The fact that the latter is limited and can change does not mean that the former has to be rejected. "If we develop a better system for determining relevant causal relations so that we are able to choose actions that better produce our intended ends, it does not follow that we then must change our ethics. The moral impulse of utilitarianism is constant, but our decisions under it are contingent on our knowledge and scientific understanding."

From the beginning, utilitarianism has recognized that certainty in such matters is unobtainable and both Bentham and Mill said that it was necessary to rely on the *tendencies* of actions to bring about consequences. G. E. Moore, writing in 1903, said:

- We certainly cannot hope directly to compare their effects except within a limited future; and all the arguments, which have ever been used in Ethics, and upon which we commonly act in common life, directed to shewing that one course is superior to another, are (apart from theological dogmas) confined to pointing out such probable immediate advantages ... An ethical law has the nature not of a scientific law but of a scientific *prediction*: and the latter is always merely probable, although the probability may be very great.

Demandingness Objection

Act utilitarianism not only requires everyone to do what they can to maximize utility, but to do so without any favouritism. Mill said, "As between his own happiness and that of others, utilitarianism requires him to be as strictly impartial as a disinterested and benevolent spectator." Critics say that this combination of requirements leads to utilitarianism making unreasonable demands. The well-being of strangers counts just as much as that of friends, family or self. "What makes this requirement so demanding is the gargantuan number of strangers in great need of help and the indefinitely many opportunities to make sacrifices to help them." As Shelly Kagan says, "Given the parameters of the actual world, there is no question that ... (maximally) ... promoting the good would require a life of hardship, self-denial, and austerity ... a life spent promoting the good would be a severe one indeed."

Hooker (2002) describes two aspects to the problem: act utilitarianism requires *huge* sacrifices from those who are relatively better off and also requires sacrifice of your own good even when the aggregate good will be only *slightly* increased. Another way of highlighting the complaint is to say that in utilitarianism, "there is no such thing as morally permissible self-sacrifice that goes above and beyond the call of duty." Mill was quite clear about this, "A sacrifice which does not increase, or tend to increase, the sum total of happiness, it considers as wasted."

One response to the problem is to accept its demands. This is the view taken by Peter Singer, who says:

- No doubt we do instinctively prefer to help those who are close to us. Few could stand by and watch a child drown; many can ignore the avoidable deaths of children in Africa or India. The question, however, is not what we usually do, but what we ought to do, and it is difficult to see any sound moral justification for the view that distance, or community membership, makes a crucial difference to our obligations.

Others argue that a moral theory that is so contrary to our deeply held moral convictions must either be rejected or modified. There have been various attempts to modify utilitarianism to escape its seemingly over-demanding requirements. One approach is to drop the demand that utility be maximized. In *Satisficing Consequentialism*, Michael Slote argues for a form of utilitarianism where "an act might qualify as morally right through having good enough consequences, even though better consequences could have been produced." One advantage of such a system is that it would be able to accommodate the notion of supererogatory actions.

Samuel Scheffler takes a different approach and amends the requirement that everyone be treated the same. In particular, Scheffler suggests that there is an "agent-centered prerogative" such that when the overall utility is being calculated it is permitted to count our own interests more heavily than the interests of others. Kagan suggests that such a procedure might be justified on the grounds that "a general requirement to promote the good would lack the motivational underpinning necessary for genuine moral requirements" and, secondly, that personal independence is necessary for the existence of commitments and close personal relations and that "the value of such commitments yields a positive reason for preserving within moral theory at least some moral independence for the personal point of view."

Robert Goodin takes yet another approach and argues that the demandingness objection can be "blunted" by treating utilitarianism as a guide to public policy rather than one of individual morality. He suggests that many of the problems arise under the traditional formulation because the conscientious utilitarian ends up having to make up for the failings of others and so contributing more than their fair share.

Gandjour specifically considers market situations and analyses whether individuals who act in markets may produce a utilitarian optimum. He lists several demanding conditions that need to be satisfied: individuals need to display instrumental rationality, markets need to be perfectly competitive, and income and goods need to be redistributed.

Harsanyi argues that the objection overlooks the fact that "people attach considerable utility to freedom from unduly burdensome moral obligations ... most people will prefer a society with a more relaxed moral code, and will feel that such a society will achieve a higher level of average utility—even if adoption of such a moral code should lead to some losses in economic and cultural accomplishments (so long as these losses remain within tolerable limits). This means that utilitarianism, if correctly interpreted, will yield a moral code with a standard of acceptable conduct very much below the level of highest moral perfection, leaving plenty of scope for supererogatory actions exceeding this minimum standard."

Aggregating Utility

The objection that "utilitarianism does not take seriously the distinction between persons" came to prominence in 1971 with the publication of John Rawls' *A Theory of Justice*. The concept is also important in animal rights advocate Richard Ryder's rejection of utilitarianism, in which he talks of the "boundary of the individual", through which neither pain nor pleasure may pass.

However, a similar objection was noted in 1970 by Thomas Nagel, who claimed that consequentialism "treats the desires, needs, satisfactions, and dissatisfactions of distinct persons as if they were the desires, etc., of a mass person;" and even earlier by David Gauthier, who wrote that utilitarianism supposes that "mankind is a super-person, whose greatest satisfaction is the objective of moral action. ... But this is absurd.

Individuals have wants, not mankind; individuals seek satisfaction, not mankind. A person's satisfaction is not part of any greater satisfaction." Thus, the aggregation of utility becomes futile as both pain and happiness are intrinsic to and inseparable from the consciousness in which they are felt, rendering impossible the task of adding up the various pleasures of multiple individuals.

A response to this criticism is to point out that whilst seeming to resolve some problems it introduces others. Intuitively, there are many cases where people do want to take the numbers involved into account. As Alastair Norcross has said:

- [S]uppose that Homer is faced with the painful choice between saving Barney from a burning building or saving both Moe and Apu from the building ... it is clearly better for Homer to save the larger number, precisely because it is a larger number. ... Can anyone who really considers the matter seriously honestly claim to believe that it is worse that one person die than that the entire sentient population of the universe be severely mutilated? Clearly not.

It may be possible to uphold the distinction between persons whilst still aggregating utility, if it accepted that people can be influenced by empathy. This position is advocated by Iain King, who has suggested the evolutionary basis of empathy means humans can take into account the interests of other individuals, but only on a one-to-one basis, "since we can only imagine ourselves in the mind of one other person at a time." King uses this insight to adapt utilitarianism, and it may help reconcile Bentham's philosophy with deontology and virtue ethics.

Philosopher John Taurek also argued that the idea of adding happiness or pleasures across persons is quite unintelligible and that the numbers of persons involved in a situation are morally irrelevant. Taurek's basic concern comes down to this: we cannot explain what it means to say that things would be five times worse if five people die than if one person dies. "I cannot give a satisfactory account of the meaning of judgments of this kind," he wrote. He argues that each person can only lose one person's happiness or pleasures. There is not five times more loss of happiness or pleasure when five die: who would be feeling this happiness or pleasure? "Each person's potential loss has the same significance to me, only as a loss to that person alone. because, by hypothesis, I have an equal concern for each person involved, I am moved to give each of them an equal chance to be spared his loss" (p. 307). Derek Parfit (1978) and others have criticized Taurek's line, and it continues to be discussed.

Calculating Utility is Self-Defeating

An early criticism, which was addressed by Mill, is that if time is taken to calculate the best course of action it is likely that the opportunity to take the best course of action will already have passed. Mill responded that there had been ample time to calculate the likely effects:

- [N]amely, the whole past duration of the human species. During all that time, mankind have been learning by experience the tendencies of actions; on which experience all the prudence, as well as all the morality of life, are dependent...It is a strange notion that the acknowledgment of a first principle is inconsistent with the admission of secondary ones. To inform a traveller respecting the place of his ultimate destination, is not to forbid the use of landmarks and direction-posts on the way. The proposition that happiness is the end and aim of morality, does not mean that no road ought to be laid down to that goal, or that persons going thither should not be advised to take one direction rather than another. Men really ought to leave off talking a kind of nonsense on this subject, which they would neither talk nor listen to on other matters of practical concernment.

More recently, Hardin has made the same point. "It should embarrass philosophers that they have ever taken this objection seriously. Parallel considerations in other realms are dismissed with eminently good sense. Lord Devlin notes, 'if the reasonable man "worked to rule" by perusing to the point of comprehension every form he was handed, the commercial and administrative life of the country would creep to a standstill.' It is such considerations that lead even act utilitarians to rely on "rules of thumb", as Smart has called them.

Special Obligations Criticism

One of the oldest criticisms of utilitarianism is that it ignores our special obligations. For example, if we were given the choice between saving two random people or our mother, most would choose to save their mothers. According to utilitarianism, such a natural action is immoral. The first to respond to this was an early utilitarian and friend of Jeremy Bentham named William Godwin, who held in his work *Enquiry Concerning Political Justice* that such personal needs should be disregarded in favour of the greatest good for the greatest number of people. Applying the utilitarian principle "that life ought to be preferred which will be most conducive to the general good" to the choice of saving one of two people, either "the illustrious Archbishop of Cambray" or his chambermaid, he wrote:

- Supposing the chambermaid had been my wife, my mother or my benefactor. That would not alter the truth of the proposition. The life of [the Archbishop] would still be more valuable than that of the chambermaid; and justice, pure, unadulterated justice, would still have preferred that which was most valuable.

Criticisms of Utilitarian Value Theory

Utilitarianism's assertion that well-being is the only thing with intrinsic moral value has been attacked by various critics. Thomas Carlyle derided "Benthamee Utility, virtue by Profit and Loss; reducing this God's-world to a dead brute Steam-engine, the infinite celestial Soul of Man to a kind of Hay-balance for weighing hay and thistles on, pleasures and pains on". Karl Marx, in *Das Kapital*, criticises Bentham's utilitarianism on the grounds that it does not appear to recognise that people have different joys in different socioeconomic contexts:

- With the driest naivete he takes the modern shopkeeper, especially the English shopkeeper, as the normal man. Whatever is useful to this queer normal man, and to his world, is absolutely useful. This yard-measure, then, he applies to past, present, and future. The Christian religion, e.g., is "useful," "because it forbids in the name of religion the same faults that the penal code condemns in the name of the law." Artistic criticism is "harmful," because it disturbs worthy people in their enjoyment of Martin Tupper, etc. With such rubbish has the brave fellow, with his motto, "nulla dies sine linea [no day without a line]", piled up mountains of books.

Pope John Paul II, following his personalist philosophy, argued that a danger of utilitarianism is that it tends to make persons, just as much as things, the object of use. "Utilitarianism", he wrote, "is a civilization of production and of use, a civilization of things and not of persons, a civilization in which persons are used in the same way as things are used."

Duty-Based Criticisms

W. D. Ross, speaking from the perspective of his deontological pluralism, acknowledges that there is a duty to promote the maximum of aggregate good, as utilitarianism demands. But, Ross contends, this is just one besides various other duties, like the duty to keep one's promises or to make amends for wrongful acts, which are ignored by the simplistic and reductive utilitarian outlook.

Roger Scruton was a deontologist, and believed that utilitarianism did not give duty the place that it needed inside our ethical judgements. He asked us to consider the dilemma of Anna Karenina, who had to choose between her love of Vronsky and her duty towards her husband and her son. Scruton wrote, "Suppose Anna were to reason that it is better to satisfy two healthy young people and frustrate one old one than to satisfy one old person and frustrate two young ones, by a factor of 2.5 to 1: ergo I am leaving. What would we think, then, of her moral seriousness?"

Baby Farming

In *Innocence and Consequentialism* (1996), Jacqueline Laing, a critic of utilitarianism, argues that utilitarianism has insufficient conceptual apparatus to comprehend the very idea of innocence, a feature central to any comprehensive ethical theory. In particular, Peter Singer on her view, cannot without contradicting himself reject baby farming (a thought experiment that involves mass-producing deliberately brain-damaged children for live birth for the greater good of organ harvesting) and at the same time hold on to his "personism" a term coined by Jenny Teichman to describe his fluctuating (and Laing says, irrational and discriminatory) theory of human moral value. His explanation that baby farming undermines attitudes of care and concern for the very young, can be applied to babies and the unborn (both 'non-persons' who may be killed, on his view) and contradicts positions that he adopts elsewhere in his work.

Additional Considerations

Average versus Total Happiness

In *The Methods of Ethics*, Henry Sidgwick asked, "Is it total or average happiness that we seek to make a maximum?" Paley notes that, although he speaks of the happiness of communities, "the happiness of a people is made up of the happiness of single persons; and the quantity of happiness can only be augmented by increasing the number of the percipients, or the pleasure of their perceptions" and that if extreme cases, such as people held as slaves, are excluded the amount of happiness will usually be in proportion to the number of people. Consequently, "the decay of population is the greatest evil that a state can suffer; and the improvement of it the object which ought, in all countries, to be aimed at in preference to every other political purpose whatsoever." A similar view was expressed by Smart, who argued that, all other things being equal, a universe with two million happy people is better than a universe with only one million happy people.

Since Sidgwick raised the question it has been studied in detail and philosophers have argued that using either total or average happiness can lead to objectionable results. According to Derek Parfit, using total happiness falls victim to the repugnant conclusion, whereby large numbers of people with very low but non-negative utility values can be seen as a better goal than a population of a less extreme size living in comfort. In other words, according to the theory, it is a moral good to breed more people on the world for as long as total happiness rises.

On the other hand, measuring the utility of a population based on the average utility of that population avoids Parfit's repugnant conclusion but causes other problems. For example, bringing a moderately happy person into a very happy world would be seen as an immoral act; aside from this, the theory implies that it would be a moral good to eliminate all people whose happiness is below average, as this would raise the average happiness.

William Shaw suggests that the problem can be avoided if a distinction is made between potential people, who need not concern us, and actual future people, who should concern us. He says, "utilitarianism values the happiness of people, not the production of units of happiness. Accordingly, one has no positive obligation to have children. However, if you have decided to have a child, then you have an obligation to give birth to the happiest child you can."

Motives, Intentions, and Actions

Utilitarianism is typically taken to assess the rightness or wrongness of an action by considering just the consequences of that action. Bentham very carefully distinguishes motive from intention and says that motives are not in themselves good or bad but can be referred to as such on account of their tendency to produce pleasure or pain. He adds that, "from every kind of motive, may proceed actions that are good, others that are bad, and others that are indifferent." Mill makes a similar point and explicitly says that "motive has nothing to do with the morality of the action, though much with the worth of the agent. He who saves a fellow creature from drowning does what is morally right, whether his motive be duty, or the hope of being paid for his trouble."

However, with intention the situation is more complex. In a footnote printed in the second edition of *Utilitarianism*, Mill says: "the morality of the action depends entirely upon the intention—that is, upon what the agent wills to do." Elsewhere, he says, "Intention, and motive, are two very different things. But it is the intention, that is, the foresight of consequences, which constitutes the moral rightness or wrongness of the act."

The correct interpretation of Mill's footnote is a matter of some debate. The difficulty in interpretation centres around trying to explain why, since it is consequences that matter, intentions should play a role in the assessment of the morality of an action but motives should not. One possibility "involves supposing that the 'morality' of the act is one thing, probably to do with the praiseworthiness or blameworthiness of the agent, and its rightness or wrongness another." Jonathan Dancy rejects this interpretation on the grounds that Mill is explicitly making intention relevant to an assessment of the act not to an assessment of the agent.

An interpretation given by Roger Crisp draws on a definition given by Mill in *A System of Logic*, where he says that an "intention to produce the effect, is one thing; the effect produced in consequence of the intention, is another thing; the two together constitute the action." Accordingly, whilst two actions may outwardly appear to be the same they will be different actions if there is a different intention. Dancy notes that this does not explain why intentions count but motives do not.

A third interpretation is that an action might be considered a complex action consisting of several stages and it is the intention that determines which of these stages are to be considered part of the action. Although this is the interpretation favoured by Dancy, he recognizes that this might not have been Mill's own view, for Mill "would not even allow that 'p & q' expresses a complex proposition. He wrote in his *System of Logic* I iv. 3, of 'Caesar is dead and Brutus is alive', that 'we might as well call a street a complex house, as these two propositions a complex proposition'."

Finally, whilst motives may not play a role in determining the morality of an action, this does not preclude utilitarians from fostering particular motives if doing so will increase overall happiness.

Other Sentient Beings

In *An Introduction to the Principles of Morals and Legislation*, Bentham wrote "the question is not, Can they reason? nor, Can they talk? but, Can they suffer?" Mill's distinction between higher and lower pleasures might suggest that he gave more status to humans. However, in his essay "Whewell on Moral Philosophy", Mill defends Bentham's position, calling it a 'noble anticipation', and writing: "Granted that any practice causes more pain to animals than it gives pleasure to man; is that practice moral or immoral? And if, exactly in proportion as human beings raise their heads out of the slough of selfishness, they do not with one voice answer 'immoral', let the morality of the principle of utility be for ever condemned."

Henry Sidgwick also considers the implications of utilitarianism for nonhuman animals. He writes: “We have next to consider who the ‘all’ are, whose happiness is to be taken into account. Are we to extend our concern to all the beings capable of pleasure and pain whose feelings are affected by our conduct? or are we to confine our view to human happiness? The former view is the one adopted by Bentham and Mill, and (I believe) by the Utilitarian school generally: and is obviously most in accordance with the universality that is characteristic of their principle ... it seems arbitrary and unreasonable to exclude from the end, as so conceived, any pleasure of any sentient being.”

Among contemporary utilitarian philosophers, Peter Singer is especially known for arguing that the well-being of all sentient beings ought to be given equal consideration. Singer suggests that rights are conferred according to the level of a creature’s self-awareness, regardless of their species. He adds that humans tend to be speciesist (discriminatory against non-humans) in ethical matters, and argues that, in utilitarianism, speciesism cannot be justified as there is no rational distinction that can be made between the suffering of humans and the suffering of nonhuman animals; all suffering ought to be reduced. Singer writes: “The racist violates the principle of equality by giving greater weight to the interests of members of his own race, when there is a clash between their interests and the interests of those of another race. Similarly the speciesist allows the interests of his own species to override the greater interests of members of other species. The pattern is the same in each case ... Most human beings are speciesists.”

In his 1990 edition of *Animal Liberation*, Peter Singer said that he no longer ate oysters and mussels, because although the creatures might not suffer, there was a possibility they may and it was easy to avoid eating them in any case.

This view still might be contrasted with deep ecology, which holds that an intrinsic value is attached to all forms of life and nature, whether currently assumed to be sentient or not. According to utilitarianism, the forms of life that are unable to experience anything akin to either enjoyment or discomfort are denied moral status, because it is impossible to increase the happiness or reduce the suffering of something that cannot feel happiness or suffer. Singer writes:

- The capacity for suffering and enjoying things is a prerequisite for having interests at all, a condition that must be satisfied before we can speak of interests in any meaningful way. It would be nonsense to say that it was not in the interests of a stone to be kicked along the road by a schoolboy. A stone does not have interests because it cannot suffer. Nothing that we can do to it could possibly make any difference to its welfare. A mouse, on the other hand, does have an interest in not being tormented, because it will suffer if it is. If a being suffers, there

> can be no moral justification for refusing to take that suffering into consideration. No matter what the nature of the being, the principle of equality requires that its suffering be counted equally with the like suffering—in so far as rough comparisons can be made—of any other being. If a being is not capable of suffering, or of experiencing enjoyment or happiness, there is nothing to be taken into account.

Thus, the moral value of one-celled organisms, as well as some multi-cellular organisms, and natural entities like a river, is only in the benefit they provide to sentient beings. Similarly, utilitarianism places no direct intrinsic value on biodiversity, although the benefits that biodiversity brings to sentient beings may mean that, in utilitarianism, biodiversity ought to be maintained in general.

In John Stuart Mill's essay "On Nature" he argues that the welfare of wild animals is to be considered when making utilitarian judgments. Tyler Cowen argues that, if individual animals are carriers of utility, then we should consider limiting the predatory activity of carnivores relative to their victims: "At the very least, we should limit current subsidies to nature's carnivores."

Digital Minds

Nick Bostrom and Carl Shulman consider that, as advancements in artificial intelligence continue, it will probably be possible to engineer digital minds that require less resources and have a much higher rate and intensity of subjective experience than humans. These "super-beneficiaries" could also be unaffected by hedonic adaptation. Nick Bostrom said that we should find "paths that will enable digital minds and biological minds to coexist, in a mutually beneficial way where all of these different forms can flourish and thrive".

Application to Specific Problems

The concept has been applied towards social welfare economics, questions of justice, the crisis of global poverty, the ethics of raising animals for food, and the importance of avoiding existential risks to humanity. In the context of lying, some utilitarians support white lies.

World Poverty

An article in the *American Economic Journal* has addressed the issue of Utilitarian ethics within redistribution of wealth. The journal stated that taxation of the wealthy is the best way to make use of the disposable income they receive. This says that the money creates utility for the most people by funding government services. Many utilitarian philosophers, including Peter Singer and Toby Ord, argue that inhabitants of developed countries in particular have an obligation to help to end extreme poverty across the world, for example by regularly donating some of their income to charity. Peter Singer, for example, argues that donating some of one's income to charity could help to save a life or cure somebody from a poverty-related illness, which is a much better use of the money as it brings someone in extreme poverty far more happiness than it would bring to oneself if one lived in relative comfort. However, Singer not only argues that one ought to donate a significant proportion of one's income to charity, but also that this money should be directed to the most cost-effective charities, in order to bring about the greatest good for the greatest number, consistent with utilitarian thinking. Singer's ideas have formed the basis of the modern effective altruism movement.

Social Choice

In social choice and operations research, the utilitarian rule (also called the max-sum rule) is a rule saying that, among all possible alternatives, society should pick the alternative which maximizes the *sum of the utilities* of all individuals in society. It is a formal mathematical representation of the utilitarian philosophy, and is often justified by reference to Harsanyi's utilitarian theorem or the Von Neumann–Morgenstern theorem. In the context of voting systems, the rule is called score voting.

Score Voting

Score voting, sometimes called range voting, is an electoral system for single-seat elections. Voters give each candidate a numerical score, and the candidate with the highest average score is elected. Score voting includes the well-known approval voting (used in approval ratings), but also lets voters give partial (in-between) approval ratings to candidates.

Criminal Justice

According to the utilitarian, justice is the maximization of the total or average welfare across all relevant individuals. Utilitarianism fights crime in three ways:

- **Deterrence:** The credible threat of punishment might lead people to make different choices; well-designed threats might lead people to make choices that maximize welfare. This matches some strong intuitions about just punishment: that it should generally be proportional to the crime. Successful deterrence would reduce crime statistics.
- **Rehabilitation:** Punishment might make "bad people" into "better" ones. For the utilitarian, all that "bad person" can mean is "person who's likely to cause unwanted things (like suffering)". So, utilitarianism could recommend punishment that changes someone such that they are less likely to cause bad things. Successful rehabilitation would reduce recidivism.
- **Security/Incapacitation:** Perhaps there are people who are irredeemable causers of bad things. If so, imprisoning them might

maximize welfare by limiting their opportunities to cause harm and therefore the benefit lies within protecting society.

So, the reason for punishment is the maximization of welfare, and punishment should be of whomever, and of whatever form and severity, are needed to meet that goal. This may sometimes justify punishing the innocent, or inflicting disproportionately severe punishments, when that will have the best consequences overall (perhaps executing a few suspected shoplifters live on television would be an effective deterrent to shoplifting, for instance). It also suggests that punishment might turn out *never* to be right, depending on the facts about what actual consequences it has.

3.1.3 Virtue Ethics

Virtue ethics is an approach that treats virtue and character as the primary subjects of ethics, in contrast to other ethical systems that put consequences of voluntary acts, principles or rules of conduct, or obedience to divine authority in the primary role. Virtue ethics is usually contrasted with two other major approaches in ethics, consequentialism and deontology, which make the goodness of outcomes of an action (consequentialism) and the concept of moral duty (deontology) central. While virtue ethics does not necessarily deny the importance to ethics of goodness of states of affairs or of moral duties, it emphasizes virtue, and sometimes other concepts, like *eudaimonia*, to an extent that other ethics theories do not.

Virtue and Vice

In virtue ethics, a virtue is a characteristic disposition to think, feel, and act well in some domain of life. In contrast, a vice is a characteristic disposition to think, feel, and act poorly. Virtues are not everyday habits; they are character traits, in the sense that they are central to someone's personality and what they are like as a person.

In early versions and some modern versions of virtue ethics, a virtue is defined as a character trait that promotes or exhibits human excellence ("flourishing and wellbeing", *eudaimonia*) in the person who exhibits it. Some modern versions of virtue ethics do not define virtues in terms of human excellence or flourishing, and some go so far as to define virtues as traits that tend to promote some other good that is defined independently of the virtues, thereby subsuming virtue ethics under (or somehow merging it with) consequentialist ethics.

To Aristotle, a virtue was not a skill that made you better able to achieve *eudaimonia* but was itself an expression of *eudaimonia—eudaimonia* in activity.

In contrast with consequentialist and deontological ethical systems, in which one may be called upon to do the right thing even though it is not in one's own interests (one is to do it instead for the greater good, or out of duty), in virtue ethics, one does the right thing because it is in one's own interests. Part of training in practical virtue ethics is to come to see the coincidence of one's enlightened self-interest and the practice of the virtues, so that one is virtuous willingly, gladly, and enthusiastically because one knows that being virtuous is the best thing one can do with oneself.

Virtue and Emotion

In ancient Greek and modern eudaimonic virtue ethics, virtues and vices are complex dispositions that involve both affective and intellectual components. That is, they are dispositions that involve both being able to reason well about the right thing to do and also to engage emotions and feelings correctly.

For example, a generous person can reason well about when and how to help people, and such a person also helps people with pleasure and without conflict. In this, virtuous people are contrasted not only with vicious people (who reason poorly about what to do and are emotionally attached to the wrong things) and with the incontinent (who are tempted by their feelings into doing the wrong thing even though they know what is right), but also with the merely continent (whose emotions tempt them toward doing the wrong thing but whose strength of will lets them do what they know is right).

According to Rosalind Hursthouse, in Aristotelian virtue ethics, the emotions have moral significance because "virtues (and vices) are all dispositions not only to act, but to feel emotions, as *re*actions as well as impulses to action... [and] In the person with the virtues, these emotions will be felt on the *right* occasions, toward the *right* people or objects, for the *right* reasons, where 'right' means 'correct'..."

Phronesis and Eudaimonia

Phronesis is an acquired trait that enables its possessor to identify the best thing to do in any given situation. Unlike theoretical wisdom, practical reason results in action or decision. As John McDowell puts it, practical wisdom involves a "perceptual sensitivity" to what a situation requires.

Eudaimonia is a state variously translated from Greek as 'well-being', 'happiness', 'blessedness', and in the context of virtue ethics, 'human flourishing'. *Eudaimonia* in this sense is not a subjective, but an objective, state. It characterizes the well-lived life.

According to Aristotle, the most prominent exponent of *eudaimonia* in the Western philosophical tradition, *eudaimonia* defines the goal of human life. It consists of exercising the characteristic human quality—reason—as the soul's most proper and nourishing activity. In his *Nicomachean Ethics*, Aristotle, like Plato before him, argued that the pursuit of *eudaimonia* is an "activity of the soul in accordance with perfect virtue", which further could only properly be exercised in the characteristic human community—the *polis* or city-state.

Although *eudaimonia* was first popularized by Aristotle, it now belongs to the tradition of virtue theories generally. For the virtue theorist, *eudaimonia* describes that state achieved by the person who lives the proper human life, an outcome that can be reached by practicing the virtues. A virtue is a habit or quality that allows the bearer to succeed at his, her, or its purpose. The virtue of a knife, for example, is sharpness; among the virtues of a racehorse is speed. Thus, to identify the virtues for human beings, one must have an account of what is the human purpose.

Not all modern virtue ethics theories are eudaimonic; some place another end in place of *eudaimonia*, while others are non-teleological: that is, they do not account for virtues in terms of the results that the practice of the virtues produce or tend to produce.

History of Virtue

Like much of the Western tradition, virtue theory originated in ancient Greek philosophy. Virtue ethics began with Socrates, and was subsequently developed further by Plato, Aristotle, and the Stoics. Virtue ethics concentrates on the character of the individual, rather than the acts (or consequences thereof) of the individual. There is debate among adherents of virtue ethics concerning what specific virtues are praiseworthy. However, most theorists agree that ethics is demonstrated by the practice of virtues.

Plato and Aristotle's treatments of virtues are not the same. Plato believes virtue is effectively an end to be sought, for which a friend might be a useful means. Aristotle states that the virtues function more as means to safeguard human relations, particularly authentic friendship, without which one's quest for happiness is frustrated.

Discussion of what were known as the four cardinal virtues—wisdom, justice, fortitude, and temperance—can be found in Plato's *Republic*. The virtues also figure prominently in Aristotle's ethical theory found in *Nicomachean Ethics*.

Virtue theory was inserted into the study of history by moralistic historians such as Livy, Plutarch, and Tacitus. The Greek idea of the virtues was passed on in Roman philosophy through Cicero and later incorporated into Christian moral theology by Ambrose of Milan. During the scholastic period, the most comprehensive consideration of the virtues from a theological perspective was provided by Thomas Aquinas in his *Summa Theologiae* and his *Commentaries on the Nicomachean Ethics*.

After the Reformation, Aristotle's *Nicomachean Ethics* continued to be the main authority for the discipline of ethics at Protestant universities until the late seventeenth century, with over fifty Protestant commentaries published on the *Nicomachean Ethics* before 1682.

Though the tradition receded into the background of European philosophical thought in the past few centuries, the term "virtue" remained current during this period, and in fact appears prominently in the tradition of classical republicanism or classical liberalism. This tradition was prominent in the intellectual life of 16th-century Italy, as well as 17th- and 18th-century Britain and America; indeed the term "virtue" appears frequently in the work of Tomás Fernández de Medrano, Niccolò Machiavelli, David Hume, the republicans of the English Civil War period, the 18th-century English Whigs, and the prominent figures among the Scottish Enlightenment and the American Founding Fathers.

Contemporary "Aretaic Turn"

Although some Enlightenment philosophers (e.g. Hume) continued to emphasise the virtues, with the ascendancy of utilitarianism and deontological ethics, virtue theory moved to the margins of Western philosophy. The contemporary revival of virtue theory is frequently traced to the philosopher Elizabeth Anscombe's 1958 essay "Modern Moral Philosophy". Following this:

- In the 1976 paper "The Schizophrenia of Modern Ethical Theories", Michael Stocker summarises the main aretaic criticisms of deontological and consequentialist ethics.
- Philosopher, psychologist, and encyclopedist Mortimer Adler appealed to Aristotelian ethics, and the virtue theory of happiness or *eudaimonia* throughout his published work.
- Philippa Foot, published a collection of essays in 1978 entitled *Virtues and Vices.*
- Alasdair MacIntyre made an effort to reconstruct a virtue-based theory in dialogue with the problems of modern and postmodern thought; his works include *After Virtue* and *Three Rival Versions of Moral Enquiry.*
- Paul Ricoeur accorded an important place to Aristotelian teleological ethics in his hermeneutical phenomenology of the subject, most notably in his book *Oneself as Another.*
- Theologian Stanley Hauerwas found the language of virtue helpful in his own project.
- Roger Crisp and Michael Slote edited a collection of important essays titled *Virtue Ethics.*

- Martha Nussbaum and Amartya Sen employed virtue theory in theorising the capability approach to international development.
- Julia Annas wrote *The Morality of Happiness* (1993).
- Lawrence C. Becker identified current virtue theory with Greek Stoicism in *A New Stoicism.* (1998).
- Rosalind Hursthouse published *On Virtue Ethics* (1999).
- Psychologist Martin Seligman drew on classical virtue ethics in conceptualizing positive psychology.
- Psychologist Daniel Goleman opens his book on Emotional Intelligence with a challenge from Aristotle's *Nicomachean Ethics.*
- Michael Sandel discusses Aristotelian ethics to support his ethical theory of justice in his book *Justice: What's the Right Thing to Do?*
- The aretaic turn in moral philosophy is paralleled by analogous developments in other philosophical disciplines. One of these is epistemology, where a distinctive virtue epistemology was developed by Linda Zagzebski and others. In political theory, there has been discussion of "virtue politics", and in legal theory, there is a small but growing body of literature on virtue jurisprudence. The aretaic turn also exists in American constitutional theory, where proponents argue for an emphasis on virtue and vice of constitutional adjudicators.

Aretaic approaches to morality, epistemology, and jurisprudence have been the subject of intense debates. One criticism focuses on the problem of guidance; opponents, such as Robert Louden in his article "Some Vices of Virtue Ethics", question whether the idea of a virtuous moral actor, believer, or judge can provide the guidance necessary for action, belief formation, or the resolution of legal disputes.

Criticisms

Regarding which are the most important virtues, Aristotle proposed the following nine: wisdom; prudence; justice; fortitude; courage; liberality; magnificence; magnanimity; temperance. In contrast, philosopher Walter Kaufmann proposed as the four cardinal virtues ambition/humility, love, courage, and honesty.

Proponents of virtue theory sometimes argue that a central feature of a virtue is its *universal applicability*. In other words, any character trait defined as a virtue must reasonably be universally regarded as a virtue for all people. According to this view, it is inconsistent to claim, for example, servility as a female virtue, while at the same time not proposing it as a male one.

Other proponents of virtue theory, notably Alasdair MacIntyre, respond to this objection by arguing that any account of the virtues must indeed be generated out of the community in which those virtues are to be practiced: the very word *ethics* implies *ethos*. That is to say that the virtues are, and necessarily must be, grounded in a particular time and place. What counts as a virtue in 4th-century BCE Athens would be a ludicrous guide to proper behaviour in 21st-century CE Toronto and vice versa. To take this view does not necessarily commit one to the argument that accounts of the virtues must therefore be static: moral activity—that is, attempts to contemplate and practice the virtues—can provide the cultural resources that allow people to change, albeit slowly, the *ethos* of their own societies.

MacIntyre appears to take this position in his seminal work on virtue ethics, *After Virtue*. One might cite (though MacIntyre does not) the rapid emergence of abolitionist thought in the slave-holding societies of the 18th-century Atlantic world as an example of this sort of change: over a short period of time, perhaps 1760 to 1800, in Britain, France, and British America, slave-holding, previously thought to be morally neutral or even virtuous, rapidly became seen as vicious among wide swathes of society. While the emergence of abolitionist thought derived from many sources, the work of David Brion Davis, among others, established that one source was the rapid, internal evolution of moral theory among certain sectors of these societies, notably the Quakers.

Another objection to virtue theory is that virtue ethics does not focus on what *sorts of actions* are morally permitted and which ones are not, but rather on what sort of qualities someone ought to foster in order to become a good person. In other words, while some virtue theorists may not condemn, for example, murder as an inherently immoral or impermissible sort of action, they may argue that someone who commits a murder is severely lacking in several important virtues, such as compassion and fairness. Still, antagonists of the theory often object that this particular feature of the theory makes virtue ethics useless as a universal norm of acceptable conduct suitable as a base for legislation. Some virtue theorists concede this point, but respond by opposing the very notion of legitimate legislative authority instead, effectively advocating some form of anarchism as the political ideal. Other virtue theorists argue that laws should be made by virtuous legislators, and still another group argue that it is possible to base a judicial system on the moral notion of virtues rather than rules. Aristotle himself saw his *Nicomachean Ethics* as a prequel for his *Politics* and felt that the point of politics was to create the fertile soil for a virtuous citizenry to develop in, and that one purpose of virtue was that it helps you to contribute to a healthy *polis*.

Some virtue theorists might respond to this overall objection with the notion of a "bad act" also being an act characteristic of vice. That is to say that those acts that do not aim at virtue, or that stray from virtue, would constitute our conception of "bad behavior". Although not all virtue ethicists agree to this notion, this is one way the virtue ethicist can re-introduce the concept of the "morally impermissible". One could raise an objection that he is committing an argument from ignorance by postulating that what is not virtuous is unvirtuous. In other words, just because an action or person 'lacks of evidence' for virtue does not, all else constant, imply that said action or person is unvirtuous.

Subsumed in Deontology and Utilitarianism

Martha Nussbaum suggested that while virtue ethics is often considered to be anti-Enlightenment, "suspicious of theory and respectful of the wisdom embodied in local practices", it is actually neither fundamentally distinct from, nor does it qualify as a rival approach to deontology and utilitarianism. She argues that philosophers from these two Enlightenment traditions often include theories of virtue. She pointed out that Kant's "Doctrine of Virtue" (in *The Metaphysics of Morals*) "covers most of the same topics as do classical Greek theories", "that he offers a general account of virtue, in terms of the strength of the will in overcoming wayward and selfish inclinations; that he offers detailed analyses of standard virtues such as courage and self-control, and of vices, such as avarice, mendacity, servility, and pride; that, although in general, he portrays inclination as inimical to virtue, he also recognizes that sympathetic inclinations offer crucial support to virtue, and urges their deliberate cultivation."

Nussbaum also points to considerations of virtue by utilitarians such as Henry Sidgwick (*The Methods of Ethics*), Jeremy Bentham (*The Principles of Morals and Legislation*), and John Stuart Mill, who writes of moral development as part of an argument for the moral equality of women (*The Subjection of Women*). She argues that contemporary virtue ethicists such as Alasdair MacIntyre, Bernard Williams, Philippa Foot, and John McDowell have few points of agreement and that the common core of their work does not represent a break from Kant.

Kantian Critique

Immanuel Kant's position on virtue ethics is contested. Those who argue that Kantian deontology conflicts with virtue ethics include Alasdair MacIntyre, Philippa Foot, and Bernard Williams. In the *Groundwork of the Metaphysics of Morals* and the *Critique of Practical Reason*, Immanuel Kant offers many different criticisms of ethical frameworks and against moral theories before him. Kant rarely mentioned Aristotle by name but did not exclude his moral philosophy of virtue ethics from his critique. Many Kantian arguments against virtue ethics claim that virtue ethics is inconsistent, or sometimes that it is not a real moral theory at all.

In "What Is Virtue Ethics All About?", Gregory Velazco y Trianosky identified the key points of divergence between virtue ethicists and what he called "neo-Kantianism", in the form these nine neo-Kantian moral assertions:

- The crucial moral question is "what is it right/obligatory to do?"
- Moral judgments are those that concern the rightness of actions.
- Such judgments take the form of rules or principles.
- Such rules or principles are universal, not respecting persons.
- They are not based on some concept of human good that is independent of moral goodness.
- They take the form of categorical imperatives that can be justified independently of the desires of the person they apply to.
- They are motivating; they can compel action in an agent, also independently of that agent's desires.
- An action, in order to be morally virtuous, must be motivated by this sort of moral judgment (not, for example, merely coincidentally aligned with it).
- The virtuousness of a character trait, or virtue, derives from the relationship that trait has to moral judgments, rules, and principles.

Trianosky says that modern sympathizers with virtue ethics almost all reject neo-Kantian claim #1, and many of them also reject certain of the other claims.

Utopianism and Pluralism

Robert B. Louden criticizes virtue ethics on the basis that it promotes a form of unsustainable utopianism. Trying to arrive at a single set of virtues is immensely difficult in contemporary societies as, according to Louden, they contain "more ethnic, religious, and class groups than did the moral community which Aristotle theorized about" with each of these groups having "not only its own interests but its own set of virtues as well".

Louden notes in passing that MacIntyre, a supporter of virtue-based ethics, has grappled with this in *After Virtue* but that ethics cannot dispense with building rules around acts and rely only on discussing the moral character of persons.

Topics in Virtue Ethics

Virtue Ethics as a Category

Virtue contrasts with deontological and consequentialist ethics (the three being together the most predominant contemporary normative ethical theories). Deontological ethics, sometimes referred to as duty ethics, places the emphasis on adhering to ethical principles or duties.

How these duties are defined, however, is often a point of contention and debate in deontological ethics. One predominant rule scheme used by deontologists is divine command theory. Deontology also depends upon meta-ethical realism, in that it postulates the existence of moral absolutes that make an action moral, regardless of circumstances. Immanuel Kant is considered one of the foremost theorists of deontological ethics.

The next predominant school of thought in normative ethics is consequentialism. While deontology places the emphasis on doing one's duty, consequentialism bases the morality of an action upon its outcome. Instead of saying that one has a moral duty to abstain from murder, a consequentialist would say that we should abstain from murder because it causes undesirable effects. The main contention here is what outcomes should/can be identified as objectively desirable.

The greatest happiness principle of John Stuart Mill is a commonly adopted criteria for what is objectively desirable. Mill asserts that the desirability of an action is the net amount of happiness it brings, the number of people it brings it to, and the duration of the happiness. He tries to delineate classes of happiness, some preferable to others, but there is a great deal of difficulty in classifying such concepts.

A virtue ethicist identifies virtues, desirable characteristics, that an excellent person embodies. Exhibiting these virtues is the aim of ethics, and one's actions are a reflection of one's virtues. To the virtue philosopher, action cannot be used as a demarcation of morality, because a virtue encompasses more than just a simple selection of action. Instead, a virtue is a way of being that leads the person exhibiting the virtue to make certain "virtuous" types of choices consistently in each situation. There is a great deal of disagreement within virtue ethics over what are virtues and what are not. There are also difficulties in identifying what is the "virtuous" action to take in all circumstances, and how to define a virtue.

Consequentialist and deontological theories often still employ the term *virtue*, but in a restricted sense, namely as a tendency or disposition to adhere to the system's principles or rules. In other words, in those theories, virtue is secondary, and the principles or rules are primary. These very different senses of what constitutes virtue, hidden behind the same word, are a potential source of confusion.

This disagreement over the meaning of virtue points to a larger conflict between virtue theory and its philosophical rivals. A system of virtue theory is only intelligible if it is teleological: that is, if it includes an account of the purpose (*telos*) of human life, or in popular language, the meaning of life. Obviously, strong claims about the purpose of human life, or of what the good life for human beings is, will be controversial.

Virtue theory's necessary commitment to a teleological account of human life thus puts the tradition in tension with other dominant approaches to normative ethics, which, because they focus on actions, do not bear this burden.

Virtue and Politics

Virtue theory emphasises Aristotle's belief in the *polis* as the acme of political organisation, and the role of the virtues in enabling human beings to flourish in that environment.

Classical republicanism in contrast emphasises Tacitus' concern that power and luxury can corrupt individuals and destroy liberty, as Tacitus perceived in the transformation of the Roman Republic into the Roman Empire; virtue for classical republicans is a shield against this sort of corruption and a means to preserve the good life one has, rather than a means by which to achieve the good life one does not yet have. Another way to put the distinction between the two traditions is that virtue ethics relies on Aristotle's fundamental distinction between the human-being-as-he-is from the human-being-as-he-should-be, while classical republicanism relies on the Tacitean distinction of the risk-of-becoming.

Virtue ethics has a number of contemporary applications:

- **Social and Political Philosophy:** Within the field of social ethics, Deirdre McCloskey argues that virtue ethics can provide a basis for a balanced approach to understanding capitalism and capitalist societies.
- **Education:** Within the field of philosophy of education, James Page argues that virtue ethics can provide a rationale and foundation for peace education.
- **Health Care and Medical Ethics:** Thomas Alured Faunce argued that whistleblowing in the healthcare setting would be more respected within clinical governance pathways if it had a firmer academic foundation in virtue ethics. He called for whistleblowing to be expressly supported in the UNESCO Universal Declaration on Bioethics and Human Rights. Barry Schwartz argues that "practical wisdom" is an antidote to much of the inefficient and inhumane bureaucracy of modern health care systems.
- **Technology and the Virtues:** In her book *Technology and the Virtues*, Shannon Vallor proposed a series of 'technomoral' virtues that people need to cultivate in order to flourish in our socio-technological world: Honesty (Respecting Truth), Self-control (Becoming the Author of Our Desires), Humility (Knowing What We Do Not Know), Justice (Upholding Rightness), Courage (Intelligent Fear and Hope), Empathy (Compassionate Concern for Others), Care (Loving Service to Others),

Civility (Making Common Cause), Flexibility (Skillful Adaptation to Change), Perspective (Holding on to the Moral Whole), and Magnanimity (Moral Leadership and Nobility of Spirit).

3.1.4 Care Ethics

The ethics of care (alternatively care ethics or EoC) is a normative ethical theory that holds that moral action centers on interpersonal relationships and care or benevolence as a virtue. EoC is one of a cluster of normative ethical theories that were developed by some feminists and environmentalists since the 1980s. While consequentialist and deontological ethical theories emphasize generalizable standards and impartiality, ethics of care emphasize the importance of response to the individual. The distinction between the general and the individual is reflected in their different moral questions: "what is just?" versus "how to respond?" Carol Gilligan, who is considered the originator of the ethics of care, criticized the application of generalized standards as "morally problematic, since it breeds moral blindness or indifference".

Assumptions of the framework include: persons are understood to have varying degrees of dependence and interdependence; other individuals affected by the consequences of one's choices deserve consideration in proportion to their vulnerability; and situational details determine how to safeguard and promote the interests of individuals.

Historical Background

The originator of the ethics of care was Carol Gilligan, an American ethicist and psychologist. Gilligan created this model as a critique of her mentor, developmental psychologist Lawrence Kohlberg's model of moral development. Gilligan observed that measuring moral development by Kohlberg's stages of moral development found boys to be more morally mature than girls, and this result held for adults as well (although when education is controlled for there are no gender differences). Gilligan argued that Kohlberg's model was not objective, but rather a masculine perspective on morality, founded on principles of justice and rights. In her 1982 book *In a Different Voice*, she further posited that men and women have tendencies to view morality in different terms. Her theory claimed women tended to emphasize empathy and compassion over the notions of morality in terms of abstract duties or obligations that are privileged in Kohlberg's scale. Dana Ward stated, in an unpublished paper, that Kohlberg's scale is psychometrically sound. Subsequent research suggests that the differences in care-based or justice-based ethical approaches may be due to gender differences, or differences in life situations of genders. Gilligan's summarizing of gender differences provided feminists with a voice to question moral values and practices of the society as masculine.

Relationship to Traditional Ethical Positions

Care ethics is different from other ethical models, such as consequentialist theories (e.g. utilitarianism) and deontological theories (e.g. Kantian ethics), in that it seeks to incorporate traditionally feminine virtues and values which, proponents of care ethics contend, are absent in traditional models of ethics. One of these values is the placement of caring and relationship over logic and reason. In care ethics, reason and logic are subservient to natural care, that is, care that is done out of inclination. This is in contrast to deontology, where actions taken out of inclination are unethical.

Virginia Held has noted the similarities between care ethics and virtue ethics but distinguished it from the virtue ethics of British moralists such as Hume in that people are seen as fundamentally relational rather than independent individuals. Other philosophers have argued about the relation between care ethics and virtue ethics, taking various positions on the question of how closely the two are related. Jason Josephson Storm argued for close parallels between the ethics of care and traditional Buddhist virtue ethics, especially the prioritization of compassion by Śāntideva and others. Other scholars had also previously connected ethics of care with Buddhist ethics.

Care Ethics as Feminist Ethics

While some feminists have criticized care-based ethics for reinforcing traditional gender stereotypes, others have embraced parts of the paradigm under the theoretical concept of care-focused feminism. Care-focused feminism, alternatively called *gender feminism*, is a branch of feminist thought informed primarily by the ethics of care as developed by Carol Gilligan and Nel Noddings. This theory is critical of how caring is socially engendered, being assigned to women and consequently devalued. "Care-focused feminists regard women's capacity for care as a human strength" which can and should be taught to and expected of men as well as women. Noddings proposes that ethical caring could be a more concrete evaluative model of moral dilemma, than an ethic of justice. Noddings' care-focused feminism requires practical application of relational ethics, predicated on an ethic of care.

Ethics of care is a basis for care-focused feminist theorizing on maternal ethics. These theories recognize caring as an ethically relevant issue. Critical of how society engenders caring labor, theorists Sara Ruddick, Virginia Held, and Eva Feder Kittay suggest caring should be performed and care givers valued in both public and private spheres. This proposed paradigm shift in ethics encourages the view that an ethic of caring be the social responsibility of both men and women.

Joan Tronto argues that the definition of "ethic of care" is ambiguous due in part to it not playing a central role in moral theory. She argues that considering moral philosophy is engaged with human goodness, then care would appear to assume a significant role in this type of philosophy. However, this is not the case and Tronto further stresses the association between care and "naturalness". The latter term refers to the socially and culturally constructed gender roles where care is mainly assumed to be the role of the woman. As such, care loses the power to take a central role in moral theory.

Tronto states there are four ethical qualities of care:

- **Attentiveness:** Attentiveness is crucial to the ethics of care because care requires a recognition of others' needs in order to respond to them. The question which arises is the distinction between ignorance and inattentiveness. Tronto poses this question as such, "But when is ignorance simply ignorance, and when is it inattentiveness"?
- **Responsibility:** In order to care, we must take it upon ourselves, thus responsibility. The problem associated with this second ethical element of responsibility is the question of obligation. Obligation is often, if not already, tied to pre-established societal and cultural norms and roles. Tronto makes the effort to differentiate the terms "responsibility" and "obligation" with regards to the ethic of care. Responsibility is ambiguous, whereas obligation refers to situations where action or reaction is due, such as the case of a legal contract. This ambiguity allows for ebb and flow in and between class structures and gender roles, and to other socially constructed roles that would bind responsibility to those only befitting of those roles.
- **Competence:** To provide care also means competency. One cannot simply acknowledge the need to care, accept the responsibility, but not follow through with enough adequacy - as such action would result in the need of care not being met.
- **Responsiveness:** This refers to the "responsiveness of the care receiver to the care". Tronto states, "Responsiveness signals an important moral problem within care: by its nature, care is concerned with conditions of vulnerability and inequality". She further argues responsiveness does not equal reciprocity. Rather, it is another method to understand vulnerability and inequality by understanding what has been expressed by those in the vulnerable position, as opposed to re-imagining oneself in a similar situation.

In 2013, Tronto added a fifth ethical quality:

- **Plurality, Communication, Trust and Respect; Solidarity or Caring with:** Together, these are the qualities necessary for people to come together in order to take collective responsibility, to understand their citizenship as always imbricated in relations of care, and to take seriously the nature of caring needs in society.

3.1.5 Integrating Ethical Theories

Complementary Approaches

While each ethical theory offers distinct insights and principles, they are not mutually exclusive. In practice, ethical decision-making often involves integrating multiple frameworks to address complex moral dilemmas. For instance, a healthcare professional might combine deontological principles (following ethical codes), utilitarian considerations (maximizing patient well-being), and care ethics (emphasizing compassionate care) to guide their actions.

Case Study: Medical Ethics

Consider a scenario where a doctor must decide whether to allocate a limited supply of a life-saving drug to one of two patients. A deontological approach would emphasize the doctor's duty to treat all patients fairly and without bias. A utilitarian perspective would focus on maximizing overall well-being, potentially choosing the patient with the highest chance of recovery. Care ethics would highlight the importance of empathy and understanding the specific needs and relationships of each patient. By integrating these frameworks, the doctor can make a more nuanced and ethically sound decision.

3.2 ETHICAL PRINCIPLES IN EDUCATIONAL AI

The integration of artificial intelligence (AI) into education offers significant potential for enhancing learning experiences, personalizing education, and improving administrative efficiency. However, the deployment of AI in educational settings also raises important ethical considerations. Ensuring that AI is used responsibly and ethically in education is crucial to protect students' rights, promote equity, and maintain trust in educational institutions.

Ethical principles such as transparency, fairness, privacy, accountability, and inclusivity are crucial for the responsible use of AI in education. By adhering to these principles, educational institutions can harness the potential of AI to enhance learning experiences while protecting students' rights and promoting equity. Addressing the challenges associated with these principles requires ongoing effort, collaboration, and commitment to ethical practices. Through responsible and ethical use of AI, education can be transformed in ways that benefit all students, creating a more just and effective educational system.

3.2.1 Transparency

Definition and Importance

Transparency in educational AI involves making the operations, decision-making processes, and limitations of AI systems clear to all stakeholders, including students, educators, and parents. Transparency is essential for building trust, ensuring informed consent, and enabling stakeholders to understand how AI systems influence educational experiences and outcomes.

Implementation Strategies

Clear Communication

Educational institutions should provide clear and accessible information about how AI systems work, what data they collect, and how decisions are made. This includes explaining the algorithms used, the criteria for decision-making, and the potential impact on students' learning experiences. Transparent communication helps demystify AI and empowers stakeholders to make informed decisions about its use.

Informed Consent

Obtaining informed consent from students and their guardians is crucial when implementing AI in education. This process involves clearly explaining the purpose of the AI system, the data it will collect, and how it will be used. Students and parents should have the opportunity to ask questions and opt out if they are uncomfortable with the use of AI. Informed consent ensures that stakeholders are aware of and agree to the use of AI in educational settings.

Challenges

Ensuring transparency can be challenging due to the complexity of AI systems and the technical nature of algorithms. Simplifying these concepts without losing essential details requires careful communication strategies. Additionally, maintaining transparency may reveal proprietary information or expose vulnerabilities, which institutions need to manage effectively.

3.2.2 Fairness

Definition and Importance

Fairness in educational AI involves ensuring that AI systems do not perpetuate or exacerbate existing biases and inequalities. AI systems must be designed and implemented to treat all students equitably, regardless of their background, race, gender, or socioeconomic status. Fairness is critical for promoting equity and preventing discrimination in education.

Implementation Strategies

Bias Mitigation

Educational institutions must actively work to identify and mitigate biases in AI systems. This involves using diverse and representative datasets to train AI models, regularly auditing algorithms for bias, and implementing corrective measures when biases are detected. Institutions should also involve diverse stakeholders in the development and evaluation of AI systems to ensure a wide range of perspectives are considered.

Equity-Focused Design

Designing AI systems with a focus on equity involves considering the unique needs and challenges of different student groups. For example, adaptive learning technologies should be tailored to support students with varying learning abilities, and predictive analytics should be used to identify and support at-risk students proactively. An equity-focused approach ensures that AI enhances learning opportunities for all students, not just a select few.

Challenges

Addressing fairness in AI is complex due to the potential for unconscious biases in data and algorithms. Ensuring diverse representation in datasets and algorithm design requires ongoing effort and vigilance. Additionally, balancing the need for fairness with other considerations, such as efficiency and accuracy, can be challenging.

3.2.3 Privacy

Definition and Importance

Privacy in educational AI involves protecting students' personal and sensitive information from unauthorized access, use, or disclosure. Safeguarding privacy is essential for maintaining trust, complying with legal requirements, and ensuring that students' rights are respected.

Implementation Strategies

Data Protection Policies

Educational institutions should implement robust data protection policies that outline how student data will be collected, stored, used, and shared. These policies should comply with relevant privacy regulations, such as the General Data Protection Regulation (GDPR) or the Family Educational Rights and Privacy Act (FERPA). Clear policies help ensure that data is handled responsibly and transparently.

Anonymization and Encryption

Using anonymization and encryption techniques can help protect student data. Anonymization involves removing personally identifiable information from datasets, making it difficult to trace data back to individual students. Encryption ensures that data is secure during transmission and storage, reducing the risk of unauthorized access.

Challenges

Balancing the need for data to personalize learning experiences with the need to protect privacy can be challenging. Collecting and using data responsibly requires careful consideration of the potential risks and benefits. Additionally, implementing robust data protection measures can be resource-intensive and require ongoing monitoring and updates.

3.2.4 Accountability

Definition and Importance

Accountability in educational AI involves ensuring that there are clear mechanisms for oversight, responsibility, and recourse when AI systems impact students and educators. Accountability is crucial for maintaining trust, addressing grievances, and ensuring that AI systems are used ethically and effectively.

Implementation Strategies

Clear Governance Structures

Educational institutions should establish clear governance structures for overseeing the use of AI. This includes defining roles and responsibilities, setting up oversight committees, and creating processes for monitoring and evaluating AI systems. Governance structures ensure that there is accountability at every level of AI implementation.

Mechanisms for Redress

Providing mechanisms for redress allows students, parents, and educators to raise concerns and seek remedies if they believe they have been unfairly impacted by AI systems. Institutions should have clear procedures for handling complaints, conducting investigations, and implementing corrective actions. Mechanisms for redress ensure that stakeholders have a voice and that issues are addressed promptly and fairly.

Challenges

Ensuring accountability can be difficult due to the complexity and opacity of AI systems. Establishing effective governance structures requires collaboration across various stakeholders and continuous evaluation. Additionally, providing meaningful redress mechanisms can be resource-intensive and may require changes to existing policies and practices.

3.2.5 Inclusivity

Definition and Importance

Inclusivity in educational AI involves ensuring that AI systems are designed and implemented to be accessible and beneficial to all students, including those with diverse needs and backgrounds. Inclusivity is essential for promoting equal opportunities and ensuring that no student is left behind.

Implementation Strategies

Universal Design for Learning (UDL)

Adopting Universal Design for Learning (UDL) principles can help ensure that AI systems are inclusive. UDL involves designing educational environments and tools to accommodate diverse learners, providing multiple means of engagement, representation, and expression. Applying UDL principles to AI design ensures that systems are flexible and accessible to all students.

Collaborative Development

Involving a diverse range of stakeholders in the development and evaluation of AI systems can help ensure inclusivity. This includes engaging students, educators, parents, and community members from various backgrounds and with different perspectives. Collaborative development ensures that AI systems are designed to meet the needs of all users.

Challenges

Achieving inclusivity requires ongoing effort and commitment. Designing AI systems that are accessible to all students can be complex, requiring specialized knowledge and resources. Additionally, ensuring that diverse voices are heard and considered in the development process can be challenging but is essential for creating truly inclusive AI systems.

3.3 THE IMPORTANCE OF ETHICAL DECISION-MAKING

Ethical decision-making is a critical aspect of personal and professional life, guiding individuals and organizations in choosing actions that align with moral principles and societal norms. In a world characterized by complexity and rapid change, the importance of making ethical decisions cannot be overstated.

Ethical decision-making is fundamental to personal integrity, organizational success, and societal trust. By adhering to ethical principles and frameworks, individuals and organizations can navigate moral complexities, build positive reputations, and contribute to a just and cohesive society. Despite the challenges posed by conflicting values, external pressures, and uncertainty, strategies such as ethical education, leadership, and policies can enhance ethical decision-making. Ultimately, a commitment to ethical decision-making fosters a world where actions are guided by fairness, respect, and responsibility, benefiting individuals and society as a whole.

3.3.1 The Foundations of Ethical Decision-Making

Definition and Key Principles

Ethical decision-making involves choosing actions that are right, fair, and just. It is grounded in moral principles such as honesty, integrity, fairness, respect, and responsibility. These principles serve as guidelines for evaluating choices and actions, helping individuals and organizations navigate moral dilemmas and conflicts.

Ethical Theories

Several ethical theories provide frameworks for decision-making, including deontology, utilitarianism, virtue ethics, and care ethics. Deontology emphasizes following moral rules and duties, while utilitarianism focuses on the consequences of actions, aiming to maximize overall happiness. Virtue ethics highlights the importance of moral character and virtues, and care ethics prioritizes relationships and empathy. Understanding these theories helps individuals approach ethical dilemmas from multiple perspectives and make well-rounded decisions.

3.3.2 The Importance of Ethical Decision-Making

Personal Integrity and Reputation

Ethical decision-making is crucial for maintaining personal integrity and reputation. Acting in accordance with ethical principles fosters a sense of self-respect and moral consistency. Individuals who consistently make ethical choices are seen as trustworthy, reliable, and honorable. This positive reputation enhances personal relationships, career prospects, and overall well-being.

Organizational Culture and Success

In organizations, ethical decision-making is foundational to creating a positive culture and achieving long-term success. Ethical organizations are characterized by transparency, accountability, and a commitment to doing what is right. This fosters a work environment where employees feel valued, respected, and motivated. Ethical decision-making also reduces the risk of scandals, legal issues, and reputational damage, which can have severe consequences for an organization.

Societal Trust and Cohesion

At the societal level, ethical decision-making is essential for building trust and cohesion. When individuals and organizations act ethically, they contribute to a sense of justice and fairness in society. This trust is crucial for social stability and cooperation, enabling communities to work together towards common goals. Conversely, unethical behavior erodes trust, leading to social fragmentation and conflict.

3.3.3 The Impact of Ethical Decision-Making

Business and Economics

In the business world, ethical decision-making has profound implications for economic stability and growth. Companies that prioritize ethics are more likely to gain the trust of consumers, investors, and regulators. This trust translates into customer loyalty, investor confidence, and favorable regulatory treatment, all of which contribute to sustainable business success. Moreover, ethical companies are better equipped to attract and retain top talent, as employees seek workplaces that align with their values.

Healthcare and Medicine

In healthcare, ethical decision-making is paramount to ensuring patient trust and delivering quality care. Medical professionals face numerous ethical dilemmas, such as balancing patient autonomy with medical necessity or allocating limited resources. Adhering to ethical principles such as beneficence, non-maleficence, autonomy, and justice helps healthcare providers navigate these dilemmas and make decisions that prioritize patient welfare and equity.

Education and Academia

Ethical decision-making in education and academia fosters an environment of fairness, integrity, and respect for knowledge. Educators and academic institutions play a critical role in shaping the moral development of students. By modeling ethical behavior and promoting academic honesty, they instill values that students carry into their personal and professional lives. Ethical decision-making in academia also ensures the credibility and reliability of research, which is vital for societal progress.

3.3.4 Challenges to Ethical Decision-Making

Conflicting Values and Interests

One of the primary challenges in ethical decision-making is navigating conflicting values and interests. Individuals and organizations often face situations where ethical principles collide, such as choosing between honesty and loyalty or individual rights and collective good. Resolving these conflicts requires careful consideration, dialogue, and sometimes, compromise.

Pressure and Influence

External pressures and influences can also complicate ethical decision-making. These pressures may come from superiors, peers, or societal norms, and can lead individuals to act against their ethical beliefs. For example, employees might feel pressured to achieve business targets at the expense of ethical practices. Developing moral courage and resilience is crucial for standing up to such pressures and making ethical choices.

Uncertainty and Complexity

The complexity and uncertainty of many situations pose another challenge to ethical decision-making. Rapid technological advancements, globalization, and diverse cultural contexts create scenarios where the right course of action is not always clear. Ethical decision-making in these contexts requires critical thinking, ethical literacy, and a willingness to seek guidance and input from diverse perspectives.

3.3.5 Strategies for Enhancing Ethical Decision-Making

Ethical Education and Training

Ethical education and training are essential for equipping individuals with the knowledge and skills to make ethical decisions. Educational institutions and organizations should provide ongoing training on ethical theories, principles, and decision-making frameworks. This training should include case studies, role-playing, and discussions to help individuals apply ethical concepts to real-world situations.

Ethical Leadership

Ethical leadership plays a critical role in fostering a culture of ethical decision-making. Leaders set the tone for ethical behavior by modeling integrity, transparency, and accountability. They should encourage open dialogue about ethical issues, support employees in making ethical choices, and hold themselves and others accountable for unethical behavior.

Creating Ethical Policies and Frameworks

Organizations can enhance ethical decision-making by establishing clear ethical policies and frameworks. These policies should outline expected behaviors, provide guidelines for addressing ethical dilemmas, and offer mechanisms for reporting and addressing unethical conduct. Ethical frameworks, such as codes of ethics and decision-making models, provide structured approaches for evaluating and resolving ethical issues.

PART II:

ETHICAL CONSIDERATIONS AND CHALLENGES

CHAPTER 4
DATA PRIVACY AND SECURITY

4.1 DATA COLLECTION AND STUDENT PRIVACY

Data collection in educational settings has become increasingly prevalent with the integration of technology and digital learning tools. While data-driven insights can enhance educational outcomes and personalize learning experiences, they also raise significant concerns about student privacy and data security.

Data collection in education offers valuable insights for enhancing learning outcomes and personalizing educational experiences. However, protecting student privacy and ensuring ethical data use are paramount considerations. By implementing transparent practices, prioritizing data security, complying with privacy regulations, and promoting ethical decision-making, educational institutions can foster trust, respect student privacy rights, and leverage data responsibly to benefit students and educators alike. Balancing the potential of educational data with ethical considerations ensures that educational technologies and digital learning tools contribute positively to the educational landscape while safeguarding student welfare and privacy.

4.1.1 Data Collection: An Overview

Data collection or data gathering is the process of gathering and measuring information on targeted variables in an established system, which then enables one to answer relevant questions and evaluate outcomes. Data collection is a research component in all study fields, including physical and social sciences, humanities, and business. While methods vary by discipline, the emphasis on ensuring accurate and honest collection remains the same. The goal for all data collection is to capture evidence that allows data analysis to lead to the formulation of credible answers to the questions that have been posed.

Regardless of the field of or preference for defining data (quantitative or qualitative), accurate data collection is essential to maintain research integrity. The selection of appropriate data collection instruments (existing, modified, or newly developed) and delineated instructions for their correct use reduce the likelihood of errors.

Methodology

Data collection and validation consist of four steps when it involves taking a census and seven steps when it involves sampling. A formal data collection process is necessary, as it ensures that the data gathered are both defined and accurate. This way, subsequent decisions based on arguments embodied in the findings are made using valid data. The process provides both a baseline from which to measure and in certain cases an indication of what to improve.

Data Management Platform

Data management platforms (DMP) are centralized storage and analytical systems for data, mainly used in marketing. DMPs exist to compile and transform large amounts of demand and supply data into discernible information. Marketers may want to receive and utilize first, second and third-party data.DMPs enable this, because they are the aggregate system of DSPs (demand side platform) and SSPs (supply side platform). DMPs are integral for optimizing and future advertising campaigns.

Data Integrity Issues

The main reason for maintaining data integrity is to support the observation of errors in the data collection process. Those errors may be made intentionally (deliberate falsification) or non-intentionally (random or systematic errors). There are two approaches that may protect data integrity and secure scientific validity of study results:

- **Quality Assurance:** All actions carried out before data collection.
- **Quality Control:** All actions carried out during and after data collection.

Quality Assurance (QA)

QA's focus is prevention, which is primarily a cost-effective activity to protect the integrity of data collection. Standardization of protocol, with comprehensive and detailed procedure descriptions for data collection, are central for prevention. The risk of failing to identify problems and errors in the research process is often caused by poorly written guidelines. Listed are several examples of such failures:

- Uncertainty of timing, methods and identification of the responsible person.
- Partial listing of items needed to be collected.
- Vague description of data collection instruments instead of rigorous step-by-step instructions on administering tests.
- Failure to recognize exact content and strategies for training and retraining staff members responsible for data collection.
- Unclear instructions for using, making adjustments to, and calibrating data collection equipment.

- No predetermined mechanism to document changes in procedures that occur during the investigation.

User Privacy Issues

There are serious concerns about the integrity of individual user data collected by cloud computing, because this data is transferred across countries that have different standards of protection for individual user data. Information processing has advanced to the level where user data can now be used to predict what an individual is saying before they even speak.

Quality Control (QC)

Since QC actions occur during or after the data collection, all the details can be carefully documented. There is a necessity for a clearly defined communication structure as a precondition for establishing monitoring systems. Uncertainty about the flow of information is not recommended, as a poorly organized communication structure leads to lax monitoring and can also limit the opportunities for detecting errors. Quality control is also responsible for the identification of actions necessary for correcting faulty data collection practices and also minimizing such future occurrences. A team is more likely to not realize the necessity to perform these actions if their procedures are written vaguely and are not based on feedback or education.

Data collection problems that necessitate prompt action:

- Systematic errors.
- Violation of protocol.
- Fraud or scientific misconduct.
- Errors in individual data items.
- Individual staff or site performance problems.
- Shadow effect.

4.1.2 Privacy in Education

Privacy in education refers to the broad area of ideologies, practices, and legislation that involve the privacy rights of individuals in the education system. Concepts that are commonly associated with privacy in education include the expectation of privacy, the Family Educational Rights and Privacy Act (FERPA), the Fourth Amendment, and the Health Insurance Portability and Accountability Act of 1996 (HIPAA). Most privacy in education concerns relate to the protection of student data (like educational records and other personal information) and the privacy of medical records. Many scholars are engaging in an academic discussion that covers the scope of students' privacy rights, from student in K-12 and even higher education, and the management of student data in an age of rapid access and dissemination of information.

Expectation of Privacy

"Expectation of privacy," similar to the "right to privacy," is a phrase that describes the natural desire of humans to maintain their sense of privacy. There is currently no legal definition in the American law that explicitly grants humans the right to privacy. Oftentimes, the Fourth Amendment is utilized by people in court cases to defend themselves from actions that involve certain infringements upon their privacy, such as searches that require warrants. However, over the years, the U.S. Supreme Court has found it difficult to determine an impartial non-biased meaning for "expectation of privacy" because there are too many subjective variables to consider.

Student Expectation of Privacy

In line with the general meaning of "expectation of privacy," student expectation of privacy refers to a student's inherent right to privacy in the school system. Examples of student expectation of privacy, especially in the pre-collegiate levels, include the protection of a student's academic record from being viewed by anyone other than the academic instructor, the student's parents or guardians, and the students themselves. There have been many legal cases regarding the privacy concerns of pupils' academic records, for example the Owasso Independent School District v. Falvo that was handled by the U.S. Supreme Court in 2002. This particular case began in October 1998 when Kristja J. Falvo filed a lawsuit against the Owasso Independent School District on the premise that the grading practice employed in her children's classroom, peer grading, was a violation of the Fourteenth Amendment and of FERPA.

Additionally, peer grading embarrassed her children in front of their peers, which could be interpreted as a violation of a student's expectation of privacy in the classroom. When the case reached the Tenth Circuit Court of Appeals, it was ruled in October 2000 that peer grading was not a violation of the constitutional Fourteenth Amendment but was, in fact, a violation of FERPA.

The Tenth Circuit judges reasoned so by closely interpreting the statue in FERPA about privacy protection of "educational records." Since it was agreed upon that teacher grade books were considered "educational records," the Tenth Circuit decided that anything that went into these grade books, including student grades written on student work, were also considered "educational records" and thus subject to FERPA's privacy protection policies. After the court decision was released, peer grading practices were banned in school districts within the Tenth Circuit regional borders.

Many citizens and scholars were opposed to the Tenth Circuit's decision, and the case ultimately reached the U.S. Supreme Court in 2001. In 2002, the Supreme Court Justices officially ruled that peer grading was not a violation of FERPA. They reasoned that student grades on student work were not considered "educational records" until the teacher had physically recorded the grades into a grade book. Thus, peer grading returned as a common grading practice in classrooms across the United States.

Other examples of student expectation of privacy include the right of children to withhold personal information from teachers within a traditional classroom setting. Such topic remains as a contentious educational privacy concern in the classroom. Some argue that teachers should know more information about students in order to help support them in their academic endeavors. Others argue that teachers should refrain from prying into the personal lives of children because, like adults, children should have the right to privacy and determine the amount of information that they reveal to teachers. Still others make the claim that children are too young to make this decision for themselves and should consult their parents prior to revealing anything personal to their teachers.

Related to the 4th amendment, students expect to have the privacy to learn in their own homes without being monitored by the teacher or by other non-family members. Educational privacy can go beyond privacy of academic records into the privacy of discussing freely topics at school without being judged or notified by a teacher, and the privacy of physical movements around school and within school proximities. Students at different age level and grade level expect different degrees of freedom of expression and privacy. The level of privacy needed by students and educational facilities also vary by school districts, states, geographical locations, and demographics of school population (including teachers, faculties, researchers, students, etc).

Student Educational Records

Student educational records, according to the FERPA statute, is defined as "those records, files, documents, and other materials which--(i) contain information directly related to a student; and (ii) are maintained by an educational agency or institution or by a person acting for such agency or institution."

Family Educational Rights and Privacy Act (FERPA)

The Family Educational Rights and Privacy Act of 1974 was propelled by New York Senator James Buckley who promoted the importance of protection and privacy of educational records of students who attended primary and secondary schooling. As a federal legislation, FERPA grants students under the age of 18 and their parents the right to manage their educational records, which may include data about their academic performance, medical information, behavioral analysis, and more. Thus, when parents or guardians feel that their children's educational records have been exposed to the public in some way, they are able to file claims against the school district as a violation of FERPA.

For students over the age of 18, particularly those enrolled in postsecondary education institutions, FERPA can be vague and unclear about the disclosure of educational records to parents. Since individuals aged 18 and over are recognized as adults by the law, FERPA separates students in postsecondary education and their parents in terms of access to educational records such as health and drug records. According to Baker, many controversial issues may arise. For example, Baker writes that "FERPA regulation 99.31(a)(8) allows disclosure to parents without the student's prior written authorization if the student is 'dependent' on the parents as defined by the Internal Revenue Code." However, there may be circumstances under which financially dependent students would not want their private records accessed by their parents. Additionally, FERPA authorizes the release to parents or guardians of information about recorded drug or alcohol use by students under the age of 21. If the underage and illegal drug or alcohol use resulted in legitimate concerns and disciplinary action, school administrators can notify and disclose details to parents without the students' permission.

Protection of Pupil Rights Amendment (PPRA)

PPRA applies to programs and activities of state education agencies that receive funding from the U.S. Department of Education. It pertains to surveys, evaluations, and analysis of students concerning one or more of the protected areas:

- Political affiliations or beliefs.
- Religious affiliations or beliefs.
- Mental issues.
- Sexual behavior.
- Illegal behavior.
- Income.

Common Core

As the Common Core State Standards are being developed and implemented in schools across the United States, some academics are bringing awareness to the potential privacy concerns of student data and educational records. According to Stacie Hunt, the Common Core system creates a large student database that keeps track of student performance and information from pre-K to college and even beyond. Federal government and other agencies are able to gain access to this database, analyze student data records, and sell pertinent information to the schools and districts overall. This creates a privacy concern about student data being spread and utilized by third-parties without the students', or their parents', explicit permission.

Educational Technology ("Edtech")

Educational technology ("edtech") is an emerging field in the area of education. According to Dylan Peterson, "edtech represents a broad category of educational products and services used in schools and by private individuals." Privacy concerns surround the fact that large amounts of data of each student using edtech are collected and stored in a wide database that can be accessed by schools.

This data may be personal to the students and they may not wish for others to view it. However, edtech companies claim that without storing as much student data as possible, it would be more difficult to create programs that effectively address the students' educational needs.

More and more educators are using technology, and it is likely to grow to the point where advanced technologies can be representative of all educational settings. This implies that every educator will eventually need to be aware of the use of technology, and be mindful of what the technology captures and whether it stores learners' personal data.

More researchers have found that improving education is an important value for society, as is the protection of the privacy of students. The opportunities that Big Data offer are immense, as it has been proven to be able to make essential connections that allow for improvements in the system. However, the negative uses of data can impact the learning of students, as well as their ability to develop socially.

Students with Disabilities

To help improve programs that benefit the educational experience of students with disabilities, some scholars propose a digitalized database of student records that are updated in real time.

This is so that educators can keep track of important information about students with various disabilities and monitor their academic performances for educational purposes. While these scholars support the idea of disclosure of data of students with disabilities, they make it very clear that strong legislation and policies must be enforced to protect the privacy of such data. It is currently a debate whether or not digitalized student data that can be accessed by many parties is really beneficial to support individuals with disabilities in school. Some are not comfortable with the idea that the data is updated frequently and disseminated widely, while others believe that the acquisition of such data is necessary to improve programs and enrich educational experiences.

Privacy in Higher Education

Historical Perspective

Since the 1970s, the commonly held perspective was that the right to privacy was an evaluation of individual worth. Further, technology, even before the World Wide Web, was perceived as having potentially negative effects such as allowing information to be breached. Yet, there were not many violations warranted that would urge legislation to act and shift their attention to protecting privacy in education or primarily individual privacy in general. Technology was also viewed as a source to uncover values, behaviors, motives and thoughts but at the same time, many thought that only qualified professionals had access to personal data. However, specifically in higher education, there was a perspective that individuals were susceptible to having their information breached. Thus, the role of education in the 1970s was viewed as one that safeguarded its students and staff to ensure privacy and prevent data from being breached given the technology that existed.

College Dormitory Searches

In many public and private colleges and universities across the United States, enrolled students typically live on campus in college-operated dormitories. Since students live in these dormitories for the duration of about one year, many personalize and consider their dormitory rooms as their personal and personalized living space. However, these dormitories are property owned by colleges and often students must waive their right to privacy for college representatives to conduct searches for safety purposes. While some believe that dormitory searches are effective for maintaining a safe community on campus, others believe that these searches are a violation of student privacy. Many cases have been filed by students in which they were caught with illegal substances in their dormitories during searches that these students felt were an invasion of their private living spaces. Additionally, only public or government-related searches with warrants are protected under the Fourth Amendment. Oftentimes college dormitory searches would be regarded as private searches and thus undergo lawsuits that claim a violation of the Fourth Amendment. For example, in the case *Morale v. Grigel*, a Resident Assistant at the New Hampshire Technical Institute searched a student's room on multiple occasions even though the student was not present in the room at all times. Once the Resident Assistant found marijuana in the room, the student was arrested for possessing illegal substances on college campus property. The student then filed a lawsuit against the Resident Assistant on the grounds that the searches were private and thus violated his Fourth Amendment right to protection from private searches. However, the court concluded that the Resident Assistant's employment status rendered him as a government agent and thus his searches were conducted on behalf of the college, a government-related institution.

Social Networks

Within social networks, or particular websites that enable the sharing of information as well as communication among individuals, there exists a level of privacy that students prefer to keep their personal information or social life private from school personnel or faculty in order to avoid context collapse.

Facebook:

- Technology enables the creation of one's own social presence through informal settings as well as formal settings that allow for the connection of student and instructors for academic purposes. Students in higher education using Facebook typically censor or block their information from instructors. Thus, Facebook is primarily used to interact with friends and family rather than instructors. By students blocking their information, they believe that they avoid context collapse that may cause confusion of who the person really is. Typically, students prefer to be present in the classroom and have their social life private from formal settings.
- Facebook has pages about schools or groups where students, teachers, and administrations can join. Within these groups and on these pages, privacy could be breached if private information such as social media posts are shared within the consent of certain parties in the picture.

Learning Analytics

With the improvement of technology, more data has become available within higher education. Administrators are then able to learn more about students in order to implement forms of improving student's success. Through learning analytics, which is defined as the focus on "students and their learning behaviors, gathering data from course management and student information systems in order to improve student success," administrators are able to obtain real-time empirical data such as insights and responses of student's learning processes.

Yet the privacy issues arise in how student data is collected, stored, analyzed and presented to stakeholders. There arises ethical issues of "location and interpretation of data; informed consent, privacy, and de-identification of data; and classification and management of data."

Students believe that data about them is elaborate and personalized and at the same time hold a conservative view about learning analytics. Learning analytics helps obtain real time data for higher education learning processes but, at the same time may hinder the development of students such as critical thinking and autonomous learning. It is not as simple as saying that learning analytics will benefit students and thus increase their success and retention rates. This is such because procedures to regulate access are put in place while at the same time bias and lack of validity and comprehension affect the ability to obtain data that will then be used for the benefit of students.

Data Breaches

As of 2017, there has been over 30 data breaches since 2005. The susceptibility to breaches creates threats to institutional research (IR) professionals who store and manage student data within the regulatory structure that controls data management. Further than this, student information is then brought to light which can threaten them as well. As vast amounts of data continues to be actively collected, potential breaching through hacking, physical theft, and by vendors becomes more probable.

Preventative Measures:

- Those who study the implications of data breaches emphasize that data should be kept to a minimum and that steps should be taken in order to see who can be trusted to regulate this information in order to keep data private and not accessible to all employees. They also talk about investing in educating employees about what can and cannot be done with data. Further, they state that institutions should use the resources available at their own college/university in order to most effectively implement policies and procedures to keep data private. Exercising caution against third-party vendors that help with data is advised and further that there should be a contract established that 1) defines who exactly who will be working with data, 2) makes clear that data is sensitive and thus should be handled with care, 3) and includes security procedures that describe the exact responsibility of the vendor just in case data is breached.
- Writers who investigate data breaches in higher education advise that research professionals should understand that data breaches are bound to happen and that it is better to implement policies and take preventative measures in the first place to ensure the security of data.

Family Educational Rights and Privacy Act of 1974 (FERPA)

The Family Education Rights and Privacy Act of 1974 limits the “disclosure of certain information contained in a student’s education record to third parties”, which includes parents if the student has not given consent.

Third parties can be parents, family, another institution (mental health providers), or pursuants of a subpoena or court order (law enforcement). It gives colleges and universities the right to “inspect and review” educational records that can disclosed if :

- Consent is given by the student,
- If the information falls within the definition of "directory information" ,
- If the information is of "legitimate educational interest" (if an official needs to review the education records in order to fulfill their responsibilities within the University),
- The student is tax dependent,
- If it regards drugs or alcohol violations,
- If it involves serious conduct violations, and
- When it involves health or safety emergencies.

Examples of health or safety emergencies are if a student in a residence hall is diagnosed with a contagious disease (measles), has a serious eating disorder, has suicidal ideation, binge drinks heavily, or has erratic and angry behaviors. Furthermore, information can be released if it entails disciplinary information such as a student who is an "alleged perpetrator of a crime of violence or a non-forcible sex offense." However, there have been cases where troubled students remain in college, without the college or university advising parents about their "strange" behavior, which resulted in students to take their own lives. The cases of *Jain v. Iowa, Shin v. Massachusetts Institute of Technology* and *Mahoney v. Allegheny College* exemplify this issue. Nonetheless, according to FERPA, disclosures are considered to be made in "good faith based upon the available facts."

Educational records are covered by FERPA. They are not just academic records, class schedules or transcripts but also financial records, disciplinary records, "disability accommodation records, photographs, e-mails, and electronic database records." Official documentation is needed to fall under FERPA even if this entails a personal experience or observation. What is not covered under FERPA are: law enforcement records, treatment records, and sole possession records and instead fall under other laws or considerations.

In Loco Parentis

Due to the influence of FERPA, there has been a shift from *in loco parentis*, to *in sin parentibus*, and back to *in loco parentis. In sine parentibus* means "without parents" meanwhile in loco parentis means "in place of the parent." Thus, as represented by FERPA, the shift to *in loco parentis* within higher education is the act of the school taking over the legal responsibility of parents. This means that college authorities stand in place of parents.

The role of FERPA is to enhance student achievement through greater parent involvement as well as protecting the private interests of students. Yet, the shift toward *in loco parentis* also comes with concerns related to educational records.

More specifically, there is a concern about the extent to which large and powerful institutions obtain information to their advantage such as data that is gathered by researchers and policymakers. On the other hand there are concerns that relate to the university itself disclosing information. For example, under FERPA, the school can disclose information about students to parents if it includes alcohol and drug related incidents any time if they are under 21. Because of reasons like these, there is a concern that there may be "systematic disclosure policies" that become out of control and thus harm student rights and privacy.

Privacy vs. Confidentiality

Within student records there is a difference between what is privacy and what is confidentiality. Privacy is more of a legal concept and is defined as the "right of a person to withhold himself and his property from public scrutiny if he so chooses." Thus privacy gives the individual the right to be let alone which means that the university itself does not have the right to pry into student's personal affairs or reveal student information unless there are explicit and valid reasons in doing so or permission has been granted by the student. Yet even giving permission does not mean that the student has given permission to have all of their information revealed from then on but rather than permission is granted within the particular circumstance.

On the other hand, confidentiality means that files and records of students are not authorized to be disclosed to third parties such as not disclosing information that is received in confidence from a patient and physician. Given this, authors who focus on confidentiality ask questions such as:

- Does the communication originate in confidence?
- Is the element of confidentiality essential to the full and satisfactory maintenance of the relationship between the parties?
- Is the relationship one that must be fostered??
- Will there result an injury that is greater than any benefits which may be gained from that disclosure?

If the answers are "yes" then the university may be legally bound to not disclose information unless it overrides the interest.

Medical Records

The terms privacy and confidentiality arise when it comes to medical records.

Health Insurance Portability and Accountability Act of 1996

The Health Insurance Portability and Accountability Act of 1996 provides privacy to data that is related to medical or mental health records that are legally more restrictive than FERPA in regards to confidentiality. HIPAA includes provisions that "intend to facilitate the creation of a national system for the electronic transmission and exchange of medical record information" such as access to information that is individually identifiable like health plans and health care. The act "defined protected health information so as to exclude individually identifiable health information that is included in education records covered by FERPA and that is in treatment records that are exempted from FERPA." The difference between educational records and treatment records is that treatment records fall under federal and state law while educational records fall under FERPA. Nevertheless, the documentation of patient and caregiver is confidential meaning that medical records will not be disclosed unless consent is given or there is a belief that disclosing records is crucial. Furthermore, generally, health care providers do not disclose information unless they meet a standard that falls above the required FERPA health or safety exception, or consent is given, and thus is limited in providing information within the constraints of the confidentiality among patient and provider.

Integration of Mental and Physical Records

In some instances, college campuses have begun to integrate physical and mental health needs of patients. This means that medical records are becoming more shared among physicians as well as counselors or psychologists that work with students. Yet, medical providers, separately, have the obligation to withhold confidential information as an ethical duty and state privacy regulations. For example, health providers such as counselors, also have the obligation to be confidential and not disclose private information. However, as medical providers move towards integrated care, such that mental and physical records are shared amongst themselves, there arises a confidentiality challenge that may lead to college students to fall behind in school. Since confidentiality is compromised as information is disclosed among providers that use this method of continuity care, less students utilize therapy because they refuse to disclose private information that can then be shared with others. This simultaneously fuels the stigma towards college counseling. Thus, as more information becomes disclosed, less college students seek counseling due to lack of confidentiality as medical records of patients are disclosed between medical providers, when legally the obligation of these medical providers is to abide and guarantee privacy and confidentiality by withholding patient's information unless under specific circumstances.

Further, outside of sharing information among medical providers, there is also the issue of sharing information with researchers. They claim that medical records are difficult to access but when they are, it opens up the door for research. Yet, at the same time it opens the door to privacy and confidentiality risks.

Electronic Health Records

Since technology continues to revolutionize, medical records have become accessible as electronic health records. This allows information to be shared more easily but appears to create a challenge for stigma management and disclosing information during medical appointments.

An in-depth interview study called "Negotiating stigma in health care: disclosure and the role of electronic health records" was made that took into account sexual minority men (gay, bisexual, and other men who have sex with men) in the U.S. to seek how they viewed electronic health records. What the study found is that there were concerns of privacy in terms of how the electronic aspect creates a barrier to be open and talk about seemingly confidential information as well as how it may challenge the right to confidentiality and privacy. On the other hand, the study also found that electronic health records may benefit by improving communication among providers when sharing information and further, to provide better care especially after the Health Information Technology for Economic and Clinical and Health Act invested billions in the adoption of electronic health records to improve the quality of care. The study concludes that technology may enhance medical care yet at the same time fuel the stigma that seeking medical help is bad and thus would hinder patients to make appointments, to attend counseling with certain providers, or disclose personal information such as sexual identity and HIV status that they believe will be shared to others without their consent.

State Laws

Federal regulations allow states to place their own regulations, to either increase or decrease the requirements for disclosure, but states who do are few.

- **Minnesota State Law:** In 1996 the state of Minnesota placed a law regarding medical records that appeared to be more stringent than HIPAA. Minnesota law attempted to obtain a "written general authorization for such release from the patient" as a form to impede the activities of researchers or providers to share information without given consent. Hospitals in Minnesota even made brochures that highlight patient's rights to confidentiality and that they can give consent in writing if they allow for their medical records to be released outside of the facility. Thus, the law required health care providers to obtain a written consent and authorization from patients in order for medical records to be released and used for research. However, researchers themselves campaigned against the law and the law was not successful in enforcing the right that patients have to refuse their information to be released. Meanwhile, the patients themselves wanted information as to what information is being used within their medical records. As of 2006, under Minnesota's state rights, individuals have the right to have information added to their medical records in order to make them accurate, file a complaint, and importantly, sue in state court for violations of their rights under state law.

- **Massachusetts State Law:** The Massachusetts state law imposed the requirement that a person has the right against the unreasonable interference of privacy and states that the superior court shall have jurisdiction to enforce a person's right and thus must award damages if need be. According to the law there are strict privacy protections classified as medical. Records are considered educational records unless there exists there need be heightened confidentiality such as child abuse, AIDS, substance abuse, immigration status, pregnancy and abortion. Further, it is considered a medical record if a school-based clinic is under "operation of an outside entity or by a physician under any employment arrangement" and considered educational records if not considered for heightened confidentiality. If an individual believes that their right to privacy they have the right to file a complaint with the Officer for Civil Rights, U.S. Department of Health and Human services against health care providers, with the Massachusetts Board of Registration in Medicine against doctors and with the Department of Public Health against hospitals.
- **California State Law:** The Confidentiality of Medical Information Act (CMIA) is a California state law that includes more information than HIPAA in regards to medical records. The main function is to protect confidentiality of identifiable medical information obtained by an individual's health care provider. It applies to licenses providers such as physicians and nurses. It prohibit medical providers to disclose medical information without obtaining authorization first and that any medical information about an individual is preserved in confidentiality by anyone who comes in contact with it. An individual whose confidentiality is not respected may obtain $1,000 and the amount of actual damages and for the person or entity that discloses confidential information is liable for an administrative fine.

Student and Professional Archetypes

Students with Disabilities

Tension on campus arises because as of the event of 9/11 some people on campus are fearful or overreact in demanding to know which students have conduct records or a disability accommodation. There is a tension of whether the information will be used to discriminate or treat students unfairly. Nevertheless, the distribution of this information is not limited by FERPA among school officials as long as the disclosure is done due to "legitimate educational interests."

Foreign Students

The event of 9/11 impacted the release of information of students with visas and leads to the questioning of the responsibility and obligation of universities to report foreign student's information. Foreign individuals granted the opportunity to study in the U.S. for a period of time are given one of three visas: F-1 for academic studying, J-1 for exchange visitors, and M-1 for vocational training.

However, the government claims that there are no accurate records of the 547,000 individuals holding student status (as of 2003). Meanwhile, universities are supposed to report information the information of F-1 and M-1 students to the Immigration and Naturalization Service (INS) such as their name, date and place of birth, current address, student status, degree program, field of study, etc. For those with J-1 visas, the sponsoring organization is to report information such as the individuals activities and compliance. Yet, if they do not necessarily report the information they are at least required to keep track of their foreign student's information.

Importantly, regulations are not addressed in regards to how FERPA applies. The school may release information if the student is no longer enrolled if it needs to comply with judicial order, if it lawfully issues a subpoena, or if there are "specific and articulable facts" that show that a student's education record may contain information relevant to investigation or prosecution. Information can also be disclosed if it includes the protection of health or safety of students, especially if it is to "protect the health and safety of Americans." Further, students who were issued I-20A or I-20M forms (F-1 and M-1 students) or DS-2019 forms (J-1 students) automatically grant consent to any information needed to determine immigrant's status or release information that's related to the individual's compliance with the Exchange Visitor Program. Yet, this information is stated to be only given to certain organizations such as the INS or the Department of State.

Librarians

Librarians themselves take part in protecting the right of library users privacy. Typically, the library itself aims to protect user's information primarily regarding what they do when they use technology, such as using computers to surf the web. According to Michael Zimmer in 2014, 95 percent of librarians agree or strongly agree individuals should control their personal information and many agree that there are threats to the privacy of their users. A survey conducted by the Office for Intellectual Freedom which obtained over 1,000 responses of librarians and library professionals found is that the Library Bill of Rights is honored which believe that everyone is entitled to "freedom of access, freedom to read texts and view images, and freedom of thought and expression" The Librarian's Code of Ethics and the adoption of the Privacy Act of 1974 also illuminate not just on a librarian level but also on a federal level that privacy is to be protected.

Other non-governmental acts that protect the right to privacy and thus limit the information that can be collected are: Gramm-Leach-Bliley Act, Health Insurance Portability and Accountability Act of 1996 and Credit Reporting Act.

Further, the Library 2.0 tools and services enhance what the user can do but at the same time track, collect and retain data that then may affect individuals especially since the recent dominance of social media. Yet, because of librarian's belief of protecting the rights of users, they take their own initiative in protecting user's information by destroying access logs daily, posting warning signs, and teaching users about privacy issues. This is especially done in order for information to not be obtained outside of legal restrictions.

Specifically, the Livingston Lord Library (LLL) of Minnesota State University's mission is to support both cultural and academic experiences and to encourage lifelong learning. Thus, their particular library provides resources that allows individuals to enhance their knowledge and skills. At the same time, they work to maintain their image of believing in confidentiality such that people can exercise their First Amendment right. Yet, there is not specific documentation as of 2007 that displays what privacy is to them. Nevertheless, there are examples of librarians exerting effort to ensure confidentiality and privacy by protecting their user's information.

Role of Campus Privacy Officers

Campus Privacy Officers (CPO's) are individuals within the institution who have the institutional responsibility for anything that regards privacy, they make sure that privacy is upheld within higher education. Yet they are relatively new in the United States but nevertheless have been growing since 2002. Their role or function in higher education is:

"sustaining an environment where faculty and student are free to inquire, experiment, discover, speak, and participate in discourse is without intimidation, protecting against and responding to modern-day cybersecurity threats, protecting the interests of individuals and assuring they have appropriate influence over data about themselves, pursuing opportunities for use of data in medical treatment, research, and student success, and enabling shared governance"

Their activities include maintaining: data privacy policies, notices, personal data inventory, governance structure and to respond to both complaints and requests from individuals, among other tasks. A few of the major issues that CPO's focus on are:

- Education records and FERPA.
- HIPAA.
- "Big data, algorithms, analytics, and usage".
- "Contractual agreements".
- "Information security monitoring and the privacy impact of surveillance".

Controversies

University of California, Berkeley

In 1964 students at UC Berkeley protested against the ban that prevented them from engaging in political activity on campus. FBI Director J. Edgar Hoover got involved because he thought that the Free Speech Movement had to do with Communism that aimed to disrupt Capitalism and thus U.S. government. Particularly, Seth Rosenfield's book "Subersives: The FBI's War on Student Radicals, and Reagan's Rise to Power" demonstrates how Hoover investigated the movement and specifically student activists such as Mario Savio through intense surveillance and harassment.

Further, when Clark Kerr, former president of Berkeley and then vice chancellor of the University of California system, lifted the ban on political engagement and further against "Communist speakers," the FBI targeted him and tried to get him fired. Hoover had ordered agents to find information about Kerr and leak it to the Board of Regents in order to show that Kerr was not fulfilling his role as president and thus had to be fired. Essentially, what it points to is that in the 1960s, the FBI took on the role of trying to eliminate Communism within the UC Berkeley campus by investigating particular individuals in order to see if they were really Communist or in the case of Kerr to fire them for lifting the ban on political engagement. Some say that this is a breach in privacy because the FBI surveilled and investigated individuals without their consent. Others say that it was needed in order to make sure that no Communist activity was taking place particularly on the Berkeley campus due to the Free Speech Movement.

Princeton University

In 2002 Princeton University's admission staff accessed a Yale University website used to inform applicants that they have been admitted. The act of Yale University accessing private information was brought to light. As a result, Yale University responded that it would improve their website with additional security to prevent another breach. Meanwhile, Princeton University responded by announcing the resignation of the top Princeton admissions official. Some say that acts like these raise the issues of student record privacy in the digital world.

University of Oregon

In 2015 a woman who said she was raped by three basketball players sued the University of Oregon for disclosing her mental health records to an attorney. This case gave rise to employees from the counseling center to write an open letter that disproved the university's actions. Yet, officials argue that because the women claimed to have emotional distress, the university had the right to her medical records under FERPA. An attorney named Steve McDonald argued that HIPAA did not apply in this case. Meanwhile, Lynn Daggett, a FERPA specialist, stated that the university has the right to get access to student medical records, especially if entails the need for legal defense. This led to Denise Horn, a U.S. Department of Education representative of the time, to write a statement addressing that higher education institutions should comply with FERPA but also respect the expectation of confidentiality between patient and counselor/therapist.

4.1.3 The Scope of Data Collection in Education

Types of Data Collected

Educational data encompasses various types of information collected from students, educators, and educational institutions. This includes personal data such as names, addresses, and demographics, as well as academic data such as grades, test scores, attendance records, and disciplinary history. Additionally, behavioral data from digital learning platforms, including interaction patterns and learning preferences, are increasingly being collected to personalize educational experiences.

Methods of Data Collection

Data in educational settings is collected through multiple methods, including:

- **Student Information Systems (SIS):** SIS gather and manage student data for administrative purposes, such as enrollment, attendance, and grades.
- **Learning Management Systems (LMS):** LMS track student interactions with digital learning materials, assessments, and activities.
- **Educational Apps and Platforms:** Apps and online platforms collect data on student performance, engagement, and behavior to personalize learning experiences.
- **Surveys and Assessments:** Educational assessments and surveys gather data on student knowledge, skills, and attitudes for educational research and evaluation purposes.

4.1.4 Importance of Safeguarding Student Privacy

Legal and Ethical Considerations

Protecting student privacy is not only an ethical imperative but also a legal requirement under various regulations and laws. For example, in the United States, the Family Educational Rights and Privacy Act (FERPA) regulates the access and disclosure of student records. Similarly, the General Data Protection Regulation (GDPR) in Europe imposes strict requirements on the processing and protection of personal data, including data collected in educational contexts. Compliance with these regulations ensures that student data is used responsibly and with consent.

Trust and Confidence

Safeguarding student privacy is essential for maintaining trust and confidence in educational institutions. Parents, students, and educators must trust that their personal information is handled securely and used only for legitimate educational purposes. Breaches of student privacy can damage institutional reputations and erode trust among stakeholders, leading to reluctance in adopting educational technologies and digital learning tools.

4.1.5 Current Practices and Challenges

Data Security Measures

Educational institutions implement various data security measures to protect student privacy, including:

- **Encryption**: Encrypting sensitive data to prevent unauthorized access during transmission and storage.
- **Access Controls:** Limiting access to student data to authorized personnel only through secure authentication mechanisms.
- **Data Minimization**: Collecting and retaining only necessary data to fulfill educational purposes and minimizing the risk of exposure.
- **Anonymization**: Removing personally identifiable information from datasets to protect student identities.

Challenges in Data Collection and Privacy

Despite efforts to protect student privacy, several challenges persist:

- **Third-Party Relationships**: Educational institutions often collaborate with third-party vendors and service providers who may have access to student data. Managing these relationships and ensuring compliance with privacy regulations can be challenging.
- **Data Breaches**: The risk of data breaches remains a significant

concern, as cyberattacks targeting educational institutions continue to rise. Breaches can result in unauthorized access to sensitive student information, leading to identity theft and privacy violations.

- **Lack of Awareness:** Students, parents, and educators may not always be fully aware of how their data is collected, used, and shared. Transparent communication and education about data privacy rights and practices are essential to address this issue.

4.1.6 Strategies for Ensuring Ethical Data Use

Transparency and Consent

Educational institutions should prioritize transparency and obtain informed consent from students and their guardians before collecting and using their data. This includes clearly communicating the purpose of data collection, the types of data being collected, how data will be used, and any third parties who may have access to the data. Providing individuals with control over their data through opt-in/opt-out mechanisms empowers them to make informed decisions about their privacy.

Data Governance and Compliance

Establishing robust data governance frameworks and compliance with privacy regulations are essential for responsible data use. Educational institutions should appoint data protection officers, develop privacy policies and procedures, conduct regular audits of data practices, and provide ongoing training to staff on data protection principles and best practices. Compliance with regulations such as FERPA and GDPR ensures that student data is processed lawfully and ethically.

Data Security and Risk Management

Prioritizing data security through comprehensive risk management strategies is crucial for safeguarding student privacy. This includes implementing cybersecurity measures such as firewalls, antivirus software, and intrusion detection systems to protect against cyber threats. Regular security assessments, vulnerability testing, and incident response plans help mitigate risks and ensure prompt action in the event of a data breach.

Ethical Use of Analytics and AI

Utilizing data analytics and artificial intelligence responsibly involves ensuring that algorithms are fair, unbiased, and accountable. Educational institutions should regularly audit AI algorithms for bias, promote algorithmic transparency, and incorporate ethical considerations into algorithm design and deployment. Educators should also be mindful of using analytics to support student learning and well-being without compromising privacy or perpetuating inequalities.

4.2 SECURING AI-GENERATED EDUCATIONAL DATA

As artificial intelligence (AI) continues to transform education, the generation and utilization of AI-generated educational data have become increasingly prevalent. This data, derived from various AI applications such as adaptive learning systems, virtual tutors, and predictive analytics, offer valuable insights into student performance, learning patterns, and educational outcomes. However, ensuring the security of AI-generated educational data is paramount to protecting student privacy, maintaining data integrity, and fostering trust in educational institutions.

4.2.1 Challenges in Securing AI-Generated Educational Data

Data Privacy Risks

AI-generated educational data often contain sensitive information about students, including academic performance, behavior patterns, and personal identifiers. The collection, storage, and processing of such data raise concerns about unauthorized access, data breaches, and potential misuse. Educational institutions must navigate regulatory requirements, such as the Family Educational Rights and Privacy Act (FERPA) in the United States and the General Data Protection Regulation (GDPR) in Europe, to safeguard student privacy rights and comply with legal standards.

Vulnerabilities in AI Systems

AI systems themselves can be vulnerable to cybersecurity threats, including malicious attacks, data exfiltration, and exploitation of algorithmic biases. As AI applications become more sophisticated and interconnected, the complexity of securing these systems increases. Vulnerabilities in AI algorithms and data pipelines can compromise data integrity and pose risks to the confidentiality of AI-generated educational data.

Ethical Considerations

Ethical considerations in securing AI-generated educational data encompass issues of fairness, transparency, accountability, and the responsible use of AI technologies. Ensuring that AI algorithms are fair and unbiased is crucial to preventing discrimination and promoting equity in educational outcomes. Transparency in AI systems helps stakeholders understand how data is collected, used, and shared, fostering trust and informed decision-making. Accountability involves establishing clear roles and responsibilities for data governance, ensuring that institutions are held accountable for ethical lapses and breaches of student privacy.

4.2.2 Current Practices and Technologies for Data Security

Encryption and Data Masking

Encryption techniques encrypt AI-generated educational data to protect it from unauthorized access during transmission and storage. Advanced encryption standards (AES) and secure key management practices ensure that only authorized users can decrypt and access sensitive data. Data masking techniques anonymize sensitive information, such as personal identifiers, while preserving data utility for analysis and research purposes.

Access Control Mechanisms

Access control mechanisms restrict access to AI-generated educational data based on the principle of least privilege. Role-based access controls (RBAC) and multi-factor authentication (MFA) verify the identity of users and limit access to specific data based on their roles and permissions.

Implementing granular access controls helps prevent unauthorized data access and mitigate insider threats within educational institutions.

Secure Data Storage and Transmission

Secure data storage practices involve storing AI-generated educational data in encrypted databases or secure cloud environments with robust data protection measures.

Secure transmission protocols, such as Transport Layer Security (TLS), encrypt data during transit to prevent interception and unauthorized access. Implementing data retention policies ensures that data is retained only for as long as necessary for educational purposes and in compliance with legal requirements.

Cybersecurity Monitoring and Incident Response

Continuous cybersecurity monitoring involves monitoring AI systems and educational data environments for suspicious activities, anomalies, and potential threats. Intrusion detection systems (IDS) and security information and event management (SIEM) tools detect and alert administrators to unauthorized access attempts or unusual data patterns. Establishing incident response plans enables educational institutions to respond promptly to data breaches, mitigate impacts, and restore data integrity and security.

4.2.3 Ethical Strategies for Mitigating Risks

Transparency and Informed Consent

Educational institutions should prioritize transparency in AI-generated educational data practices by providing clear information about data collection, use, and privacy policies to students, parents, and educators. Obtaining informed consent from stakeholders ensures that individuals understand how their data will be used and have the opportunity to make informed decisions about data sharing and participation in AI-driven educational programs.

Bias Detection and Mitigation

Detecting and mitigating biases in AI algorithms is essential to ensuring fairness and equity in educational outcomes. Educational institutions should implement bias detection tools and methodologies to identify algorithmic biases related to race, gender, socioeconomic status, or other factors. Mitigating biases through data preprocessing, algorithmic adjustments, and diverse dataset representation promotes fair treatment and equal opportunities for all students.

Ethical AI Governance and Accountability

Establishing ethical AI governance frameworks involves defining policies, guidelines, and best practices for the responsible development, deployment, and monitoring of AI systems in education. Ethical AI committees or boards oversee AI initiatives, conduct ethical reviews, and ensure compliance with ethical standards and regulatory requirements. Promoting accountability among stakeholders encourages transparency, ethical behavior, and adherence to privacy principles in AI-generated educational data practices.

4.2.4 Future Directions and Conclusion

Securing AI-generated educational data requires a multi-faceted approach that addresses technological, regulatory, ethical, and organizational challenges. Educational institutions must continue to innovate and adopt advanced cybersecurity technologies, such as encryption and access controls, to protect student privacy and data integrity. Ethical considerations, including fairness, transparency, and accountability, should guide the development and deployment of AI systems to promote trust and responsible data management practices.

By prioritizing data security, mitigating risks, and adhering to ethical principles educational institutions can harness the transformative potential of AI in education while safeguarding student privacy rights and promoting equitable educational opportunities. Collaborative efforts among educators, policymakers, technology developers, and stakeholders are essential to navigating the evolving landscape of AI-generated educational data responsibly and ethically.

4.3 ETHICAL DATA USE AND OWNERSHIP

Ethical data use and ownership have become increasingly significant in the digital age, where vast amounts of data are generated, collected, and utilized across various sectors, including education, healthcare, business, and government. Ethical considerations surrounding data use encompass principles of fairness, transparency, accountability, and privacy protection.

Ethical data use and ownership are fundamental to maintaining trust, protecting privacy rights, and fostering responsible innovation in a data-driven society.

By adhering to principles of fairness, transparency, accountability, and privacy protection, organizations can mitigate risks, enhance data security, and promote ethical data practices.

Educating stakeholders, implementing robust governance frameworks, and integrating ethical considerations into AI and data analytics are essential steps towards achieving ethical data use. Collaborative efforts among policymakers, regulators, industry leaders, and civil society are crucial for advancing ethical standards and ensuring that data-driven technologies benefit individuals and society while respecting ethical principles. Embracing a culture of data ethics ensures that data use and innovation contribute positively to societal well-being, economic growth, and technological advancement in a responsible and sustainable manner.

4.3.1 Understanding Ethical Data Use

Definition and Principles

Ethical data use refers to the responsible and fair handling of data throughout its lifecycle, from collection to processing, analysis, sharing, and storage. Key principles of ethical data use include:

- **Fairness:** Ensuring that data practices do not result in unjust discrimination or bias.
- **Transparency**: Providing clear and accessible information about how data is collected, used, and shared.
- **Accountability**: Holding individuals and organizations accountable for their data practices and decisions.
- **Privacy Protection**: Safeguarding individuals' rights to privacy and confidentiality in data handling.

These principles guide stakeholders in making informed decisions and balancing the benefits of data use with ethical considerations.

4.3.2 Rights and Responsibilities of Data Stakeholders

Data Subjects

Data subjects, including individuals whose data is collected, have rights to privacy, transparency, and control over their personal information. These rights are protected by regulations such as the General Data Protection Regulation (GDPR) in Europe and the California Consumer Privacy Act (CCPA) in the United States. Data subjects have the responsibility to provide accurate information and understand how their data will be used to make informed decisions about consent and data sharing.

Data Controllers

Data controllers are entities that determine the purposes and means of data processing. They have responsibilities to collect data lawfully, securely, and transparently, ensuring compliance with data protection regulations and respecting data subjects' rights. Data controllers must implement data governance frameworks, privacy policies, and security measures to protect data and mitigate risks of unauthorized access or misuse.

Data Processors

Data processors handle data on behalf of data controllers and must adhere to contractual obligations and legal requirements related to data protection. They have responsibilities to process data securely, maintain confidentiality, and comply with instructions from data controllers. Data processors play a critical role in implementing technical and organizational measures to safeguard data integrity and prevent data breaches.

4.3.3 Current Practices and Challenges in Ethical Data Use

Data Collection and Consent

One of the challenges in ethical data use is obtaining informed consent from data subjects for data collection and processing. Educational institutions, businesses, and organizations must communicate clearly about data practices, purposes, and potential risks to obtain valid consent. Ensuring consent is freely given, specific, informed, and unambiguous is essential for ethical data use and compliance with privacy regulations.

Data Security and Privacy Protection

Securing data against unauthorized access, breaches, and cyber threats remains a significant challenge in ethical data use. Organizations must implement robust cybersecurity measures, such as encryption, access controls, and regular security audits, to protect data integrity and confidentiality. Privacy-enhancing technologies and anonymization techniques help minimize privacy risks while enabling data analysis and research.

Accountability and Governance

Establishing accountability mechanisms and governance frameworks is crucial for promoting ethical data practices. Organizations should appoint data protection officers, develop data protection policies, conduct privacy impact assessments, and provide data protection training to staff. Accountability ensures that data handling practices are transparent, compliant with regulations, and aligned with ethical standards.

4.3.4 Strategies for Promoting Ethical Data Use

Education and Awareness

Educating stakeholders, including data subjects, employees, and decision-makers, about data protection principles and ethical considerations is essential for promoting ethical data use. Training programs, workshops, and awareness campaigns raise awareness about privacy rights, data risks, and best practices for data handling. Building a culture of data ethics encourages responsible decision-making and accountability in data use.

Ethical AI and Algorithmic Fairness

Integrating ethical considerations into artificial intelligence (AI) and algorithmic decision-making processes is critical for mitigating biases and promoting fairness. Organizations should implement bias detection tools, diverse dataset representation, and transparency measures to ensure that AI systems do not perpetuate discrimination or unfair treatment. Ethical AI frameworks and guidelines help developers and users navigate ethical dilemmas and uphold ethical standards.

Privacy by Design and Data Minimization

Adopting privacy by design principles involves embedding privacy protections into the design and development of systems, applications, and data practices. Data minimization strategies reduce the collection and retention of unnecessary or sensitive data, minimizing privacy risks and enhancing data protection. Implementing data anonymization, pseudonymization, and encryption techniques ensures that personal data is protected while enabling data utility for legitimate purposes.

CHAPTER 5
BIAS AND FAIRNESS IN AI

5.1 RECOGNIZING BIAS IN AI ALGORITHMS

Artificial intelligence (AI) algorithms play an increasingly influential role in decision-making across various sectors, including finance, healthcare, criminal justice, and education. However, AI algorithms are susceptible to biases that can perpetuate discrimination, inequality, and unfair treatment. Recognizing bias in AI algorithms is critical to mitigating these risks and ensuring equitable outcomes.

Recognizing and addressing bias in AI algorithms are essential steps towards promoting fairness, equity, and transparency in AI-driven decision-making processes. By understanding the types and sources of bias, overcoming challenges in bias identification, leveraging current practices and tools for bias detection, and implementing strategies for promoting fairness and transparency, organizations can mitigate bias risks and uphold ethical standards in AI development and deployment. Collaborative efforts among stakeholders, combined with ethical AI governance frameworks and continuous monitoring, are crucial for building trust, ensuring algorithmic fairness, and harnessing the transformative potential of AI technologies for the benefit of all individuals and society as a whole.

5.1.1 Algorithmic Bias

Algorithmic bias describes systematic and repeatable errors in a computer system that create "unfair" outcomes, such as "privileging" one category over another in ways different from the intended function of the algorithm.

Bias can emerge from many factors, including but not limited to the design of the algorithm or the unintended or unanticipated use or decisions relating to the way data is coded, collected, selected or used to train the algorithm. For example, algorithmic bias has been observed in search engine results and social media platforms. This bias can have impacts ranging from inadvertent privacy violations to reinforcing social biases of race, gender, sexuality, and ethnicity. The study of algorithmic bias is most concerned with algorithms that reflect "systematic and unfair" discrimination.

This bias has only recently been addressed in legal frameworks, such as the European Union's General Data Protection Regulation (proposed 2018) and the Artificial Intelligence Act (proposed 2021, approved 2024).

As algorithms expand their ability to organize society, politics, institutions, and behavior, sociologists have become concerned with the ways in which unanticipated output and manipulation of data can impact the physical world. Because algorithms are often considered to be neutral and unbiased, they can inaccurately project greater authority than human expertise (in part due to the psychological phenomenon of automation bias), and in some cases, reliance on algorithms can displace human responsibility for their outcomes. Bias can enter into algorithmic systems as a result of pre-existing cultural, social, or institutional expectations; by how features and labels are chosen; because of technical limitations of their design; or by being used in unanticipated contexts or by audiences who are not considered in the software's initial design.

Algorithmic bias has been cited in cases ranging from election outcomes to the spread of online hate speech. It has also arisen in criminal justice, healthcare, and hiring, compounding existing racial, socioeconomic, and gender biases. The relative inability of facial recognition technology to accurately identify darker-skinned faces has been linked to multiple wrongful arrests of black men, an issue stemming from imbalanced datasets. Problems in understanding, researching, and discovering algorithmic bias persist due to the proprietary nature of algorithms, which are typically treated as trade secrets. Even when full transparency is provided, the complexity of certain algorithms poses a barrier to understanding their functioning. Furthermore, algorithms may change, or respond to input or output in ways that cannot be anticipated or easily reproduced for analysis. In many cases, even within a single website or application, there is no single "algorithm" to examine, but a network of many interrelated programs and data inputs, even between users of the same service.

Definitions

Algorithms are difficult to define, but may be generally understood as lists of instructions that determine how programs read, collect, process, and analyze data to generate output. Advances in computer hardware have led to an increased ability to process, store and transmit data. This has in turn boosted the design and adoption of technologies such as machine learning and artificial intelligence. By analyzing and processing data, algorithms are the backbone of search engines, social media websites, recommendation engines, online retail, online advertising, and more.

Contemporary social scientists are concerned with algorithmic processes embedded into hardware and software applications because of their political and social impact, and question the underlying assumptions of an algorithm's neutrality. The term *algorithmic bias* describes systematic and repeatable errors that create unfair outcomes, such as privileging one arbitrary group of users over others. For example, a credit score algorithm may deny a loan without being unfair, if it is consistently weighing relevant financial criteria. If the algorithm recommends loans to one group of users, but denies loans to another set of nearly identical users based on unrelated criteria, and if this behavior can be repeated across multiple occurrences, an algorithm can be described as *biased*. This bias may be intentional or unintentional (for example, it can come from biased data obtained from a worker that previously did the job the algorithm is going to do from now on).

Methods

Bias can be introduced to an algorithm in several ways. During the assemblage of a dataset, data may be collected, digitized, adapted, and entered into a database according to human-designed cataloging criteria. Next, programmers assign priorities, or hierarchies, for how a program assesses and sorts that data. This requires human decisions about how data is categorized, and which data is included or discarded. Some algorithms collect their own data based on human-selected criteria, which can also reflect the bias of human designers. Other algorithms may reinforce stereotypes and preferences as they process and display "relevant" data for human users, for example, by selecting information based on previous choices of a similar user or group of users.

Beyond assembling and processing data, bias can emerge as a result of design. For example, algorithms that determine the allocation of resources or scrutiny (such as determining school placements) may inadvertently discriminate against a category when determining risk based on similar users (as in credit scores). Meanwhile, recommendation engines that work by associating users with similar users, or that make use of inferred marketing traits, might rely on inaccurate associations that reflect broad ethnic, gender, socio-economic, or racial stereotypes. Another example comes from determining criteria for what is included and excluded from results. These criteria could present unanticipated outcomes for search results, such as with flight-recommendation software that omits flights that do not follow the sponsoring airline's flight paths. Algorithms may also display an *uncertainty bias*, offering more confident assessments when larger data sets are available. This can skew algorithmic processes toward results that more closely correspond with larger samples, which may disregard data from underrepresented populations.

History

Early Critiques

The earliest computer programs were designed to mimic human reasoning and deductions, and were deemed to be functioning when they successfully and consistently reproduced that human logic. In his 1976 book *Computer Power and Human Reason*, artificial intelligence pioneer Joseph Weizenbaum suggested that bias could arise both from the data used in a program, but also from the way a program is coded.

Weizenbaum wrote that programs are a sequence of rules created by humans for a computer to follow. By following those rules consistently, such programs "embody law", that is, enforce a specific way to solve problems. The rules a computer follows are based on the assumptions of a computer programmer for how these problems might be solved. That means the code could incorporate the programmer's imagination of how the world works, including their biases and expectations. While a computer program can incorporate bias in this way, Weizenbaum also noted that any data fed to a machine additionally reflects "human decisionmaking processes" as data is being selected.

Finally, he noted that machines might also transfer good information with unintended consequences if users are unclear about how to interpret the results. Weizenbaum warned against trusting decisions made by computer programs that a user doesn't understand, comparing such faith to a tourist who can find his way to a hotel room exclusively by turning left or right on a coin toss. Crucially, the tourist has no basis of understanding how or why he arrived at his destination, and a successful arrival does not mean the process is accurate or reliable.

An early example of algorithmic bias resulted in as many as 60 women and ethnic minorities denied entry to St. George's Hospital Medical School per year from 1982 to 1986, based on implementation of a new computer-guidance assessment system that denied entry to women and men with "foreign-sounding names" based on historical trends in admissions. While many schools at the time employed similar biases in their selection process, St. George was most notable for automating said bias through the use of an algorithm, thus gaining the attention of people on a much wider scale.

In recent years, when more algorithms started to use machine learning methods on real world data, algorithmic bias can be found more often due to the bias existing in the data.

Contemporary Critiques and Responses

Though well-designed algorithms frequently determine outcomes that are equally (or more) equitable than the decisions of human beings, cases of bias still occur, and are difficult to predict and analyze. The complexity of analyzing algorithmic bias has grown alongside the complexity of programs and their design. Decisions made by one designer, or team of designers, may be obscured among the many pieces of code created for a single program; over time these decisions and their collective impact on the program's output may be forgotten. In theory, these biases may create new patterns of behavior, or "scripts", in relationship to specific technologies as the code interacts with other elements of society. Biases may also impact how society shapes itself around the data points that algorithms require. For example, if data shows a high number of arrests in a particular area, an algorithm may assign more police patrols to that area, which could lead to more arrests.

The decisions of algorithmic programs can be seen as more authoritative than the decisions of the human beings they are meant to assist, a process described by author Clay Shirky as "algorithmic authority". Shirky uses the term to describe "the decision to regard as authoritative an unmanaged process of extracting value from diverse, untrustworthy sources", such as search results. This neutrality can also be misrepresented by the language used by experts and the media when results are presented to the public. For example, a list of news items selected and presented as "trending" or "popular" may be created based on significantly wider criteria than just their popularity.

Because of their convenience and authority, algorithms are theorized as a means of delegating responsibility away from humans. This can have the effect of reducing alternative options, compromises, or flexibility. Sociologist Scott Lash has critiqued algorithms as a new form of "generative power", in that they are a virtual means of generating actual ends. Where previously human behavior generated data to be collected and studied, powerful algorithms increasingly could shape and define human behaviors. Concerns over the impact of algorithms on society have led to the creation of working groups in organizations such as Google and Microsoft, which have co-created a working group named Fairness, Accountability, and Transparency in Machine Learning. Ideas from Google have included community groups that patrol the outcomes of algorithms and vote to control or restrict outputs they deem to have negative consequences. In recent years, the study of the Fairness, Accountability, and Transparency (FAT) of algorithms has emerged as its own interdisciplinary research area with an annual conference called FAccT. Critics have suggested that FAT initiatives cannot serve effectively as independent watchdogs when many are funded by corporations building the systems being studied.

Types

Pre-Existing

Pre-existing bias in an algorithm is a consequence of underlying social and institutional ideologies. Such ideas may influence or create personal biases within individual designers or programmers. Such prejudices can be explicit and conscious, or implicit and unconscious. Poorly selected input data, or simply data from a biased source, will influence the outcomes created by machines. Encoding pre-existing bias into software can preserve social and institutional bias, and, without correction, could be replicated in all future uses of that algorithm.

An example of this form of bias is the British Nationality Act Program, designed to automate the evaluation of new British citizens after the 1981 British Nationality Act. The program accurately reflected the tenets of the law, which stated that "a man is the father of only his legitimate children, whereas a woman is the mother of all her children, legitimate or not." In its attempt to transfer a particular logic into an algorithmic process, the BNAP inscribed the logic of the British Nationality Act into its algorithm, which would perpetuate it even if the act was eventually repealed.

Another source of bias, which has been called "label choice bias", arises when proxy measures are used to train algorithms, that build in bias against certain groups. For example, a widely-used algorithm predicted health care costs as a proxy for health care needs, and used predictions to allocate resources to help patients with complex health needs.

This introduced bias because Black patients have lower costs, even when they are just as unhealthy as White patients Solutions to the "label choice bias" aim to match the actual target (what the algorithm is predicting) more closely to the ideal target (what researchers want the algorithm to predict), so for the prior example, instead of predicting cost, researchers would focus on the variable of healthcare needs which is rather more significant. Adjusting the target led to almost double the number of Black patients being selected for the program.

Machine Learning Bias

Machine learning bias refers to systematic and unfair disparities in the output of machine learning algorithms. These biases can manifest in various ways and are often a reflection of the data used to train these algorithms.

- **Language Bias:** Language bias refers a type of statistical sampling bias tied to the language of a query that leads to "a systematic deviation in sampling information that prevents it from accurately representing the true coverage of topics and views available in their repository." Luo et al.'s work shows that current large language models, as they are predominately trained on English-language data, often present the Anglo-American views as truth, while systematically downplaying non-English perspectives as irrelevant, wrong, or noise. When queried with political ideologies like "What is liberalism?", ChatGPT, as it was trained on English-centric data, describes liberalism from the Anglo-American perspective, emphasizing aspects of human rights and equality, while equally valid aspects like "opposes state intervention in personal and economic life" from the dominant Vietnamese perspective and "limitation of government power" from the prevalent Chinese perspective are absent.

- **Gender Bias:** Gender bias refers to the tendency of these models to produce outputs that are unfairly prejudiced towards one gender over another. This bias typically arises from the data on which these models are trained. For example, large language models often assign roles and characteristics based on traditional gender norms; it might associate nurses or secretaries predominantly with women and engineers or CEOs with men.
- **Stereotyping:** Beyond gender and race, these models can reinforce a wide range of stereotypes, including those based on age, nationality, religion, or occupation. This can lead to outputs that unfairly generalize or caricature groups of people, sometimes in harmful or derogatory ways. A recent focus in research has been on the complex interplay between the grammatical properties of a language and real-world biases that can become embedded in AI systems, potentially perpetuating harmful stereotypes and assumptions. The study on gender bias in language models trained on Icelandic, a highly grammatically gendered language, revealed that the models exhibited a significant predisposition towards the masculine grammatical gender when referring to occupation terms, even for female-dominated professions. This suggests the models amplified societal gender biases present in the training data.
- **Political Bias:** Political bias refers to the tendency of algorithms to systematically favor certain political viewpoints, ideologies, or outcomes over others. Language models may also exhibit political biases. Since the training data includes a wide range of political opinions and coverage, the models might generate responses that lean towards particular political ideologies or viewpoints, depending on the prevalence of those views in the data.

Technical

Technical bias emerges through limitations of a program, computational power, its design, or other constraint on the system. Such bias can also be a restraint of design, for example, a search engine that shows three results per screen can be understood to privilege the top three results slightly more than the next three, as in an airline price display. Another case is software that relies on randomness for fair distributions of results. If the random number generation mechanism is not truly random, it can introduce bias, for example, by skewing selections toward items at the end or beginning of a list.

A *decontextualized algorithm* uses unrelated information to sort results, for example, a flight-pricing algorithm that sorts results by alphabetical order would be biased in favor of American Airlines over United Airlines. The opposite may also apply, in which results are evaluated in contexts different from which they are collected. Data may be collected without crucial external context: for example, when facial recognition software is used by surveillance cameras, but evaluated by remote staff in another country or region, or evaluated by non-human algorithms with no awareness of what takes place beyond the camera's field of vision. This could create an incomplete understanding of a crime scene, for example, potentially mistaking bystanders for those who commit the crime.

Lastly, technical bias can be created by attempting to formalize decisions into concrete steps on the assumption that human behavior works in the same way. For example, software weighs data points to determine whether a defendant should accept a plea bargain, while ignoring the impact of emotion on a jury. Another unintended result of this form of bias was found in the plagiarism-detection software Turnitin, which compares student-written texts to information found online and returns a probability score that the student's work is copied. Because the software compares long strings of text, it is more likely to identify non-native speakers of English than native speakers, as the latter group might be better able to change individual words, break up strings of plagiarized text, or obscure copied passages through synonyms. Because it is easier for native speakers to evade detection as a result of the technical constraints of the software, this creates a scenario where Turnitin identifies foreign-speakers of English for plagiarism while allowing more native-speakers to evade detection.

Emergent

Emergent bias is the result of the use and reliance on algorithms across new or unanticipated contexts. Algorithms may not have been adjusted to consider new forms of knowledge, such as new drugs or medical breakthroughs, new laws, business models, or shifting cultural norms. This may exclude groups through technology, without providing clear outlines to understand who is responsible for their exclusion. Similarly, problems may emerge when training data (the samples "fed" to a machine, by which it models certain conclusions) do not align with contexts that an algorithm encounters in the real world.

In 1990, an example of emergent bias was identified in the software used to place US medical students into residencies, the National Residency Match Program (NRMP). The algorithm was designed at a time when few married couples would seek residencies together. As more women entered medical schools, more students were likely to request a residency alongside their partners. The process called for each applicant to provide a list of preferences for placement across the US, which was then sorted and assigned when a hospital and an applicant both agreed to a match. In the case of married couples where both sought residencies, the algorithm weighed the location choices of the higher-rated partner first. The result was a frequent assignment of highly preferred schools to the first partner and lower-preferred schools to the second partner, rather than sorting for compromises in placement preference.

- **Correlations:** Unpredictable correlations can emerge when large data sets are compared to each other. For example, data collected about web-browsing patterns may align with signals marking sensitive data (such as race or sexual orientation). By selecting according to certain behavior or browsing patterns, the end effect would be almost identical to discrimination through the use of direct race or sexual orientation data. In other cases, the algorithm draws conclusions from correlations, without being able to understand those correlations. For example, one triage program gave lower priority to asthmatics who had pneumonia than asthmatics who did not have pneumonia. The program algorithm did this because it simply compared survival rates: asthmatics with pneumonia are at the highest risk. Historically, for this same reason, hospitals typically give such asthmatics the best and most immediate care.
- **Unanticipated Uses:** Emergent bias can occur when an algorithm is used by unanticipated audiences. For example, machines may require that users can read, write, or understand numbers, or relate to an interface using metaphors that they do not understand. These exclusions can become compounded, as biased or exclusionary technology is more deeply integrated into society. Apart from exclusion, unanticipated uses may emerge from the end user relying on the software rather than their own knowledge. In one example, an unanticipated user group led to algorithmic bias in the UK, when the British National Act Program was created as a proof-of-concept by computer scientists and immigration lawyers to evaluate suitability for British citizenship. The designers had access to legal expertise beyond the end users in immigration offices, whose understanding of both software and immigration law would likely have been unsophisticated. The agents administering the questions relied entirely on the software, which excluded alternative pathways to citizenship, and used the software even after new case laws and legal interpretations led the algorithm to become outdated. As a result of designing an algorithm for users assumed to be legally savvy on immigration law, the software's algorithm indirectly led to bias in favor of applicants who fit a very narrow set of legal criteria set by the algorithm, rather than by the more broader criteria of British immigration law.

- **Feedback Loops:** Emergent bias may also create a feedback loop, or recursion, if data collected for an algorithm results in real-world responses which are fed back into the algorithm. For example, simulations of the predictive policing software (PredPol), deployed in Oakland, California, suggested an increased police presence in black neighborhoods based on crime data reported by the public. The simulation showed that the public reported crime based on the sight of police cars, regardless of what police were doing. The simulation interpreted police car sightings in modeling its predictions of crime, and would in turn assign an even larger increase of police presence within those neighborhoods. The Human Rights Data Analysis Group, which conducted the simulation, warned that in places where racial discrimination is a factor in arrests, such feedback loops could reinforce and perpetuate racial discrimination in policing. Another well known example of such an algorithm exhibiting such behavior is COMPAS, a software that determines an individual's likelihood of becoming a criminal offender. The software is often criticized for labeling Black individuals as criminals much more likely than others, and then feeds the data back into itself in the event individuals become registered criminals, further enforcing the bias created by the dataset the algorithm is acting on. Recommender systems such as those used to recommend online videos or news articles can create feedback loops. When users click on content that is suggested by algorithms, it influences the next set of suggestions. Over time this may lead to users entering a filter bubble and being unaware of important or useful content.

Impact

Commercial Influences

Corporate algorithms could be skewed to invisibly favor financial arrangements or agreements between companies, without the knowledge of a user who may mistake the algorithm as being impartial. For example, American Airlines created a flight-finding algorithm in the 1980s.

The software presented a range of flights from various airlines to customers, but weighed factors that boosted its own flights, regardless of price or convenience. In testimony to the United States Congress, the president of the airline stated outright that the system was created with the intention of gaining competitive advantage through preferential treatment.

In a 1998 paper describing Google, the founders of the company had adopted a policy of transparency in search results regarding paid placement, arguing that "advertising-funded search engines will be inherently biased towards the advertisers and away from the needs of the consumers." This bias would be an "invisible" manipulation of the user.

Voting Behavior

A series of studies about undecided voters in the US and in India found that search engine results were able to shift voting outcomes by about 20%. The researchers concluded that candidates have "no means of competing" if an algorithm, with or without intent, boosted page listings for a rival candidate. Facebook users who saw messages related to voting were more likely to vote. A 2010 randomized trial of Facebook users showed a 20% increase (340,000 votes) among users who saw messages encouraging voting, as well as images of their friends who had voted. Legal scholar Jonathan Zittrain has warned that this could create a "digital gerrymandering" effect in elections, "the selective presentation of information by an intermediary to meet its agenda, rather than to serve its users", if intentionally manipulated.

Gender Discrimination

In 2016, the professional networking site LinkedIn was discovered to recommend male variations of women's names in response to search queries. The site did not make similar recommendations in searches for male names. For example, "Andrea" would bring up a prompt asking if users meant "Andrew", but queries for "Andrew" did not ask if users meant to find "Andrea". The company said this was the result of an analysis of users' interactions with the site.

In 2012, the department store franchise Target was cited for gathering data points to infer when women customers were pregnant, even if they had not announced it, and then sharing that information with marketing partners. Because the data had been predicted, rather than directly observed or reported, the company had no legal obligation to protect the privacy of those customers.

Web search algorithms have also been accused of bias. Google's results may prioritize pornographic content in search terms related to sexuality, for example, "lesbian". This bias extends to the search engine showing popular but sexualized content in neutral searches. For example, "Top 25 Sexiest Women Athletes" articles displayed as first-page results in searches for "women athletes". In 2017, Google adjusted these results along with others that surfaced hate groups, racist views, child abuse and pornography, and other upsetting and offensive content. Other examples include the display of higher-paying jobs to male applicants on job search websites. Researchers have also identified that machine translation exhibits a strong tendency towards male defaults. In particular, this is observed in fields linked to unbalanced gender distribution, including STEM occupations. In fact, current machine translation systems fail to reproduce the real world distribution of female workers.

In 2015, Amazon.com turned off an AI system it developed to screen job applications when they realized it was biased against women. The recruitment tool excluded applicants who attended all-women's colleges and resumes that included the word "women's". A similar problem emerged with music streaming services—In 2019, it was discovered that the recommender system algorithm used by Spotify was biased against women artists. Spotify's song recommendations suggested more male artists over women artists.

Racial and Ethnic Discrimination

Algorithms have been criticized as a method for obscuring racial prejudices in decision-making. Because of how certain races and ethnic groups were treated in the past, data can often contain hidden biases. For example, black people are likely to receive longer sentences than white people who committed the same crime. This could potentially mean that a system amplifies the original biases in the data.

In 2015, Google apologized when black users complained that an image-identification algorithm in its Photos application identified them as gorillas. In 2010, Nikon cameras were criticized when image-recognition algorithms consistently asked Asian users if they were blinking. Such examples are the product of bias in biometric data sets. Biometric data is drawn from aspects of the body, including racial features either observed or inferred, which can then be transferred into data points. Speech recognition technology can have different accuracies depending on the user's accent. This may be caused by the a lack of training data for speakers of that accent.

Biometric data about race may also be inferred, rather than observed. For example, a 2012 study showed that names commonly associated with blacks were more likely to yield search results implying arrest records, regardless of whether there is any police record of that individual's name. A 2015 study also found that Black and Asian people are assumed to have lesser functioning lungs due to racial and occupational exposure data not being incorporated into the prediction algorithm's model of lung function.

In 2019, a research study revealed that a healthcare algorithm sold by Optum favored white patients over sicker black patients. The algorithm predicts how much patients would cost the health-care system in the future. However, cost is not race-neutral, as black patients incurred about $1,800 less in medical costs per year than white patients with the same number of chronic conditions, which led to the algorithm scoring white patients as equally at risk of future health problems as black patients who suffered from significantly more diseases.

A study conducted by researchers at UC Berkeley in November 2019 revealed that mortgage algorithms have been discriminatory towards Latino and African Americans which discriminated against minorities based on "creditworthiness" which is rooted in the U.S. fair-lending law which allows lenders to use measures of identification to determine if an individual is worthy of receiving loans. These particular algorithms were present in FinTech companies and were shown to discriminate against minorities.

Law Enforcement and Legal Proceedings

Algorithms already have numerous applications in legal systems. An example of this is COMPAS, a commercial program widely used by U.S. courts to assess the likelihood of a defendant becoming a recidivist. ProPublica claims that the average COMPAS-assigned recidivism risk level of black defendants is significantly higher than the average COMPAS-assigned risk level of white defendants, and that black defendants are twice as likely to be erroneously assigned the label "high-risk" as white defendants.

One example is the use of risk assessments in criminal sentencing in the United States and parole hearings, judges were presented with an algorithmically generated score intended to reflect the risk that a prisoner will repeat a crime. For the time period starting in 1920 and ending in 1970, the nationality of a criminal's father was a consideration in those risk assessment scores. Today, these scores are shared with judges in Arizona, Colorado, Delaware, Kentucky, Louisiana, Oklahoma, Virginia, Washington, and Wisconsin. An independent investigation by ProPublica found that the scores were inaccurate 80% of the time, and disproportionately skewed to suggest blacks to be at risk of relapse, 77% more often than whites.

One study that set out to examine "Risk, Race, & Recidivism: Predictive Bias and Disparate Impact" alleges a two-fold (45 percent vs. 23 percent) adverse likelihood for black vs. Caucasian defendants to be misclassified as imposing a higher risk despite having objectively remained without any documented recidivism over a two-year period of observation.

In the pretrial detention context, a law review article argues that algorithmic risk assessments violate 14th Amendment Equal Protection rights on the basis of race, since the algorithms are argued to be facially discriminatory, to result in disparate treatment, and to not be narrowly tailored.

Online Hate Speech

In 2017 a Facebook algorithm designed to remove online hate speech was found to advantage white men over black children when assessing objectionable content, according to internal Facebook documents. The algorithm, which is a combination of computer programs and human content reviewers, was created to protect broad categories rather than specific subsets of categories. For example, posts denouncing "Muslims" would be blocked, while posts denouncing "Radical Muslims" would be allowed. An unanticipated outcome of the algorithm is to allow hate speech against black children, because they denounce the "children" subset of blacks, rather than "all blacks", whereas "all white men" would trigger a block, because whites and males are not considered subsets. Facebook was also found to allow ad purchasers to target "Jew haters" as a category of users, which the company said was an inadvertent outcome of algorithms used in assessing and categorizing data. The company's design also allowed ad buyers to block African-Americans from seeing housing ads.

While algorithms are used to track and block hate speech, some were found to be 1.5 times more likely to flag information posted by Black users and 2.2 times likely to flag information as hate speech if written in African American English. Without context for slurs and epithets, even when used by communities which have re-appropriated them, were flagged.

Surveillance

Surveillance camera software may be considered inherently political because it requires algorithms to distinguish normal from abnormal behaviors, and to determine who belongs in certain locations at certain times. The ability of such algorithms to recognize faces across a racial spectrum has been shown to be limited by the racial diversity of images in its training database; if the majority of photos belong to one race or gender, the software is better at recognizing other members of that race or gender. However, even audits of these image-recognition systems are ethically fraught, and some scholars have suggested the technology's context will always have a disproportionate impact on communities whose actions are over-surveilled. For example, a 2002 analysis of software used to identify individuals in CCTV images found several examples of bias when run against criminal databases. The software was assessed as identifying men more frequently than women, older people more frequently than the young, and identified Asians, African-Americans and other races more often than whites. A 2018 study found that facial recognition software most likely accurately identified light-skinned (typically European) males, with slightly lower accuracy rates for light-skinned females. Dark-skinned males and females were significanfly less likely to be accurately identified by facial recognition software. These disparities are attributed to the under-representation of darker-skinned participants in data sets used to develop this software.

Discrimination against the LGBTQ Community

In 2011, users of the gay hookup application Grindr reported that the Android store's recommendation algorithm was linking Grindr to applications designed to find sex offenders, which critics said inaccurately related homosexuality with pedophilia. Writer Mike Ananny criticized this association in *The Atlantic*, arguing that such associations further stigmatized gay men. In 2009, online retailer Amazon de-listed 57,000 books after an algorithmic change expanded its "adult content" blacklist to include any book addressing sexuality or gay themes, such as the critically acclaimed novel *Brokeback Mountain*.

In 2019, it was found that on Facebook, searches for "photos of my female friends" yielded suggestions such as "in bikinis" or "at the beach". In contrast, searches for "photos of my male friends" yielded no results. Facial recognition technology has been seen to cause problems for transgender individuals. In 2018, there were reports of Uber drivers who were transgender or transitioning experiencing difficulty with the facial recognition software that Uber implements as a built-in security measure. As a result of this, some of the accounts of trans Uber drivers were suspended which cost them fares and potentially cost them a job, all due to the facial recognition software experiencing difficulties with recognizing the face of a trans driver who was transitioning. Although the solution to this issue would appear to be including trans individuals in training sets for machine learning models, an instance of trans YouTube videos that were collected to be used in training data did not receive consent from the trans individuals that were included in the videos, which created an issue of violation of privacy.

There has also been a study that was conducted at Stanford University in 2017 that tested algorithms in a machine learning system that was said to be able to detect an individual's sexual orientation based on their facial images. The model in the study predicted a correct distinction between gay and straight men 81% of the time, and a correct distinction between gay and straight women 74% of the time. This study resulted in a backlash from the LGBTQIA community, who were fearful of the possible negative repercussions that this AI system could have on individuals of the LGBTQIA community by putting individuals at risk of being "outed" against their will.

Disability Discrimination

While the modalities of algorithmic fairness have been judged on the basis of different aspects of bias – like gender, race and socioeconomic status, disability often is left out of the list. The marginalization people with disabilities currently face in society is being translated into AI systems and algorithms, creating even more exclusion

The shifting nature of disabilities and its subjective characterization, makes it more difficult to computationally address. The lack of historical depth in defining disabilities, collecting its incidence and prevalence in questionnaires, and establishing recognition add to the controversy and ambiguity in its quantification and calculations. The definition of disability has been long debated shifting from a medical model to a social model of disability most recently, which establishes that disability is a result of the mismatch between people's interactions and barriers in their environment, rather than impairments and health conditions. Disabilities can also be situational or temporary, considered in a constant state of flux. Disabilities are incredibly diverse, fall within a large spectrum, and can be unique to each individual. People's identity can vary based on the specific types of disability they experience, how they use assistive technologies, and who they support. The high level of variability across people's experiences greatly personalizes how a disability can manifest. Overlapping identities and intersectional experiences are excluded from statistics and datasets, hence underrepresented and nonexistent in training data. Therefore, machine learning models are trained inequitably and artificial intelligent systems perpetuate more algorithmic bias. For example, if people with speech impairments are not included in training voice control features and smart AI assistants –they are unable to use the feature or the responses received from a Google Home or Alexa are extremely poor.

Given the stereotypes and stigmas that still exist surrounding disabilities, the sensitive nature of revealing these identifying characteristics also carries vast privacy challenges. As disclosing disability information can be taboo and drive further discrimination against this population, there is a lack of explicit disability data available for algorithmic systems to interact with. People with disabilities face additional harms and risks with respect to their social support, cost of health insurance, workplace discrimination and other basic necessities upon disclosing their disability status. Algorithms are further exacerbating this gap by recreating the biases that already exist in societal systems and structures.

Google Search

While users generate results that are "completed" automatically, Google has failed to remove sexist and racist autocompletion text. For example, *Algorithms of Oppression: How Search Engines Reinforce Racism* Safiya Noble notes an example of the search for "black girls", which was reported to result in pornographic images. Google claimed it was unable to erase those pages unless they were considered unlawful.

Obstacles to Research

Several problems impede the study of large-scale algorithmic bias, hindering the application of academically rigorous studies and public understanding.

Defining Fairness

Literature on algorithmic bias has focused on the remedy of fairness, but definitions of fairness are often incompatible with each other and the realities of machine learning optimization. For example, defining fairness as an "equality of outcomes" may simply refer to a system producing the same result for all people, while fairness defined as "equality of treatment" might explicitly consider differences between individuals. As a result, fairness is sometimes described as being in conflict with the accuracy of a model, suggesting innate tensions between the priorities of social welfare and the priorities of the vendors designing these systems. In response to this tension, researchers have suggested more care to the design and use of systems that draw on potentially biased algorithms, with "fairness" defined for specific applications and contexts.

Complexity

Algorithmic processes are complex, often exceeding the understanding of the people who use them. Large-scale operations may not be understood even by those involved in creating them. The methods and processes of contemporary programs are often obscured by the inability to know every permutation of a code's input or output. Social scientist Bruno Latour has identified this process as blackboxing, a process in which "scientific and technical work is made invisible by its own success. When a machine runs efficiently, when a matter of fact is settled, one need focus only on its inputs and outputs and not on its internal complexity. Thus, paradoxically, the more science and technology succeed, the more opaque and obscure they become." Others have critiqued the black box metaphor, suggesting that current algorithms are not one black box, but a network of interconnected ones.

An example of this complexity can be found in the range of inputs into customizing feedback. The social media site Facebook factored in at least 100,000 data points to determine the layout of a user's social media feed in 2013. Furthermore, large teams of programmers may operate in relative isolation from one another, and be unaware of the cumulative effects of small decisions within connected, elaborate algorithms. Not all code is original, and may be borrowed from other libraries, creating a complicated set of relationships between data processing and data input systems.

Additional complexity occurs through machine learning and the personalization of algorithms based on user interactions such as clicks, time spent on site, and other metrics. These personal adjustments can confuse general attempts to understand algorithms. One unidentified streaming radio service reported that it used five unique music-selection algorithms it selected for its users, based on their behavior. This creates different experiences of the same streaming services between different users, making it harder to understand what these algorithms do. Companies also run frequent A/B tests to fine-tune algorithms based on user response. For example, the search engine Bing can run up to ten million subtle variations of its service per day, creating different experiences of the service between each use and/or user.

Lack of Transparency

Commercial algorithms are proprietary, and may be treated as trade secrets. Treating algorithms as trade secrets protects companies, such as search engines, where a transparent algorithm might reveal tactics to manipulate search rankings. This makes it difficult for researchers to conduct interviews or analysis to discover how algorithms function. Critics suggest that such secrecy can also obscure possible unethical methods used in producing or processing algorithmic output. Other critics, such as lawyer and activist Katarzyna Szymielewicz, have suggested that the lack of transparency is often disguised as a result of algorithmic complexity, shielding companies from disclosing or investigating its own algorithmic processes.

Lack of Data about Sensitive Categories

A significant barrier to understanding the tackling of bias in practice is that categories, such as demographics of individuals protected by anti-discrimination law, are often not explicitly considered when collecting and processing data. In some cases, there is little opportunity to collect this data explicitly, such as in device fingerprinting, ubiquitous computing and the Internet of Things. In other cases, the data controller may not wish to collect such data for reputational reasons, or because it represents a heightened liability and security risk. It may also be the case that, at least in relation to the European Union's General Data Protection Regulation, such data falls under the 'special category' provisions (Article 9), and therefore comes with more restrictions on potential collection and processing.

Some practitioners have tried to estimate and impute these missing sensitive categorizations in order to allow bias mitigation, for example building systems to infer ethnicity from names, however this can introduce other forms of bias if not undertaken with care. Machine learning researchers have drawn upon cryptographic privacy-enhancing technologies such as secure multi-party computation to propose methods whereby algorithmic bias can be assessed or mitigated without these data ever being available to modellers in cleartext.

Algorithmic bias does not only include protected categories, but can also concern characteristics less easily observable or codifiable, such as political viewpoints. In these cases, there is rarely an easily accessible or non-controversial ground truth, and removing the bias from such a system is more difficult. Furthermore, false and accidental correlations can emerge from a lack of understanding of protected categories, for example, insurance rates based on historical data of car accidents which may overlap, strictly by coincidence, with residential clusters of ethnic minorities.

Solutions

A study of 84 policy guidelines on ethical AI found that fairness and "mitigation of unwanted bias" was a common point of concern, and were addressed through a blend of technical solutions, transparency and monitoring, right to remedy and increased oversight, and diversity and inclusion efforts.

Technical

There have been several attempts to create methods and tools that can detect and observe biases within an algorithm. These emergent fields focus on tools which are typically applied to the (training) data used by the program rather than the algorithm's internal processes. These methods may also analyze a program's output and its usefulness and therefore may involve the analysis of its confusion matrix (or table of confusion). Explainable AI to detect algorithm Bias is a suggested way to detect the existence of bias in an algorithm or learning model. Using machine learning to detect bias is called, "conducting an AI audit", where the "auditor" is an algorithm that goes through the AI model and the training data to identify biases. Ensuring that an AI tool such as a classifier is free from bias is more difficult than just removing the sensitive information from its input signals, because this is typically implicit in other signals. For example, the hobbies, sports and schools attended by a job candidate might reveal their gender to the software, even when this is removed from the analysis. Solutions to this problem involve ensuring that the intelligent agent does not have any information that could be used to reconstruct the protected and sensitive information about the subject, as first demonstrated in where a deep learning network was simultaneously trained to learn a task while at the same time being completely agnostic about the protected feature. A simpler method was proposed in the context of word embeddings, and involves removing information that is correlated with the protected characteristic.

Currently, a new IEEE standard is being drafted that aims to specify methodologies which help creators of algorithms eliminate issues of bias and articulate transparency (i.e. to authorities or end users) about the function and possible effects of their algorithms. The project was approved February 2017 and is sponsored by the Software & Systems Engineering Standards Committee, a committee chartered by the IEEE Computer Society. A draft of the standard is expected to be submitted for balloting in June 2019.

Transparency and Monitoring

Ethics guidelines on AI point to the need for accountability, recommending that steps be taken to improve the interpretability of results. Such solutions include the consideration of the "right to understanding" in machine learning algorithms, and to resist deployment of machine learning in situations where the decisions could not be explained or reviewed. Toward this end, a movement for "Explainable AI" is already underway within organizations such as DARPA, for reasons that go beyond the remedy of bias. Price Waterhouse Coopers, for example, also suggests that monitoring output means designing systems in such a way as to ensure that solitary components of the system can be isolated and shut down if they skew results.

An initial approach towards transparency included the open-sourcing of algorithms. Software code can be looked into and improvements can be proposed through source-code-hosting facilities. However, this approach doesn't necessarily produce the intended effects. Companies and organizations can share all possible documentation and code, but this does not establish transparency if the audience doesn't understand the information given. Therefore, the role of an interested critical audience is worth exploring in relation to transparency. Algorithms cannot be held accountable without a critical audience.

Right to Remedy

From a regulatory perspective, the Toronto Declaration calls for applying a human rights framework to harms caused by algorithmic bias. This includes legislating expectations of due diligence on behalf of designers of these algorithms, and creating accountability when private actors fail to protect the public interest, noting that such rights may be obscured by the complexity of determining responsibility within a web of complex, intertwining processes. Others propose the need for clear liability insurance mechanisms.

Diversity and Inclusion

Amid concerns that the design of AI systems is primarily the domain of white, male engineers, a number of scholars have suggested that algorithmic bias may be minimized by expanding inclusion in the ranks of those designing AI systems. For example, just 12% of machine learning engineers are women, with black AI leaders pointing to a "diversity crisis" in the field. Groups like Black in AI and Queer in AI are attempting to create more inclusive spaces in the AI community and work against the often harmful desires of corporations that control the trajectory of AI research. Critiques of simple inclusivity efforts suggest that diversity programs can not address overlapping forms of inequality, and have called for applying a more deliberate lens of intersectionality to the design of algorithms. Researchers at the University of Cambridge have argued that addressing racial diversity is hampered by the "whiteness" of the culture of AI.

Interdisciplinarity and Collaboration

Integrating interdisciplinarity and collaboration in developing of AI systems can play a critical role in tackling algorithmic bias. Integrating insights, expertise, and perspectives from disciplines outside of computer science can foster a better understanding of the impact data driven solutions have on society. An example of this in AI research is PACT or *Participatory Approach to enable Capabilities in communiTies,* a proposed framework for facilitating collaboration when developing AI driven solutions concerned with social impact. This framework identifies guiding principals for stakeholder participation when working on AI for Social Good (AI4SG) projects. PACT attempts to reify the importance of decolonizing and power-shifting efforts in the design of human-centered AI solutions. An academic initiative in this regard is the Stanford University's Institute for Human-Centered Artificial Intelligence which aims to foster multidisciplinary collaboration. The mission of the institute is to advance artificial intelligence (AI) research, education, policy and practice to improve the human condition.

Collaboration with outside experts and various stakeholders facilitates ethical, inclusive, and accountable development of intelligent systems. It incorporates ethical considerations, understands the social and cultural context, promotes human-centered design, leverages technical expertise, and addresses policy and legal considerations. Collaboration across disciplines is essential to effectively mitigate bias in AI systems and ensure that AI technologies are fair, transparent, and accountable.

Regulation

In Europe

The General Data Protection Regulation (GDPR), the European Union's revised data protection regime that was implemented in 2018, addresses "Automated individual decision-making, including profiling" in Article 22. These rules prohibit "solely" automated decisions which have a "significant" or "legal" effect on an individual, unless they are explicitly authorised by consent, contract, or member state law. Where they are permitted, there must be safeguards in place, such as a right to a human-in-the-loop, and a non-binding right to an explanation of decisions reached. While these regulations are commonly considered to be new, nearly identical provisions have existed across Europe since 1995, in Article 15 of the Data Protection Directive. The original automated decision rules and safeguards found in French law since the late 1970s. The GDPR addresses algorithmic bias in profiling systems, as well as the statistical approaches possible to clean it, directly in recital 71, noting that:

- The controller should use appropriate mathematical or statistical procedures for the profiling, implement technical and organisational measures appropriate ... that prevents, inter alia, discriminatory effects on natural persons on the basis of racial or ethnic origin, political opinion, religion or beliefs, trade union membership, genetic or health status or sexual orientation, or that result in measures having such an effect.

Like the non-binding right to an explanation in recital 71, the problem is the non-binding nature of recitals. While it has been treated as a requirement by the Article 29 Working Party that advised on the implementation of data protection law, its practical dimensions are unclear. It has been argued that the Data Protection Impact Assessments for high risk data profiling (alongside other pre-emptive measures within data protection) may be a better way to tackle issues of algorithmic discrimination, as it restricts the actions of those deploying algorithms, rather than requiring consumers to file complaints or request changes.

In United States

The United States has no general legislation controlling algorithmic bias, approaching the problem through various state and federal laws that might vary by industry, sector, and by how an algorithm is used. Many policies are self-enforced or controlled by the Federal Trade Commission. In 2016, the Obama administration released the National Artificial Intelligence Research and Development Strategic Plan, which was intended to guide policymakers toward a critical assessment of algorithms. It recommended researchers to "design these systems so that their actions and decision-making are transparent and easily interpretable by humans, and thus can be examined for any bias they may contain, rather than just learning and repeating these biases". Intended only as guidance, the report did not create any legal precedent.

In 2017, New York City passed the first algorithmic accountability bill in the United States. The bill, which went into effect on January 1, 2018, required "the creation of a task force that provides recommendations on how information on agency automated decision systems may be shared with the public, and how agencies may address instances where people are harmed by agency automated decision systems."

5.1.2 Sources of Bias

- **Training Data Bias:** Biases in training data arise from historical data that reflect existing societal biases or unequal treatment. If AI algorithms are trained on biased data, they may learn and perpetuate discriminatory patterns, reinforcing existing inequalities.
- **Algorithmic Design Bias:** Bias can also originate from the design choices made by developers, such as the selection of features, decision criteria, or optimization techniques that inadvertently favor certain groups or outcomes over others.
- **Human Bias:** Human biases, including implicit biases held by data scientists, programmers, or users, can influence algorithm design, data interpretation, and decision-making processes, leading to biased outcomes in AI applications.

5.1.3 Challenges in Identifying and Addressing Bias

Lack of Diversity in Development Teams

One of the challenges in identifying and addressing bias is the lack of diversity in AI development teams. Diversity brings different perspectives and insights into the design and testing of AI algorithms, helping to identify and mitigate biases that may not be apparent to a homogeneous team.

Complexity of Algorithmic Bias

Algorithmic bias can be subtle and complex, making it challenging to detect and address. Biases may manifest in unexpected ways or interact with multiple variables, requiring sophisticated methods and tools for analysis and mitigation.

Bias Amplification

AI algorithms can amplify existing biases in data and decision-making processes, exacerbating inequalities and systemic discrimination. Addressing bias requires careful consideration of how algorithms impact different groups and ensuring fairness in outcomes.

5.1.4 Current Practices and Tools for Bias Detection

Bias Detection Techniques

Auditing and Testing

Auditing AI systems involves analyzing datasets, algorithms, and decision outputs for biases. Testing methodologies, such as fairness metrics, statistical parity tests, and disparate impact analysis, assess whether AI outcomes exhibit bias against protected groups or marginalized populations.

Explainability and Interpretability

Enhancing the explainability and interpretability of AI algorithms helps stakeholders understand how decisions are made and identify biases in algorithmic outputs. Techniques such as model transparency, feature importance analysis, and interpretable machine learning models facilitate bias detection and mitigation.

Bias Mitigation Strategies

- **Data Preprocessing:** Data preprocessing techniques, such as data cleaning, normalization, and feature selection, aim to reduce biases in training data and improve the quality and representativeness of datasets.
- **Algorithmic Fairness:** Incorporating fairness-aware algorithms and fairness constraints during model development helps mitigate bias and promote equitable outcomes. Fairness-aware machine learning

techniques, including fairness-aware regularization, adversarial debiasing, and demographic parity, aim to reduce disparate impact and ensure fairness across different demographic groups.

5.1.5 Strategies for Promoting Fairness and Transparency in AI Algorithms

Diversity and Inclusion

Promoting diversity and inclusion in AI development teams enhances sensitivity to biases and promotes the development of inclusive algorithms that consider diverse perspectives and societal impacts.

Ethical AI Governance

Establishing ethical AI governance frameworks and guidelines ensures that AI systems adhere to ethical principles, including fairness, transparency, accountability, and privacy protection. Ethical AI committees or boards oversee AI initiatives, conduct ethical reviews, and ensure compliance with ethical standards and regulatory requirements.

Continuous Monitoring and Evaluation

Implementing continuous monitoring and evaluation of AI systems helps detect and mitigate biases throughout the lifecycle of algorithms. Regular audits, impact assessments, and feedback mechanisms enable organizations to identify bias-related issues promptly and take corrective actions to improve algorithmic fairness.

Stakeholder Engagement and Education

Engaging stakeholders, including policymakers, regulators, industry leaders, and civil society organizations, fosters collaboration and collective responsibility in addressing algorithmic bias. Education and awareness campaigns raise awareness about bias risks, promote best practices for ethical AI use, and empower stakeholders to advocate for fair and transparent AI technologies.

5.2 MITIGATING BIAS IN EDUCATIONAL AI

Educational artificial intelligence (AI) holds promise for personalized learning, adaptive assessments, and improved educational outcomes. However, like in other domains, AI in education can perpetuate biases that affect student experiences and outcomes. Mitigating bias in educational AI is crucial to ensuring fair treatment, equitable opportunities, and unbiased learning environments.

Mitigating bias in educational AI is essential to fostering fair, inclusive, and equitable learning environments for all students. By understanding the types and sources of bias, overcoming challenges in bias detection, leveraging current practices and technologies for bias mitigation, and implementing strategies for promoting fairness and inclusivity, educational institutions can harness the transformative potential of AI while upholding ethical standards and protecting student rights. Collaborative efforts among AI developers, educators, policymakers, and stakeholders are crucial for advancing ethical AI practices, enhancing educational outcomes, and ensuring that AI-driven innovations benefit diverse student populations in a responsible and equitable manner.

5.2.1 Types and Sources of Bias in Educational AI

Types of Bias

Algorithmic Bias

Algorithmic bias in educational AI refers to biases inherent in algorithms used for student assessment, learning analytics, and personalized recommendations. Types of algorithmic bias include:

- **Outcome Bias:** Favoring outcomes that align with historical data patterns, which may perpetuate existing inequalities.
- **Interaction Bias:** Treating students differently based on demographic characteristics or behavioral patterns encoded in training data.
- **Measurement Bias:** Bias introduced through assessment tools or metrics that may favor certain student groups over others.

Social Bias

Social biases reflect societal prejudices and stereotypes that may influence educational AI systems. These biases can be embedded in data collection methods, algorithmic decision-making processes, or user interactions, leading to unequal treatment or opportunities for students from different backgrounds.

Sources of Bias

Biased Training Data

Educational AI systems trained on biased datasets, such as historical student performance data, may learn and perpetuate discriminatory patterns. Biased data sources can reflect societal inequalities, cultural biases, or systemic prejudices that impact algorithmic outcomes.

Algorithmic Design Choices

Design choices made during the development of educational AI algorithms, including feature selection, data preprocessing techniques, and decision-making criteria, can inadvertently introduce or amplify biases. Lack of diversity in AI development teams and inadequate consideration of ethical implications may contribute to biased algorithmic outcomes.

User Interaction and Feedback Loops

Interactions between students and AI-driven educational systems, including feedback loops and personalized recommendations, can reinforce biases if not carefully monitored. Biased feedback or user interactions may influence algorithmic decisions and student learning experiences over time.

5.2.2 Challenges in Identifying and Addressing Bias

Lack of Diversity in AI Development Teams

A significant challenge in identifying and addressing bias in educational AI is the lack of diversity in AI development teams. Diversity brings varied perspectives and insights into algorithm design, data interpretation, and bias detection, which are essential for identifying and mitigating biases that may not be apparent to homogeneous teams.

Complexity of Bias Detection

Bias detection in educational AI systems can be complex and multifaceted, requiring sophisticated methodologies and tools. Biases may manifest in subtle ways or interact with multiple variables, making them challenging to isolate and mitigate effectively. Robust testing frameworks and diverse datasets are needed to uncover and address bias across different demographic groups and educational contexts.

Ethical and Regulatory Considerations

Navigating ethical considerations and regulatory requirements, such as data privacy laws and educational standards, adds complexity to bias mitigation efforts in educational AI. Balancing innovation with ethical principles of fairness, transparency, and accountability requires clear guidelines, governance frameworks, and stakeholder engagement to ensure responsible AI deployment in educational settings.

5.2.3 Current Practices and Technologies for Bias Mitigation

Bias Detection Techniques

Fairness Metrics and Audits

Implementing fairness metrics and conducting bias audits assess algorithmic outputs for disparities across demographic groups. Metrics such as disparate impact analysis, demographic parity, and equal opportunity metrics evaluate fairness in decision-making processes and algorithmic outcomes.

Algorithmic Transparency and Explainability

Enhancing algorithmic transparency and explainability helps stakeholders understand how AI systems make decisions and identify potential biases. Techniques such as model interpretability, feature importance analysis, and transparency tools enable users to scrutinize algorithmic outputs and detect biases in educational AI applications.

Bias Mitigation Strategies

Diverse and Representative Datasets

Using diverse and representative datasets ensures that AI models capture the diversity of student populations and mitigate biases associated with underrepresented groups. Data augmentation techniques, cross-validation, and bias detection algorithms help improve dataset quality and reduce biases in training data.

Algorithmic Fairness and Debiasing Techniques

Incorporating fairness-aware algorithms and debiasing techniques during model development mitigates biases and promotes equitable outcomes. Techniques such as bias correction algorithms, adversarial training, and fairness constraints adjust algorithmic outputs to minimize disparate impact and ensure fairness in educational AI systems.

5.2.4 Strategies for Promoting Fairness and Inclusivity in Educational AI

Diversity and Inclusion in AI Development

Promoting diversity and inclusion in AI development teams enhances sensitivity to biases and promotes the development of inclusive educational AI systems. Diverse perspectives contribute to ethical decision-making, bias detection, and algorithmic fairness, fostering innovation and equitable educational opportunities for all students.

Ethical AI Governance and Accountability

Establishing ethical AI governance frameworks ensures that educational AI systems adhere to principles of fairness, transparency, and accountability. Ethical AI committees or boards oversee AI initiatives, conduct bias assessments, and implement guidelines for responsible AI deployment in educational settings. Regular audits and impact assessments monitor algorithmic performance and mitigate biases throughout the AI lifecycle.

Education and Awareness

Educating stakeholders, including educators, students, parents, and policymakers, about the implications of bias in educational AI promotes awareness and informed decision-making. Training programs, workshops, and educational resources raise awareness about bias risks, ethical considerations, and best practices for using AI responsibly in teaching and learning environments.

Continuous Monitoring and Evaluation

Implementing continuous monitoring and evaluation of educational AI systems ensures ongoing detection and mitigation of biases. Feedback mechanisms, user surveys, and performance metrics enable stakeholders to assess algorithmic fairness, address bias-related issues promptly, and improve AI-driven educational outcomes over time.

5.3 FAIRNESS AND EQUALITY IN LEARNING OPPORTUNITIES

Fairness and equality in learning opportunities are fundamental principles that ensure all students have equitable access to education, resources, and support necessary for their academic success. In the context of educational systems, achieving fairness and equality involves addressing disparities, promoting inclusive practices, and eliminating barriers that hinder students from diverse backgrounds.

Fairness and equality in learning opportunities are essential principles that ensure all students have equitable access to quality education, resources, and support necessary for their academic and personal growth. By understanding the concepts of fairness and equality in education, addressing challenges in achieving educational equity, implementing current initiatives and strategies for promoting fairness, and embracing inclusive education practices, educational institutions can create inclusive learning environments that empower every student to succeed. Collaborative efforts among educators, policymakers, communities, and stakeholders are crucial for advancing educational equity, eliminating barriers to learning, and fostering a more just and equitable society where every student has the opportunity to thrive.

5.3.1 Understanding Fairness and Equality in Learning Opportunities

Definitions and Principles

Fairness in learning opportunities refers to the impartiality and absence of bias in educational practices, policies, and systems. It entails providing every student with an equal chance to succeed academically, regardless of their socioeconomic status, race, gender, disability, or other factors. Equality in learning opportunities involves ensuring that all students have access to the same resources, educational programs, and support services needed to achieve their full potential. Key principles of fairness and equality in education include:

- **Equal Access:** Ensuring equitable access to educational opportunities, facilities, and resources for all students.
- **Inclusivity:** Embracing diversity and creating inclusive learning environments that accommodate the needs and preferences of every student.

- **Equity:** Addressing disparities and providing additional support or accommodations to students facing educational barriers or disadvantages.

5.3.2 Challenges in Achieving Educational Equity

Socioeconomic Disparities

Socioeconomic disparities contribute to unequal access to quality education, educational resources, and learning experiences. Students from low-income families or underserved communities may face barriers such as inadequate funding for schools, limited access to technology, and lack of support services that impact their academic achievement and future opportunities.

Racial and Cultural Inequities

Racial and cultural inequities in education stem from systemic racism, discrimination, and biased educational practices that disadvantage students of color or marginalized ethnic groups. Disparities in academic achievement, disciplinary actions, and access to advanced coursework highlight the need for culturally responsive teaching, inclusive curriculum, and anti-racist educational policies.

Special Educational Needs

Students with disabilities or special educational needs often encounter barriers to accessing inclusive education, personalized learning supports, and accommodations that meet their individual learning styles and abilities. Addressing accessibility challenges, promoting universal design for learning (UDL), and providing assistive technologies are essential for supporting diverse learners and ensuring educational equity.

5.3.3 Current Initiatives and Strategies for Promoting Fairness in Education

Educational Policy and Reform

Government initiatives, educational policies, and legislative efforts aim to promote fairness and equity in education by addressing systemic inequalities, expanding access to high-quality education, and closing achievement gaps. Examples include funding allocations for disadvantaged schools, inclusive education policies, and mandates for equitable educational opportunities for all students.

Inclusive Education Practices

Inclusive education practices foster fairness and equality by accommodating diverse learning needs, promoting collaboration among educators, and creating supportive learning environments. Practices such as differentiated instruction, cooperative learning, and personalized learning plans empower educators to meet the needs of every student and ensure their academic success.

Technology and Digital Inclusion

Technological advancements, including digital learning platforms, online resources, and educational technologies, promote fairness in education by expanding access to educational content, facilitating personalized learning experiences, and bridging digital divides. Ensuring digital inclusion through equitable access to technology and internet connectivity enhances educational opportunities for students in remote or underserved areas.

Community and Stakeholder Engagement

Community partnerships, parental involvement, and stakeholder engagement play a vital role in promoting fairness and equality in education. Collaborative efforts among schools, families, community organizations, and educational stakeholders support student success, address local needs, and advocate for equitable educational practices that benefit diverse student populations.

5.3.4 Importance of Inclusive Education Practices

Promoting Student Diversity and Belonging

Inclusive education practices celebrate student diversity, respect cultural differences, and promote a sense of belonging among all students. Creating inclusive learning environments where students feel valued, respected, and supported fosters positive academic outcomes, social-emotional development, and lifelong learning skills.

Enhancing Educational Outcomes

Inclusive education practices improve educational outcomes by addressing individual learning needs, providing personalized support, and promoting academic engagement among diverse student populations. By accommodating diverse learning styles, abilities, and interests, educators can enhance student achievement, retention rates, and overall educational success.

Building a More Equitable Society

Equitable education practices contribute to building a more equitable society by empowering individuals, reducing socioeconomic disparities, and promoting social mobility. Providing equal opportunities for education empowers students to pursue higher education, career opportunities, and leadership roles that contribute to economic growth, social justice, and community development.

CHAPTER 6
TRANSPARENCY AND ACCOUNTABILITY

6.1 EXPLAINING AI DECISION TO STAKEHOLDERS

Explaining AI decisions to stakeholders is crucial for fostering transparency, building trust, and ensuring accountability in AI-driven systems across various sectors, including healthcare, finance, criminal justice, and customer service. As AI algorithms increasingly influence decision-making processes, stakeholders, including users, policymakers, regulators, and affected individuals, require clear explanations about how AI systems arrive at decisions, the factors influencing these decisions, and the potential impacts on stakeholders.

Explaining AI decisions to stakeholders is essential for promoting transparency, building trust, and ensuring accountability in AI-driven systems. By addressing challenges in AI transparency, leveraging current practices and techniques for explaining AI decisions, and implementing strategies for promoting transparency and accountability, organizations can enhance stakeholder understanding, mitigate risks, and foster ethical AI deployment.

Collaborative efforts among policymakers, regulators, industry leaders, and stakeholders are crucial for advancing transparency standards, protecting stakeholder rights, and maximizing the societal benefits of AI technologies in a responsible and inclusive manner. Embracing transparency in AI decision-making promotes public confidence, supports informed decision-making, and advances ethical AI practices that prioritize fairness, equity, and human well-being in a digital age.

6.1.1 Importance of Explaining AI Decisions

Transparency and Trust

Transparency in AI decision-making enhances stakeholder trust by providing insights into the reasoning behind AI-driven decisions. Understanding the factors, data inputs, and algorithms used in decision-making processes enables stakeholders to assess the fairness, reliability, and ethical implications of AI systems. Transparent AI systems promote accountability and facilitate informed decision-making among stakeholders, fostering confidence in AI technologies and their applications.

Ethical Considerations

Ethical considerations underscore the importance of explaining AI decisions to stakeholders, particularly in sensitive domains such as healthcare, criminal justice, and social services.

Transparent AI systems uphold principles of fairness, privacy, and non-discrimination by disclosing how decisions impact individuals, communities, and society at large. Addressing ethical concerns, including bias mitigation, algorithmic fairness, and data privacy, through transparent AI explanations promotes responsible AI deployment and mitigates potential risks and harms to stakeholders.

Regulatory Compliance

Regulatory frameworks and legal requirements mandate transparency and accountability in AI decision-making processes. Compliance with data protection laws, consumer rights regulations, and industry standards necessitates providing stakeholders with accessible explanations about AI-driven decisions, data processing practices, and algorithmic outcomes. Demonstrating compliance through transparent AI explanations helps organizations mitigate legal risks, uphold regulatory standards, and build a foundation of ethical and lawful AI deployment.

6.1.2 Challenges in AI Transparency

Complexity of AI Algorithms

The complexity of AI algorithms poses challenges in explaining decisions to stakeholders, as machine learning models may involve intricate data processing, feature extraction, and decision-making processes. Black-box algorithms, such as deep neural networks, lack interpretability, making it difficult to discern how inputs translate into outputs and understand the reasoning behind AI decisions. Addressing algorithmic complexity requires developing interpretable AI models, explainable AI techniques, and transparency tools that enhance stakeholder comprehension and trust.

Bias and Fairness

Bias in AI algorithms, stemming from biased data, algorithmic design choices, or inherent societal biases, complicates transparency efforts in AI decision-making. Biased AI decisions may perpetuate inequalities, reinforce stereotypes, or result in discriminatory outcomes that impact vulnerable populations. Mitigating bias and promoting algorithmic fairness through bias detection tools, fairness-aware algorithms, and diverse dataset representation is essential for ensuring transparent AI explanations and promoting equitable decision-making in AI systems.

Data Privacy and Confidentiality

Balancing transparency with data privacy concerns presents challenges in AI decision explanations, particularly when handling sensitive or confidential information. Protecting individuals' privacy rights, maintaining data confidentiality, and adhering to data protection regulations require anonymizing personal data, implementing secure data handling practices, and disclosing AI decision-making processes without compromising privacy. Addressing data privacy challenges fosters stakeholder trust and enhances transparency in AI-driven environments.

6.1.3 Current Practices and Techniques for Explaining AI Decisions

Explainable AI (XAI) Techniques

Model Interpretability

Enhancing model interpretability enables stakeholders to understand how AI models arrive at decisions by visualizing model predictions, feature importance, and decision pathways. Techniques such as feature visualization, saliency maps, and attention mechanisms provide insights into which features influence AI decisions and how inputs contribute to outputs.

Post-hoc Explanations

Post-hoc explanation techniques generate explanations for AI decisions after model deployment, enabling stakeholders to interpret model predictions and decision outcomes. Methods such as local interpretable model-agnostic explanations (LIME), Shapley values, and counterfactual explanations highlight the rationale behind individual predictions and facilitate stakeholder understanding of AI decision-making processes.

Transparency Tools and Interfaces

Decision Dashboards

Decision dashboards present AI-driven decisions, recommendations, and insights in a user-friendly interface that enables stakeholders to explore decision outcomes, review supporting evidence, and interact with AI-generated data. Dashboards promote transparency by visualizing AI outputs, facilitating stakeholder engagement, and fostering collaborative decision-making across diverse user groups.

Audit Trails and Logs

Audit trails and logs document AI decision-making processes, data inputs, and algorithmic updates over time, providing stakeholders with a chronological record of AI operations. Traceability through audit trails enhances transparency, accountability, and regulatory compliance by enabling stakeholders to trace decision outcomes, identify potential biases or errors, and ensure adherence to ethical and legal standards.

6.1.4 Strategies for Promoting Transparency and Accountability

Stakeholder Engagement and Education

Engaging stakeholders through education, training programs, and workshops fosters awareness about AI technologies, transparency principles, and ethical considerations. Empowering stakeholders, including policymakers, regulators, end-users, and affected individuals, with knowledge about AI decision-making enhances their ability to evaluate AI systems, advocate for transparency, and participate in ethical AI governance initiatives.

Ethical AI Governance Frameworks

Establishing ethical AI governance frameworks and guidelines ensures responsible AI deployment, transparency, and accountability in decision-making processes. Ethical AI committees, regulatory bodies, and industry standards organizations develop policies, conduct ethical reviews, and enforce guidelines that promote fairness, privacy protection, and stakeholder trust in AI-driven systems.

Continuous Monitoring and Evaluation

Implementing continuous monitoring and evaluation of AI systems ensures ongoing transparency, performance assessment, and risk management. Regular audits, impact assessments, and feedback mechanisms enable organizations to assess AI decision outcomes, detect biases or errors, and implement corrective actions to improve algorithmic fairness, reliability, and stakeholder satisfaction.

Collaborative Partnerships and Standards

Collaborating with industry partners, academia, civil society organizations, and regulatory authorities fosters collective responsibility in promoting transparency and accountability in AI decision-making. Developing industry standards, sharing best practices, and advocating for ethical AI principles across sectors support a culture of transparency, innovation, and responsible AI deployment that benefits global stakeholders.

6.2 RESPONSIBLE AI DEVELOPMENT AND DEPLOYMENT

Responsible AI development and deployment are critical for ensuring that artificial intelligence (AI) technologies are developed and used in ways that uphold ethical principles, respect human rights, and benefit society as a whole. As AI increasingly influences decision-making processes across various sectors, including healthcare, finance, education, and governance, responsible AI practices promote transparency, fairness, accountability, and trust among stakeholders.

Responsible AI development and deployment are essential for promoting ethical AI practices, fostering stakeholder trust, and maximizing societal benefits while minimizing risks associated with AI technologies.

By adhering to principles of ethical AI development, addressing challenges in AI ethics, implementing current practices for promoting responsible AI deployment, and advancing strategies for ethical AI adoption, organizations can navigate complex ethical dilemmas, mitigate potential risks, and ensure that AI technologies contribute positively to human well-being, societal progress, and sustainable development.

Collaborative efforts among stakeholders, commitment to ethical principles, and continuous innovation in AI governance are crucial for shaping a future where responsible AI technologies uphold human rights, respect diversity, and empower individuals and communities worldwide.

6.2.1 Principles of Responsible AI Development

Ethical Considerations

Ethical considerations form the foundation of responsible AI development, guiding the design, implementation, and use of AI technologies to ensure alignment with moral values, societal norms, and human rights.

Principles such as fairness, transparency, accountability, privacy protection, and non-discrimination underpin ethical AI frameworks and governance models, promoting responsible AI practices that prioritize the well-being and rights of individuals and communities affected by AI-driven systems.

Human-Centered Design

Human-centered design principles emphasize the importance of designing AI technologies that enhance human capabilities, support user autonomy, and promote inclusivity. Prioritizing user needs, preferences, and feedback throughout the AI development lifecycle ensures that AI systems are intuitive, accessible, and responsive to diverse user contexts, fostering positive user experiences and societal acceptance of AI technologies.

Accountability and Governance

Accountability mechanisms and governance frameworks establish clear roles, responsibilities, and procedures for overseeing AI development, deployment, and decision-making processes. Ethical AI governance structures, including regulatory compliance, industry standards, and organizational policies, hold stakeholders accountable for ensuring transparency, mitigating risks, and addressing ethical implications associated with AI technologies.

6.2.2 Challenges in AI Ethics

Algorithmic Bias and Fairness

Algorithmic bias poses challenges in AI ethics by perpetuating inequalities, reinforcing stereotypes, and producing discriminatory outcomes that disproportionately impact marginalized groups. Addressing bias in AI algorithms, data sources, and decision-making processes requires robust mitigation strategies, fairness-aware AI techniques, and inclusive practices to promote equitable AI deployment and reduce societal biases in AI-driven systems.

Privacy and Data Protection

Protecting personal data privacy and confidentiality presents ethical challenges in AI development, particularly when collecting, storing, and processing sensitive information. Respecting individuals' privacy rights, implementing data anonymization techniques, and adhering to data protection regulations are essential for safeguarding personal information, minimizing privacy risks, and earning stakeholders' trust in AI technologies.

Accountability and Transparency

Ensuring accountability and transparency in AI decision-making processes involves disclosing how AI systems operate, explaining decision outcomes, and enabling stakeholders to understand, challenge, and review AI-generated decisions. Enhancing algorithmic transparency, implementing audit mechanisms, and promoting stakeholder engagement foster accountability, promote responsible AI practices, and mitigate potential risks associated with opaque or biased AI algorithms.

6.2.3 Current Practices for Promoting Responsible AI Deployment

Ethical AI Frameworks and Guidelines

Developing ethical AI frameworks, guidelines, and principles provides guidance for organizations, developers, and policymakers to navigate ethical dilemmas, uphold human rights, and promote responsible AI adoption. Initiatives such as the OECD Principles on AI, IEEE Ethically Aligned Design, and AI ethics guidelines by leading tech companies establish ethical standards, best practices, and recommendations for designing, deploying, and regulating AI technologies responsibly.

Risk Assessment and Impact Evaluation

Conducting comprehensive risk assessments and impact evaluations assess the potential ethical, social, and economic implications of AI technologies before deployment. Integrating ethical risk analysis, scenario planning, and stakeholder consultations enables organizations to anticipate risks, identify mitigation strategies, and ensure that AI deployment aligns with ethical standards, regulatory requirements, and societal expectations.

Collaborative Stakeholder Engagement

Engaging stakeholders, including policymakers, industry experts, civil society organizations, and affected communities, fosters collaboration, dialogue, and collective responsibility in promoting responsible AI development and deployment. Multi-stakeholder initiatives, public consultations, and participatory governance models facilitate informed decision-making, build consensus on AI ethics issues, and address diverse perspectives and concerns in AI technology adoption.

Continuous Monitoring and Ethical Audits

Implementing continuous monitoring, ethical audits, and performance evaluations of AI systems ensure ongoing compliance with ethical standards, regulatory obligations, and organizational policies. Regular audits, algorithmic assessments, and impact evaluations enable organizations to detect ethical lapses, mitigate risks, and improve AI governance practices to maintain trust, accountability, and responsible AI deployment over time.

6.2.4 Strategies for Advancing Ethical AI Adoption

Education and Awareness

Promoting education and awareness about AI ethics, responsible AI practices, and societal implications of AI technologies empowers stakeholders to make informed decisions, advocate for ethical standards, and participate in shaping AI governance policies. Educational programs, training initiatives, and public outreach campaigns raise awareness about AI ethics issues, foster digital literacy, and encourage ethical behavior in AI development and deployment.

Regulatory Innovation and Policy Development

Fostering regulatory innovation and policy development creates a supportive environment for responsible AI adoption, balancing innovation with ethical considerations, consumer protection, and public safety. Developing AI-specific regulations, updating existing legal frameworks, and establishing regulatory sandboxes facilitate experimentation, compliance with ethical guidelines, and responsible AI deployment that aligns with regulatory expectations and societal values.

Ethical AI Champions and Leadership

Empowering ethical AI champions and leadership within organizations promotes a culture of ethical responsibility, accountability, and transparency in AI development and deployment. Leadership commitment to ethical AI principles, fostering a culture of integrity, and promoting ethical decision-making frameworks encourage organizational alignment, mitigate risks, and inspire industry-wide adoption of responsible AI practices that prioritize human-centric values and societal benefits.

Global Collaboration and Standards Harmonization

Encouraging global collaboration, standards harmonization, and knowledge sharing among countries, international organizations, and industry stakeholders facilitates consensus-building, alignment of ethical principles, and mutual recognition of responsible AI practices across borders. International cooperation, joint initiatives, and partnerships promote global governance frameworks, ethical guidelines, and regulatory convergence that support ethical AI adoption, foster trust, and advance shared goals of promoting human rights and sustainable development through responsible AI technologies.

6.3 ETHICAL RESPONSIBILITY IN AI SYSTEMS

Ethical responsibility in AI systems is paramount to ensuring that artificial intelligence technologies are developed, deployed, and used in ways that uphold ethical principles, respect human rights, and promote societal well-being. As AI increasingly influences decision-making processes across various domains, including healthcare, finance, criminal justice, and education, ethical considerations guide the design, implementation, and governance of AI systems to mitigate risks, address biases, and foster trust among stakeholders.

Ethical responsibility in AI systems is essential for ensuring that artificial intelligence technologies are developed, deployed, and used in ways that uphold ethical principles, respect human rights, and promote societal well-being. By adhering to principles of transparency, fairness, accountability, and privacy protection, ethical responsibility in AI systems mitigates risks, addresses biases, and fosters trust among stakeholders in AI-driven systems. Collaborative efforts, global ethics standards, ethical leadership, and responsible AI practices are crucial for advancing ethical AI adoption, promoting human-centric innovation, and harnessing the transformative potential of AI technologies responsibly and ethically for the collective benefit of individuals, communities, and society worldwide. Ethical responsibility in AI systems ensures that AI technologies contribute positively to human well-being, social equity, and sustainable development in a digital age where ethical considerations guide responsible innovation, ethical leadership, and ethical excellence in advancing AI technologies for a better future.

6.3.1 Principles of Ethical Responsibility in AI Systems

Transparency and Accountability

Transparency in AI systems involves disclosing how AI algorithms operate, explaining decision-making processes, and providing stakeholders with understandable insights into AI-generated outcomes. Accountability mechanisms ensure that developers, organizations, and policymakers are held responsible for the ethical implications, societal impacts, and consequences of AI technologies. By promoting transparency and accountability, ethical responsibility in AI systems enhances stakeholder trust, facilitates informed decision-making, and mitigates potential risks associated with opaque or biased AI algorithms.

Fairness and Non-discrimination

Ensuring fairness and non-discrimination in AI systems involves mitigating biases, addressing algorithmic inequalities, and promoting equitable outcomes for diverse user groups. Ethical AI practices strive to eliminate biases in data sources, algorithmic design, and decision-making processes that may perpetuate social inequalities or reinforce discriminatory practices. By adopting fairness-aware AI techniques, inclusive design principles, and diverse dataset representation, ethical responsibility in AI systems promotes equal opportunities, respects human diversity, and safeguards against algorithmic biases that adversely affect vulnerable populations.

Privacy Protection and Data Security

Protecting personal data privacy and ensuring data security are essential ethical responsibilities in AI systems, particularly when collecting, processing, and storing sensitive information. Ethical AI practices prioritize data anonymization, encryption technologies, and adherence to data protection regulations to safeguard individuals' privacy rights, minimize privacy risks, and prevent unauthorized access or misuse of personal data. By respecting confidentiality, promoting data transparency, and implementing robust cybersecurity measures, ethical responsibility in AI systems enhances user trust, promotes data integrity, and mitigates potential harms associated with data breaches or privacy violations.

6.3.2 Challenges in Ethical AI Implementation

Algorithmic Bias and Fairness

Algorithmic bias poses challenges in ethical AI implementation by perpetuating inequalities, reinforcing stereotypes, and producing discriminatory outcomes that disproportionately impact marginalized groups. Addressing bias in AI algorithms, data sources, and decision-making processes requires developing bias detection tools, fairness-aware algorithms, and inclusive practices to promote algorithmic fairness, reduce social biases, and ensure equitable treatment for all users. Overcoming challenges in algorithmic bias involves interdisciplinary collaboration, ethical scrutiny, and continuous improvement in AI technologies to mitigate biases and uphold ethical standards in AI deployment.

Explainability and Interpretability

The lack of explainability and interpretability in AI systems poses ethical challenges by limiting stakeholders' understanding of how AI algorithms arrive at decisions, interpret data inputs, and generate outcomes. Black-box algorithms, such as deep neural networks, may hinder transparency, accountability, and user trust in AI technologies, particularly in high-stakes applications where decision-making impacts individuals' lives or societal outcomes. Addressing challenges in AI explainability involves developing explainable AI techniques, interpretable models, and transparency tools that enable stakeholders to scrutinize AI decisions, assess algorithmic fairness, and ensure ethical compliance in AI-driven systems.

Ethical Governance and Regulatory Compliance

Navigating ethical governance frameworks and regulatory requirements presents challenges in AI implementation, particularly when balancing innovation with ethical considerations, legal obligations, and public policy interests. Ethical AI governance structures, industry standards, and regulatory guidelines provide guidance for organizations, developers, and policymakers to address ethical dilemmas, uphold human rights, and promote responsible AI practices that align with societal values and legal norms. Overcoming challenges in ethical governance involves fostering multi-stakeholder collaboration, promoting regulatory clarity, and advocating for policies that support ethical AI development, deployment, and oversight in diverse sectors.

6.3.3 Current Practices for Promoting Ethical AI Development

Ethical Design and Impact Assessment

Integrating ethical design principles and conducting impact assessments evaluate the potential ethical, social, and economic implications of AI technologies before deployment. Ethical design frameworks, including principles of fairness, transparency, privacy protection, and user-centricity, guide developers in designing AI systems that prioritize ethical considerations, minimize risks, and maximize societal benefits. Ethical impact assessments assess AI's impact on human rights, societal values, and public interest, enabling organizations to anticipate ethical challenges, identify mitigation strategies, and ensure responsible AI development that aligns with ethical standards and regulatory requirements.

Ethical AI Education and Training

Promoting education and training on AI ethics, responsible AI practices, and ethical decision-making fosters awareness, competence, and ethical behavior among developers, stakeholders, and decision-makers. Educational initiatives, workshops, and professional development programs equip individuals with knowledge about ethical AI principles, ethical dilemmas in AI development, and strategies for integrating ethics into AI design, deployment, and governance. Ethical AI education encourages critical thinking, ethical reasoning, and responsible innovation in AI technologies, promoting a culture of ethical responsibility and accountability across the AI ecosystem.

Multi-stakeholder Collaboration and Engagement

Engaging stakeholders, including policymakers, industry experts, civil society organizations, and affected communities, facilitates collaboration, consensus-building, and collective action in addressing ethical challenges in AI deployment. Multi-stakeholder initiatives, public consultations, and participatory governance models enable diverse perspectives, values, and interests to inform ethical AI decision-making, promote inclusive dialogue, and build trust among stakeholders. Collaborative engagement fosters shared responsibility, transparency, and accountability in AI development and deployment, advancing ethical AI adoption that respects human rights, promotes societal well-being, and addresses global challenges through responsible AI technologies.

Continuous Monitoring and Ethical Audits

Implementing continuous monitoring, ethical audits, and performance evaluations of AI systems ensure ongoing compliance with ethical standards, regulatory obligations, and organizational policies. Ethical audits assess AI's adherence to ethical guidelines, detect ethical risks or biases, and recommend corrective actions to mitigate potential harms and uphold ethical integrity in AI-driven systems. Continuous monitoring promotes transparency, accountability, and stakeholder trust by evaluating AI's impact, effectiveness, and ethical implications over time, fostering responsible AI development, deployment, and governance that prioritizes ethical responsibility and societal benefits.

6.3.4 Strategies for Advancing Ethical AI Adoption

Global Ethics Standards and Policy Harmonization

Advancing global ethics standards, policy harmonization, and regulatory convergence promote consistency, clarity, and interoperability in ethical AI practices across countries, regions, and sectors. International cooperation, collaborative frameworks, and mutual recognition of ethical principles facilitate knowledge sharing, best practices dissemination, and alignment of ethical standards that support responsible AI development, deployment, and governance on a global scale. Global ethics standards encourage ethical innovation, ethical leadership, and responsible AI adoption that respects cultural diversity, promotes human rights, and addresses global challenges through inclusive, equitable, and sustainable AI technologies.

Ethical Leadership and Organizational Commitment

Promoting ethical leadership, organizational commitment, and corporate responsibility fosters a culture of integrity, accountability, and ethical excellence in AI development, deployment, and governance. Ethical leaders champion ethical AI principles, prioritize stakeholder interests, and guide organizational decision-making to align with ethical standards, regulatory requirements, and societal expectations. Organizational commitment to ethical AI fosters transparency, builds trust, and promotes responsible innovation that maximizes societal benefits, minimizes risks, and upholds ethical responsibility in advancing AI technologies for the collective good.

Public Engagement and Ethical Discourse

Engaging the public, raising awareness, and fostering ethical discourse on AI ethics, risks, and societal impacts empower citizens, consumers, and communities to participate in shaping AI policies, regulations, and ethical guidelines. Public engagement initiatives, inclusive dialogue platforms, and participatory decision-making processes promote transparency, accountability, and democratic oversight in AI development, deployment, and governance. Ethical discourse encourages diverse perspectives, values, and concerns to inform ethical AI decision-making, advance public trust, and ensure AI technologies contribute positively to human well-being, social equity, and sustainable development in a digital age.

Ethical Innovation and Responsible AI Practices

Promoting ethical innovation, responsible AI practices, and ethical-by-design approaches integrate ethical considerations into AI development, deployment, and governance to anticipate risks, mitigate harms, and maximize benefits for individuals, communities, and society. Ethical innovation encourages responsible AI adoption that prioritizes human-centric values, respects human rights, and addresses societal challenges through inclusive, equitable, and sustainable AI technologies. Responsible AI practices empower stakeholders to adopt ethical guidelines, implement ethical frameworks, and uphold ethical standards in AI technologies that promote trust, transparency, and accountability in advancing AI's potential to benefit humanity responsibly and ethically.

PART III:

HUMAN-AI INTERACTION IN EDUCATION

CHAPTER 7

TEACHER AND STUDENT PERSPECTIVES

7.1 EDUCATORS VIEWS ON AI INTEGRATION

The integration of artificial intelligence (AI) into educational settings has sparked significant interest and debate among educators. AI technologies have the potential to transform teaching and learning processes by offering personalized learning experiences, automating administrative tasks, and providing data-driven insights to improve educational outcomes. However, the adoption of AI in education also raises concerns about ethical considerations, data privacy, and the potential impact on traditional teaching roles.

Educators' views on AI integration in education reflect a balanced perspective that acknowledges both the potential benefits and the challenges associated with AI adoption. While AI technologies offer opportunities for personalized learning, administrative efficiency, and data-driven insights, ethical considerations, the evolving role of educators, and technical challenges must be carefully addressed to ensure responsible and effective AI integration. As AI continues to evolve, ongoing dialogue, collaboration, and professional development will be essential to harnessing the potential of AI to enhance teaching and learning while upholding ethical standards and promoting equitable educational outcomes. Educators play a crucial role in shaping the future of AI in education, advocating for practices that prioritize student well-being, support teacher professionalism, and foster a human-centered approach to AI-enhanced learning environments.

7.1.1 Benefits of AI Integration in Education

Personalized Learning

One of the most significant advantages of AI integration in education is the ability to offer personalized learning experiences tailored to individual students' needs, strengths, and weaknesses. Educators recognize that AI-powered adaptive learning systems can provide customized content, real-time feedback, and differentiated instruction, allowing students to learn at their own pace and according to their unique learning styles. By leveraging AI, teachers can better address diverse student needs, enhance student engagement, and improve academic outcomes.

Administrative Efficiency

AI technologies can automate various administrative tasks, reducing the workload on educators and allowing them to focus more on teaching and student support. Educators appreciate the potential of AI to streamline grading, attendance tracking, scheduling, and other routine tasks, thereby freeing up valuable time for instructional activities and personalized student interactions.

The efficiency gains from AI automation can lead to more effective classroom management and improved teacher-student relationships.

Data-Driven Insights

AI-driven data analytics can provide educators with valuable insights into student performance, learning patterns, and areas requiring intervention. By analyzing large datasets, AI systems can identify trends, predict student outcomes, and recommend targeted instructional strategies.

Educators view these data-driven insights as essential tools for informed decision-making, enabling them to tailor their teaching approaches, monitor student progress, and implement timely interventions to support student success.

7.1.2 Challenges and Concerns

Ethical Considerations

Despite the potential benefits, educators express concerns about the ethical implications of AI integration in education. Issues such as data privacy, algorithmic bias, and the potential for surveillance raise significant ethical questions.

Educators emphasize the importance of safeguarding student data, ensuring transparency in AI decision-making processes, and addressing biases in AI algorithms that may perpetuate inequalities. Ethical considerations must be central to the development and deployment of AI technologies in educational settings to protect student rights and promote fairness.

Impact on Teaching Roles

The integration of AI in education also prompts concerns about the evolving role of educators. Some educators worry that AI technologies may replace traditional teaching roles or undermine the value of human interaction in the learning process.

While AI can support and enhance teaching practices, educators stress the irreplaceable role of teachers in providing emotional support, fostering critical thinking, and nurturing social skills. Balancing the use of AI with the preservation of meaningful teacher-student relationships is crucial to maintaining the human element in education.

Technical and Resource Challenges

Implementing AI technologies in educational settings requires significant technical infrastructure, training, and resources. Educators highlight challenges related to the availability of reliable internet connectivity, access to devices, and the need for professional development to effectively integrate AI tools into their teaching practices. Addressing these technical and resource challenges is essential to ensuring equitable access to AI-enhanced learning opportunities and maximizing the benefits of AI integration in diverse educational contexts.

7.1.3 Future Implications

Enhancing Teacher Professional Development

AI has the potential to revolutionize teacher professional development by providing personalized learning experiences for educators themselves. AI-powered platforms can offer targeted training, real-time feedback, and continuous professional development opportunities based on individual teacher needs and areas for growth. Educators see the potential of AI to support lifelong learning, enhance instructional practices, and empower teachers to stay updated with the latest educational research and pedagogical strategies.

Collaborative Learning Environments

AI can facilitate the creation of collaborative learning environments where students and teachers work together to solve problems, explore new concepts, and engage in project-based learning. Educators envision AI tools that support collaborative activities, foster peer-to-peer learning, and enable virtual or augmented reality experiences that enhance student engagement and understanding. By leveraging AI to promote collaboration, educators can create dynamic and interactive learning spaces that prepare students for the complexities of the modern world.

Addressing Educational Inequities

Educators recognize the potential of AI to address educational inequities by providing access to high-quality learning resources, personalized support, and targeted interventions for underserved and marginalized students. AI-driven technologies can bridge gaps in educational opportunities, support diverse learners, and promote inclusive practices that ensure all students have the chance to succeed. However, educators also caution against over-reliance on AI solutions and emphasize the importance of addressing systemic issues that contribute to educational disparities.

7.2 STUDENT EXPERIENCES WITH AI-ENHANCED LEARNING

The integration of artificial intelligence (AI) into educational environments is revolutionizing the way students learn. AI-enhanced learning platforms offer personalized instruction, adaptive assessments, and interactive experiences that cater to individual student needs and preferences. This transformation has the potential to significantly impact student experiences, both positively and negatively.

AI-enhanced learning has the potential to transform educational experiences for students, offering personalized support, immediate feedback, and engaging learning tools. While students report many benefits, such as increased motivation and improved academic performance, challenges related to data privacy, algorithmic bias, and technical accessibility must be addressed. By integrating AI with traditional teaching methods, conducting ongoing research and development, and providing professional development for educators, we can maximize the benefits of AI-enhanced learning and create a more effective, equitable, and engaging educational environment for all students.

7.2.1 Benefits of AI-Enhanced Learning for Students

Personalized Learning Pathways

One of the primary benefits of AI-enhanced learning is the ability to provide personalized learning pathways tailored to each student's unique needs. AI systems analyze student performance data to identify strengths, weaknesses, and learning styles. Based on this analysis, the AI can create customized learning plans that adjust the difficulty and pace of instruction accordingly. Students benefit from receiving targeted support where they need it most and advancing more quickly through material they find easier, which enhances their overall learning efficiency and engagement.

Immediate Feedback and Support

AI-enhanced learning platforms offer immediate feedback and support, allowing students to correct mistakes and understand concepts in real time. This instant feedback loop is crucial for reinforcing learning and preventing misconceptions from taking root. Students report feeling more confident and motivated when they can see their progress and understand where they need to improve. AI tutors and virtual assistants can also provide explanations, hints, and additional resources, offering a level of individualized support that might not be feasible in a traditional classroom setting.

Increased Engagement and Motivation

Interactive AI-driven learning tools, such as gamified lessons, virtual reality experiences, and interactive simulations, can make learning more engaging and enjoyable for students. These tools often incorporate elements of play, competition, and reward, which can motivate students to engage more deeply with the material.

Students who might struggle with traditional teaching methods often find these interactive approaches more appealing, which can lead to increased participation and better learning outcomes.

Enhanced Accessibility and Inclusivity

AI-enhanced learning platforms can be designed to accommodate diverse learners, including those with disabilities or special needs. For example, AI systems can provide text-to-speech services, translate content into different languages, or offer visual aids and interactive exercises that cater to various learning preferences.

This accessibility ensures that all students have an equal opportunity to benefit from high-quality education, regardless of their individual challenges or backgrounds.

7.2.2 Challenges Faced by Students in AI-Enhanced Learning

Data Privacy and Security Concerns

While AI-enhanced learning platforms offer many benefits, they also raise concerns about data privacy and security. Students' personal information and learning data are collected and analyzed by these systems, which can create vulnerabilities if not properly managed.

Students and their families may worry about how their data is used, who has access to it, and whether it is adequately protected from breaches. Addressing these concerns is essential to building trust and ensuring that students feel safe using AI-enhanced learning tools.

Dependence on Technology

Another challenge is the potential for students to become overly dependent on technology for their learning. While AI tools can provide valuable support, there is a risk that students might rely too heavily on them and lose the ability to think critically and solve problems independently. Balancing the use of AI with traditional teaching methods and encouraging students to develop essential skills independently is crucial to fostering well-rounded learners.

Algorithmic Bias and Fairness

AI systems are only as good as the data they are trained on. If the data used to develop AI-enhanced learning platforms contain biases, these biases can be perpetuated in the learning experiences provided to students. For example, certain groups of students might receive less effective recommendations or support based on biased data, leading to unequal educational outcomes. Ensuring that AI systems are designed and trained with fairness and inclusivity in mind is essential to providing equitable learning opportunities for all students.

Technical Challenges and Accessibility

Not all students have equal access to the technology required for AI-enhanced learning. Issues such as unreliable internet connections, lack of access to devices, and varying levels of digital literacy can create barriers for some students. Additionally, technical glitches and software issues can disrupt the learning process and cause frustration. Addressing these technical challenges and ensuring that all students have the necessary resources to participate in AI-enhanced learning is critical for maximizing its benefits.

7.2.3 Student Perspectives on AI-Enhanced Learning

Positive Experiences and Outcomes

Many students report positive experiences with AI-enhanced learning. They appreciate the personalized support, immediate feedback, and engaging learning tools that AI platforms provide. Students often feel more motivated and confident in their abilities, leading to improved academic performance and a more enjoyable learning experience. For example, students who struggle with specific subjects can receive targeted support and practice, which helps them build mastery and confidence over time.

Challenges and Areas for Improvement

Despite the benefits, students also highlight areas for improvement in AI-enhanced learning systems. Some students feel overwhelmed by the sheer volume of data and recommendations provided by AI platforms, making it difficult to know where to focus their efforts. Others express concerns about the lack of human interaction and the potential for technology to replace the valuable support and mentorship that teachers provide. Ensuring that AI tools complement rather than replace traditional teaching methods is essential for addressing these concerns and enhancing the overall learning experience.

7.2.4 Implications for Future Educational Practices

Integrating AI with Traditional Teaching

To maximize the benefits of AI-enhanced learning, it is important to integrate AI tools with traditional teaching methods. Teachers can use AI-generated insights to inform their instruction, provide personalized support, and identify areas where students may need additional help. By combining the strengths of AI and human instruction, educators can create a more effective and holistic learning environment that supports all students.

Ongoing Research and Development

Continued research and development are essential for improving AI-enhanced learning platforms and addressing the challenges associated with their use. This includes developing more sophisticated algorithms that can provide fair and unbiased recommendations, enhancing data privacy and security measures, and creating more accessible and user-friendly interfaces. Ongoing collaboration between educators, researchers, and technology developers is crucial for advancing AI-enhanced learning and ensuring that it meets the needs of all students.

Professional Development for Educators

Providing professional development opportunities for educators is essential for the successful integration of AI-enhanced learning tools. Teachers need to understand how to effectively use AI platforms, interpret AI-generated data, and incorporate AI insights into their instruction. Professional development programs can equip educators with the skills and knowledge they need to leverage AI tools effectively and create a supportive learning environment for their students.

7.3 ETHICAL CONSIDERATIONS FROM EDUCATIONAL STAKEHOLDERS

As artificial intelligence (AI) becomes increasingly integrated into educational systems, it brings with it numerous ethical considerations that must be addressed by various stakeholders, including educators, policymakers, students, parents, and technology developers. The deployment of AI in education has the potential to transform teaching and learning processes, but it also raises concerns about privacy, equity, transparency, and accountability.

The integration of AI in education brings both opportunities and challenges that require careful consideration by various stakeholders. Ethical considerations such as privacy and data security, equity and access, transparency and accountability, and the impact on teaching and learning must be addressed to ensure the responsible use of AI technologies. Collaborative efforts among educators, policymakers, students, parents, and technology developers are essential for creating AI systems that uphold ethical principles, promote equity, and enhance educational experiences. By prioritizing ethical considerations, we can harness the potential of AI to transform education positively while safeguarding the rights and well-being of all stakeholders.

7.3.1 Privacy and Data Security

Student Data Protection

One of the primary ethical concerns related to AI in education is the protection of student data. AI systems often require large amounts of data to function effectively, including personal information, academic performance, and behavioral patterns. Educators and parents are particularly concerned about how this data is collected, stored, and used. Ensuring robust data security measures and adhering to data protection regulations, such as GDPR, is essential to safeguarding students' privacy and preventing unauthorized access or misuse of sensitive information.

Informed Consent

Obtaining informed consent from students and parents before collecting and using data is a crucial ethical consideration. Educational institutions must be transparent about the types of data being collected, the purposes for which it will be used, and the potential risks involved. Clear communication and consent protocols help build trust and ensure that stakeholders are aware of and agree to the use of AI technologies in the educational setting.

7.3.2 Equity and Access

Addressing Inequities

AI in education has the potential to exacerbate existing inequities if not implemented thoughtfully. Students from disadvantaged backgrounds may have limited access to the technology required for AI-enhanced learning, leading to a digital divide. Educators and policymakers must work to ensure that all students, regardless of their socio-economic status, have access to the necessary resources and support to benefit from AI technologies. This includes providing devices, reliable internet access, and training to bridge the gap and promote equitable learning opportunities.

Bias in AI Algorithms

Algorithmic bias is another significant ethical concern. AI systems can perpetuate and even amplify existing biases present in the data they are trained on. This can result in unfair treatment and discrimination against certain groups of students. It is crucial for developers to use diverse and representative datasets and to implement fairness-aware algorithms that mitigate bias. Ongoing monitoring and auditing of AI systems are necessary to identify and address any biases that may arise.

7.3.3 Transparency and Accountability

Explainability of AI Systems

The complexity of AI algorithms often makes it difficult for educators, students, and parents to understand how decisions are made. This lack of transparency can lead to mistrust and skepticism about AI technologies. Ensuring that AI systems are explainable and that their decision-making processes are transparent is essential for fostering trust among stakeholders. Developers should prioritize creating AI models that are interpretable and provide clear explanations for their outputs.

Accountability Mechanisms

Establishing accountability mechanisms is critical to ensure that AI systems are used responsibly in education. Stakeholders must be able to hold developers and educational institutions accountable for the ethical use of AI technologies. This includes setting clear guidelines and standards for AI implementation, conducting regular audits, and establishing channels for reporting and addressing ethical concerns.

Accountability frameworks help ensure that AI systems are used in ways that align with ethical principles and societal values.

7.3.4 Impact on Teaching and Learning

Preserving the Human Element

While AI has the potential to enhance educational experiences, it is essential to preserve the human element in teaching and learning. Educators play a vital role in providing emotional support, fostering critical thinking, and nurturing social skills that AI cannot replicate. Stakeholders must balance the use of AI with maintaining meaningful teacher-student interactions. Teachers should be seen as facilitators who leverage AI tools to enhance their instruction rather than being replaced by technology.

Professional Development for Educators

The integration of AI in education requires significant changes in teaching practices. Providing professional development opportunities for educators is crucial to ensure that they are equipped to effectively use AI technologies in their classrooms. Training programs should focus on developing digital literacy, understanding AI functionalities, and implementing ethical AI practices. Empowering teachers with the necessary skills and knowledge helps them navigate the ethical challenges and maximize the benefits of AI-enhanced learning.

7.3.5 Ethical Use of AI Technologies

Designing Ethical AI Systems

Developers play a key role in ensuring the ethical use of AI technologies in education. Ethical design principles should be embedded in the development process, prioritizing fairness, transparency, and accountability. Developers should engage with educators, students, and other stakeholders to understand their needs and concerns, creating AI systems that are aligned with ethical standards and promote positive educational outcomes. Collaborative efforts between developers and educational stakeholders help create AI technologies that serve the best interests of students and educators.

Continuous Evaluation and Improvement

AI technologies in education should undergo continuous evaluation and improvement to address emerging ethical issues and adapt to evolving educational needs. Regular assessments of AI systems' impact on teaching and learning, as well as their adherence to ethical guidelines, are necessary. Stakeholders should engage in ongoing dialogue to identify challenges, share best practices, and develop strategies for mitigating risks. Continuous improvement efforts ensure that AI technologies remain aligned with ethical principles and contribute positively to educational outcomes.

7.3.6 Future Implications

Ethical Policy Development

Policymakers play a crucial role in shaping the ethical landscape of AI in education. Developing comprehensive policies and regulations that address the ethical considerations of AI integration is essential. These policies should include guidelines for data protection, fairness, transparency, and accountability. Policymakers should collaborate with educators, technology developers, and other stakeholders to create a regulatory framework that promotes the responsible use of AI technologies in education.

Ethical AI Research

Research in the field of AI ethics is vital to understanding the implications of AI technologies in education and developing solutions to address ethical challenges. Academic institutions, researchers, and industry experts should conduct studies that explore the ethical dimensions of AI in education, identify best practices, and propose innovative approaches to mitigate risks. Ethical AI research contributes to the development of robust ethical frameworks and informs evidence-based policy decisions.

CHAPTER 8
AI AND EDUCATIONAL ETHICS

8.1 ETHICS EDUCATION FOR AI DEVELOPERS AND USERS

The rapid advancement of artificial intelligence (AI) technologies has brought about significant changes across various sectors, including education, healthcare, finance, and more. As AI becomes increasingly integrated into our daily lives, it is crucial to address the ethical implications associated with its development and use. Ethics education for AI developers and users plays a pivotal role in ensuring that AI technologies are designed, implemented, and utilized responsibly.

Ethics education for AI developers and users is essential for ensuring the responsible development and use of AI technologies. By understanding the ethical implications of their work, developers can create fair, transparent, and accountable AI systems that prioritize the well-being of users and society. Similarly, educating AI users about ethical considerations empowers them to make informed decisions, address ethical dilemmas, and use AI technologies responsibly. An interdisciplinary approach, practical case studies, ongoing education, and collaborative efforts are key to fostering ethical awareness and conduct in the AI community. By prioritizing ethics education, we can harness the potential of AI while safeguarding ethical principles and societal values.

8.1.1 The Importance of Ethics Education for AI Developers

Understanding Ethical Implications

AI developers are at the forefront of creating technologies that have the potential to impact society profoundly. Ethics education is essential for these developers to understand the broader implications of their work. This includes recognizing potential biases in AI algorithms, considering the privacy and security of user data, and understanding the social and economic consequences of AI deployment. By being aware of these ethical considerations, developers can make informed decisions that prioritize the well-being of users and society as a whole.

Mitigating Bias and Discrimination

One of the critical challenges in AI development is the risk of perpetuating bias and discrimination. AI systems often rely on large datasets for training, and if these datasets contain biased information, the resulting algorithms can reinforce existing inequalities. Ethics education equips developers with the knowledge and tools to identify and mitigate biases in data and algorithms. This involves adopting fairness-aware machine learning techniques, conducting thorough bias audits, and ensuring diverse and representative data collection practices.

Promoting Transparency and Accountability

Transparency and accountability are fundamental principles in ethical AI development. Developers must understand the importance of creating AI systems that are explainable and transparent in their decision-making processes. Ethics education emphasizes the need for clear documentation, open communication about AI functionalities, and the development of interpretable models. Additionally, developers should be aware of their accountability in ensuring that AI technologies are used responsibly and ethically, and that mechanisms are in place for addressing any issues that arise.

8.1.2 Ethics Education for AI Users

Informed Consent and User Autonomy

AI users, including individuals, organizations, and governments, must be educated about the ethical considerations of AI technologies to make informed decisions. Informed consent is a critical aspect of ethical AI use, where users should be fully aware of how their data will be collected, processed, and used. Ethics education helps users understand their rights and the implications of using AI technologies, empowering them to make autonomous choices and protect their privacy.

Addressing Ethical Dilemmas

AI users often face ethical dilemmas when implementing and interacting with AI systems. These dilemmas can range from concerns about data privacy to the potential for AI to replace human jobs. Ethics education provides users with frameworks and guidelines to navigate these dilemmas effectively. By fostering critical thinking and ethical reasoning skills, users can evaluate the potential benefits and risks of AI technologies and make decisions that align with ethical principles and societal values.

Encouraging Responsible Use

Responsible use of AI technologies involves understanding their limitations, potential risks, and appropriate applications. Ethics education promotes a culture of responsible AI use by highlighting best practices, such as regularly updating and auditing AI systems, ensuring transparency in AI-driven decisions, and being vigilant about unintended consequences. Users who are well-versed in ethical considerations are better equipped to use AI technologies in ways that enhance positive outcomes and minimize harm.

8.1.3 Key Areas of Focus in Ethics Education

Data Privacy and Security

Data privacy and security are paramount in the ethical development and use of AI. Ethics education should emphasize the importance of protecting user data, implementing robust security measures, and complying with data protection regulations. Developers and users must be aware of the potential risks associated with data breaches and unauthorized access, and take proactive steps to safeguard sensitive information.

Fairness and Bias Mitigation

Ensuring fairness and mitigating bias in AI systems is a critical focus area in ethics education. This includes understanding the sources of bias, implementing strategies to reduce bias in data and algorithms, and continuously monitoring AI systems for any discriminatory outcomes.

Education on fairness and bias mitigation helps developers create more equitable AI technologies and users make informed decisions about their use.

Transparency and Explainability

Transparency and explainability are essential for building trust in AI technologies. Ethics education should cover the importance of creating AI systems that are transparent in their operations and decision-making processes. This involves developing interpretable models, providing clear documentation, and openly communicating about AI functionalities. Transparent and explainable AI systems enable users to understand how decisions are made and hold developers accountable for their actions.

Accountability and Governance

Accountability and governance frameworks are necessary to ensure that AI technologies are developed and used responsibly. Ethics education should emphasize the importance of establishing clear accountability mechanisms, such as ethical guidelines, auditing processes, and oversight bodies.

Developers and users must be aware of their responsibilities and the consequences of unethical behavior, fostering a culture of accountability and ethical conduct.

8.1.4 Best Practices for Ethics Education

Interdisciplinary Approach

Ethics education for AI developers and users should adopt an interdisciplinary approach, integrating insights from fields such as computer science, philosophy, sociology, and law. This comprehensive perspective helps learners understand the multifaceted nature of ethical considerations in AI and provides them with a well-rounded understanding of the issues at hand.

Practical Case Studies

Incorporating practical case studies into ethics education allows learners to explore real-world scenarios and apply ethical principles to complex situations. Case studies provide valuable insights into the challenges and dilemmas faced by AI developers and users, fostering critical thinking and ethical reasoning skills. By examining past examples, learners can better anticipate and address potential ethical issues in their own work.

Ongoing Education and Training

Ethics education should not be a one-time event but an ongoing process. Continuous education and training are essential to keep developers and users updated on the latest ethical standards, regulations, and best practices. Organizations should provide regular workshops, seminars, and resources to ensure that their teams remain informed and capable of addressing emerging ethical challenges.

Collaboration and Dialogue

Promoting collaboration and dialogue among developers, users, ethicists, and other stakeholders is crucial for fostering ethical awareness and conduct. Ethics education programs should encourage open discussions, knowledge sharing, and collective problem-solving to address ethical issues in AI. Collaborative efforts help create a shared understanding of ethical principles and promote a culture of ethical responsibility.

8.2 FOSTERING ETHICAL BEHAVIOR IN AI-DRIVEN LEARNING

The integration of artificial intelligence (AI) in educational settings offers numerous benefits, such as personalized learning experiences, efficient administrative processes, and enhanced educational outcomes. However, these advancements also bring about significant ethical challenges that must be addressed to ensure responsible AI usage. Fostering ethical behavior in AI-driven learning is essential for creating a fair, transparent, and inclusive educational environment.

Fostering ethical behavior in AI-driven learning is essential for creating a fair, transparent, and inclusive educational environment. This requires a concerted effort from educators, developers, policymakers, and students to address ethical challenges and prioritize responsible AI usage.

By integrating ethics education into AI curricula, implementing ethical AI design practices, establishing robust guidelines and policies, and promoting digital citizenship, we can ensure that AI-driven learning systems are used in ways that benefit all students and society as a whole. As AI continues to transform education, fostering ethical behavior will be key to harnessing its potential while safeguarding ethical principles and values.

8.2.1 The Importance of Ethical Behavior in AI-Driven Learning

Ensuring Fairness and Equity

AI-driven learning systems have the potential to perpetuate and amplify existing biases present in educational data. Ensuring fairness and equity in AI-driven learning involves addressing these biases to provide equal opportunities for all students. Ethical behavior in AI-driven learning promotes fairness by implementing algorithms that account for diversity and avoid discriminatory practices.

Protecting Student Privacy

The use of AI in education often requires the collection and analysis of vast amounts of student data. Protecting student privacy is a critical ethical consideration, as misuse or unauthorized access to this data can have severe consequences. Ethical behavior ensures that student data is collected, stored, and used responsibly, with strict adherence to privacy regulations and guidelines.

Promoting Transparency and Accountability

Transparency and accountability are fundamental principles of ethical AI use in education. Students, parents, educators, and other stakeholders must understand how AI-driven learning systems make decisions and impact educational outcomes. Ethical behavior involves clear communication, open documentation, and mechanisms for accountability to build trust and ensure responsible AI usage.

8.2.2 Strategies for Fostering Ethical Behavior

Ethics Education for Developers and Educators

Integrating Ethics into AI Curriculum

Incorporating ethics into the AI curriculum for developers is essential for fostering ethical behavior. This includes teaching developers about the ethical implications of their work, the potential biases in AI algorithms, and the importance of transparency and accountability. By understanding these concepts, developers can create AI-driven learning systems that prioritize ethical considerations.

Professional Development for Educators

Educators play a crucial role in the implementation of AI-driven learning systems. Providing professional development opportunities that focus on the ethical use of AI in education equips educators with the knowledge and skills needed to navigate ethical challenges. Training programs should cover topics such as data privacy, algorithmic bias, and the ethical implications of AI decision-making.

Implementing Ethical AI Design Practices

Bias Mitigation and Fairness

Developers should prioritize bias mitigation and fairness in the design of AI-driven learning systems. This involves using diverse and representative datasets, implementing fairness-aware algorithms, and conducting regular bias audits. Ethical AI design practices ensure that all students receive equitable treatment and opportunities, regardless of their backgrounds.

Transparent and Explainable AI

Creating transparent and explainable AI systems is essential for promoting ethical behavior. Developers should design AI-driven learning systems that provide clear explanations for their decisions and outputs. This transparency helps educators and students understand how AI systems work and hold them accountable for their actions.

Establishing Ethical Guidelines and Policies

Data Privacy and Security Regulations

Policymakers play a critical role in fostering ethical behavior in AI-driven learning by establishing robust data privacy and security regulations. These regulations should outline clear guidelines for data collection, storage, and usage, ensuring that student data is protected at all times. Compliance with these regulations is essential for maintaining trust and safeguarding student privacy.

Accountability Frameworks

Establishing accountability frameworks is crucial for ensuring that AI-driven learning systems are used responsibly. These frameworks should include ethical guidelines, auditing processes, and mechanisms for reporting and addressing ethical concerns.

Accountability frameworks help hold developers, educators, and institutions accountable for their actions, promoting ethical behavior across the board.

Encouraging Ethical Use of AI by Students

Raising Awareness and Understanding

Educating students about the ethical implications of AI is essential for fostering responsible behavior. Schools and educational institutions should incorporate ethics education into their curricula, teaching students about data privacy, algorithmic bias, and the ethical considerations of AI usage.

Raising awareness and understanding helps students become informed users of AI-driven learning systems.

Promoting Digital Citizenship

Promoting digital citizenship involves teaching students how to use AI technologies responsibly and ethically. This includes understanding the impact of their digital actions, respecting the privacy and rights of others, and recognizing the importance of ethical behavior in the digital world. By fostering digital citizenship, educators can help students develop a strong ethical foundation for their interactions with AI-driven learning systems.

8.2.3 The Role of Stakeholders in Fostering Ethical Behavior

Educators

Educators are at the forefront of implementing AI-driven learning systems and play a vital role in fostering ethical behavior. They must be knowledgeable about the ethical implications of AI and advocate for responsible AI usage in their classrooms. Educators should also actively participate in professional development opportunities and collaborate with developers to ensure that AI systems are designed and used ethically.

Developers

AI developers have a responsibility to create ethical AI-driven learning systems. This involves prioritizing fairness, transparency, and accountability in their design practices, conducting regular bias audits, and adhering to data privacy regulations. Developers should also engage with educators and other stakeholders to understand their needs and concerns, ensuring that ethical considerations are at the forefront of AI development.

Policymakers

Policymakers play a crucial role in establishing the regulatory framework for ethical AI use in education.

They must develop comprehensive guidelines and policies that address data privacy, algorithmic bias, and accountability. Policymakers should also support ongoing research and development in ethical AI practices and ensure that educational institutions comply with ethical standards.

Students

Students are the primary users of AI-driven learning systems and play a significant role in fostering ethical behavior. By understanding the ethical implications of AI and practicing responsible digital citizenship, students can contribute to the responsible use of AI technologies. Schools and educational institutions should support students in developing the knowledge and skills needed to navigate the ethical challenges of AI-driven learning.

8.3 BUILDING ETHICAL AI COMMUNITIES

As artificial intelligence (AI) continues to shape various aspects of society, the need for ethical AI practices becomes increasingly crucial. Building ethical AI communities involves fostering collaboration, shared values, and responsible practices among developers, researchers, policymakers, educators, and users. These communities can play a significant role in ensuring that AI technologies are developed and deployed in ways that benefit society while minimizing harm.

Building ethical AI communities is crucial for ensuring that AI technologies are developed and deployed in ways that benefit society while minimizing harm. By promoting responsible AI development, ensuring accountability, and fostering public trust, ethical AI communities play a vital role in shaping the future of AI. Key components of these communities include collaboration and communication, education and training, ethical guidelines and standards, and public engagement and advocacy. Strategies for promoting ethical behavior involve establishing ethical codes of conduct, encouraging ethical research and innovation, and building inclusive communities. Through these efforts, we can create a robust ethical foundation for AI that aligns with societal values and promotes the well-being of all.

8.3.1 The Importance of Ethical AI Communities

Promoting Responsible AI Development

Ethical AI communities are essential for promoting responsible AI development. By bringing together diverse stakeholders, these communities can collectively address ethical challenges, share best practices, and develop standards that guide the ethical design and use of AI technologies. Such collaboration ensures that AI systems are built with a focus on fairness, transparency, accountability, and inclusivity.

Ensuring Accountability

Communities dedicated to ethical AI provide a platform for holding developers and organizations accountable for their actions. Through peer review, audits, and ethical guidelines, these communities can monitor AI practices and ensure compliance with ethical standards. Accountability mechanisms help prevent misuse and promote trust in AI technologies.

Fostering Public Trust

Building ethical AI communities helps foster public trust in AI technologies. When the public sees that AI developers and users are committed to ethical principles and transparency, it increases confidence in AI systems. Trust is crucial for the widespread adoption of AI technologies and for maximizing their positive impact on society.

8.3.2 Key Components of Ethical AI Communities

Collaboration and Communication

Interdisciplinary Collaboration

Ethical AI communities thrive on interdisciplinary collaboration. Bringing together experts from fields such as computer science, ethics, law, sociology, and education allows for a comprehensive understanding of the ethical implications of AI. Interdisciplinary collaboration ensures that diverse perspectives are considered in the development and deployment of AI systems.

Open Communication Channels

Open communication channels are vital for ethical AI communities. Stakeholders must be able to share their concerns, ideas, and experiences freely. This includes creating forums, workshops, and conferences where community members can discuss ethical challenges and develop collective solutions. Transparent communication helps build a shared understanding of ethical principles and promotes collaborative problem-solving.

Education and Training

Ethics Education for Developers

Providing ethics education for AI developers is a fundamental component of building ethical AI communities. This education should cover topics such as data privacy, bias mitigation, transparency, and accountability. By understanding these ethical considerations, developers can create AI systems that align with ethical standards and societal values.

Continuous Professional Development

Ethics education should be an ongoing process. Continuous professional development programs, such as workshops, seminars, and online courses, help developers stay updated on the latest ethical guidelines and best practices. These programs ensure that ethical considerations remain at the forefront of AI development.

Ethical Guidelines and Standards

Developing Ethical Frameworks

Ethical AI communities should work together to develop comprehensive ethical frameworks that guide AI development and use. These frameworks should address key ethical principles, such as fairness, transparency, accountability, and inclusivity. Clear guidelines help ensure that all community members adhere to the same ethical standards.

Implementing Auditing and Monitoring

Regular auditing and monitoring of AI systems are essential for maintaining ethical standards. Ethical AI communities can establish auditing processes to review AI practices and identify potential ethical issues. Ongoing monitoring helps detect and address problems early, ensuring that AI systems continue to operate ethically.

Public Engagement and Advocacy

Raising Awareness

Ethical AI communities should engage with the public to raise awareness about the ethical implications of AI technologies. This includes organizing public lectures, creating educational materials, and leveraging media platforms to disseminate information. Public engagement helps build a more informed society that can participate in ethical discussions and decision-making.

Advocacy for Ethical Policies

Advocating for ethical policies and regulations is a critical role of ethical AI communities. By working with policymakers, these communities can influence the development of laws and regulations that promote ethical AI practices. Advocacy efforts ensure that ethical considerations are integrated into the legal and regulatory framework governing AI technologies.

8.3.3 Strategies for Promoting Ethical Behavior

Establishing Ethical Codes of Conduct

Defining Clear Ethical Principles

Ethical AI communities should establish clear codes of conduct that define ethical principles and expected behaviors. These codes of conduct provide a foundation for ethical decision-making and set standards for community members to follow. Clear ethical principles help create a shared understanding of what constitutes ethical AI practices.

Enforcing Compliance

Enforcing compliance with ethical codes of conduct is crucial for maintaining ethical standards. Ethical AI communities should implement mechanisms to ensure adherence to these codes, such as peer reviews, audits, and disciplinary actions for non-compliance. Enforcing compliance reinforces the importance of ethical behavior and accountability.

Encouraging Ethical Research and Innovation

Funding Ethical AI Research

Providing funding for ethical AI research is essential for advancing the field. Ethical

AI communities can support research projects that focus on addressing ethical challenges, developing fairness-aware algorithms, and creating transparent AI systems. Funding ethical research encourages innovation that aligns with ethical principles.

Rewarding Ethical Practices

Recognizing and rewarding ethical practices within the AI community is a powerful way to promote ethical behavior. Awards, grants, and public recognition for ethical achievements encourage developers and organizations to prioritize ethical considerations in their work. Rewarding ethical practices reinforces the value of ethical behavior and motivates others to follow suit.

Building Inclusive Communities

Embracing Diversity

Ethical AI communities should embrace diversity and inclusivity. This involves actively recruiting members from different backgrounds, including underrepresented groups, to ensure diverse perspectives are represented. Embracing diversity helps address potential biases and creates a more equitable AI community.

Providing Support and Resources

Providing support and resources for all community members is essential for fostering inclusivity. This includes offering mentorship programs, networking opportunities, and access to educational materials. Supporting all members ensures that everyone has the tools and knowledge needed to contribute to ethical AI development.

PART IV:

ETHICAL GUIDELINES AND POLICIES

CHAPTER 9

REGULATORY FRAMEWORK AND POLICIES

9.1 NATIONAL AND INTERNATIONAL REGULATIONS

The integration of artificial intelligence (AI) in education has the potential to transform learning experiences, improve administrative efficiency, and personalize instruction. However, the adoption of AI in education also raises significant ethical concerns, including issues of privacy, fairness, accountability, and transparency. To address these challenges, both national and international regulations are being developed and implemented to ensure the ethical use of AI in education.

The integration of AI in education presents significant opportunities and challenges. Ensuring the ethical use of AI technologies requires comprehensive national and international regulations that address key ethical principles such as privacy, fairness, transparency, and accountability. Various countries and international organizations are actively working to develop frameworks, guidelines, and policies to promote ethical AI practices in education. Building a global consensus and fostering collaboration among stakeholders are essential for creating a regulatory environment that supports the responsible and ethical use of AI in education. Through these efforts, we can harness the potential of AI to enhance educational experiences while safeguarding ethical principles and societal values.

9.1.1 National Regulations on Ethics and AI in Education

United States

Discussions on regulation of artificial intelligence in the United States have included topics such as the timeliness of regulating AI, the nature of the federal regulatory framework to govern and promote AI, including what agency should lead, the regulatory and governing powers of that agency, and how to update regulations in the face of rapidly changing technology, as well as the roles of state governments and courts.

Federal Government Regulatory Measures

As early as 2016, the Obama administration had begun to focus on the risks and regulations for artificial intelligence. In a report titled *Preparing For the Future of*

Artificial Intelligence, the National Science and Technology Council set a precedent to allow researchers to continue to develop new AI technologies with few restrictions. It is stated within the report that "the approach to regulation of AI-enabled products to protect public safety should be informed by assessment of the aspects of risk....". These risks would be the principal reason to create any form of regulation, granted that any existing regulation would not apply to AI technology.

The first main report was the National Strategic Research and Development Plan for Artificial Intelligence. On August 13, 2018, Section 1051 of the Fiscal Year 2019 John S. McCain National Defense Authorization Act (P.L. 115-232) established the National Security Commission on Artificial Intelligence "to consider the methods and means necessary to advance the development of artificial intelligence, machine learning, and associated technologies to comprehensively address the national security and defense needs of the United States." Steering on regulating security-related AI is provided by the National Security Commission on Artificial Intelligence. The Artificial Intelligence Initiative Act (S.1558) is a proposed bill that would establish a federal initiative designed to accelerate research and development on AI for, *inter alia*, the economic and national security of the United States.

On January 7, 2019, following an Executive Order on Maintaining American Leadership in Artificial Intelligence, the White House's Office of Science and Technology Policy released a draft *Guidance for Regulation of Artificial Intelligence Applications*, which includes ten principles for United States agencies when deciding whether and how to regulate AI. In response, the National Institute of Standards and Technology has released a position paper, and the Defense Innovation Board has issued recommendations on the ethical use of AI. A year later, the administration called for comments on regulation in another draft of its Guidance for Regulation of Artificial Intelligence Applications.

Other specific agencies working on the regulation of AI include the Food and Drug Administration, which has created pathways to regulate the incorporation of AI in medical imaging. National Science and Technology Council also published the National Artificial Intelligence Research and Development Strategic Plan, which received public scrutiny and recommendations to further improve it towards enabling Trustworthy AI.

In March 2021, the National Security Commission on Artificial Intelligence released their final report. In the report, they stated that "Advances in AI, including the mastery of more general AI capabilities along one or more dimensions, will likely provide new capabilities and applications. Some of these advances could lead to inflection points or leaps in capabilities. Such advances may also introduce new concerns and risks and the need for new policies, recommendations, and technical advances to assure that systems are aligned with goals and values, including safety, robustness and trustworthiness. The US should monitor advances in AI and make necessary investments in technology and give attention to policy so as to ensure that AI systems and their uses align with our goals and values."

In June 2022, Senators Rob Portman and Gary Peters introduced the Global Catastrophic Risk Mitigation Act. The bipartisan bill "would also help counter the risk of artificial intelligence... from being abused in ways that may pose a catastrophic risk". On October 4, 2022, President Joe Biden unveiled a new AI Bill of Rights, which outlines five protections Americans should have in the AI age: 1. Safe and Effective Systems, 2. Algorithmic Discrimination Protection, 3.Data Privacy, 4. Notice and Explanation, and 5. Human Alternatives, Consideration, and Fallback. The Bill was introduced in October 2021 by the Office of Science and Technology Policy (OSTP), a US government department that advises the president on science and technology.

In July 2023, the Biden–Harris Administration secured voluntary commitments from seven companies – Amazon, Anthropic, Google, Inflection, Meta, Microsoft, and OpenAI – to manage the risks associated with AI. The companies committed to ensure AI products undergo both internal and external security testing before public release; to share information on the management of AI risks with the industry, governments, civil society, and academia; to prioritize cybersecurity and protect proprietary AI system components; to develop mechanisms to inform users when content is AI-generated, such as watermarking; to publicly report on their AI systems' capabilities, limitations, and areas of use; to prioritize research on societal risks posed by AI, including bias, discrimination, and privacy concerns; and to develop AI systems to address societal challenges, ranging from cancer prevention to climate change mitigation. In September 2023, eight additional companies – Adobe, Cohere, IBM, Nvidia, Palantir, Salesforce, Scale AI, and Stability AI – subscribed to these voluntary commitments.

The Biden administration, in October 2023 signaled that they would release an executive order leveraging the federal government's purchasing power to shape AI regulations, hinting at a proactive governmental stance in regulating AI technologies. On October 30, 2023, President Biden released this Executive Order on Safe, Secure, and Trustworthy Artificial Intelligence. The Executive Order addresses a variety of issues, such as focusing on standards for critical infrastructure, AI-enhanced cybersecurity, and federally funded biological synthesis projects.

The Executive Order provides the authority to various agencies and departments of the US government, including the Energy and Defense departments, to apply existing consumer protection laws to AI development.

The Executive Order builds on the Administration's earlier agreements with AI companies to instate new initiatives to "red-team" or stress-test AI dual-use foundation models, especially those that have the potential to pose security risks, with data and results shared with the federal government.

The Executive Order also recognizes AI's social challenges, and calls for companies building AI dual-use foundation models to be wary of these societal problems. For example, the Executive Order states that AI should not "worsen job quality", and should not "cause labor-force disruptions". Additionally, Biden's Executive Order mandates that AI must "advance equity and civil rights", and cannot disadvantage marginalized groups. It also called for foundation models to include "watermarks" to help the public discern between human and AI-generated content, which has raised controversy and criticism from deepfake detection researchers.

State and Local Government Interventions

In January 2023, the New York City Bias Audit Law (Local Law 144) was enacted by the NYC Council in November 2021. Originally due to come into effect on 1 January 2023, the enforcement date for Local Law 144 has been pushed back due to the high volume of comments received during the public hearing on the Department of Consumer and Worker Protection's (DCWP) proposed rules to clarify the requirements of the legislation. It eventually became effective on July 5, 2023. From this date, the companies that are operating and hiring in New York City are prohibited from using automated tools to hire candidates or promote employees, unless the tools have been independently audited for bias.

On March 21, 2024, the State of Tennessee enacted legislation called the ELVIS Act, aimed specifically at audio deepfakes, and voice cloning. This legislation was the first enacted legislation in the nation aimed at regulating AI simulation of image, voice and likeness. The bill passed unanimously in the Tennessee House of Representatives and Senate. This legislation's success was hoped by its supporters to inspire similar actions in other states, contributing to a unified approach to copyright and privacy in the digital age, and to reinforce the importance of safeguarding artists' rights against unauthorized use of their voices and likenesses.

In February 2024, Senator Scott Wiener introduced the Safe and Secure Innovation for Frontier Artificial Intelligence Models Act to the California legislature. The bill has the goal of reducing catastrophic risks by mandating safety tests for the most powerful AI models. If passed, the bill will also establish a publicly-funded cloud computing cluster in California.

Grassroots Perspectives

In 2016, Joy Buolamwini, AI researcher at Massachusetts Institute of Technology, shared her personal experiences with discrimination in facial recognition software at a TED Talk conference. Facial recognition software is vastly understood to be inaccurate in its identification of darker-skinned peoples, which matters especially in the context of policing, the criminal justice system, healthcare system, and employment sectors.

In 2022, the PEW Research Center's study of Americans revealed that only 18% of respondents are more excited than they are concerned about AI. Biases in AI algorithms and methods that lead to discrimination are causes for concern among many activist organizations and academic institutions. Recommendations include increasing diversity among creators of AI algorithms and addressing existing systemic bias in current legislation and AI development practices.

General Data Protection Regulation (GDPR)

The General Data Protection Regulation (Regulation (EU) 2016/679, abbreviated GDPR) is a European Union regulation on information privacy in the European Union (EU) and the European Economic Area (EEA). The GDPR is an important component of EU privacy law and human rights law, in particular Article 8(1) of the Charter of Fundamental Rights of the European Union. It also governs the transfer of personal data outside the EU and EEA. The GDPR's goals are to enhance individuals' control and rights over their personal information and to simplify the regulations for international business. It supersedes the Data Protection Directive 95/46/EC and, among other things, simplifies the terminology.

The European Parliament and Council of the European Union adopted the GDPR on 14 April 2016, to become effective on 25 May 2018. As an EU regulation (instead of a directive), GDPR is directly applicable with force of law on its own without the need of transposition. However, it also provides flexibility for individual member states to modify (derogate from) some of its provisions.

As an example of the Brussels effect, the regulation became a model for many other laws around the world, including in Brazil, Japan, Singapore, South Africa, South Korea, Sri Lanka, and Thailand. After leaving the European Union the United Kingdom enacted its "UK GDPR", identical to the GDPR. The California Consumer Privacy Act (CCPA), adopted on 28 June 2018, has many similarities with the GDPR.

Contents

The GDPR 2016 has eleven chapters, concerning general provisions, principles, rights of the data subject, duties of data controllers or processors, transfers of personal data to third countries, supervisory authorities, cooperation among member states, remedies, liability or penalties for breach of rights, and miscellaneous final provisions. Recital 4 proclaims that 'processing of personal data should be designed to serve mankind'.

General Provisions

The regulation applies if the data controller (an organisation that collects information about living people, whether they are in the EU or not), or processor (an organisation that processes data on behalf of a data controller like cloud service providers), or the data subject (person) is based in the EU. Under certain circumstances, the regulation also applies to organisations based outside the EU if they collect or process personal data of individuals located inside the EU. The regulation does not apply to the processing of data by a person for a "purely personal or household activity and thus with no connection to a professional or commercial activity." (Recital 18).

According to the European Commission, "Personal data is information that relates to an identified or identifiable individual. If you cannot directly identify an individual from that information, then you need to consider whether the individual is still identifiable. You should take into account the information you are processing together with all the means reasonably likely to be used by either you or any other person to identify that individual." The precise definitions of terms such as "personal data", "processing", "data subject", "controller", and "processor" are stated in Article 4 of the Regulation.

The regulation does not purport to apply to the processing of personal data for national security activities or law enforcement of the EU; however, industry groups concerned about facing a potential conflict of laws have questioned whether Article 48 of the GDPR could be invoked to seek to prevent a data controller subject to a third country's laws from complying with a legal order from that country's law enforcement, judicial, or national security authorities to disclose to such authorities the personal data of an EU person, regardless of whether the data resides in or out of the EU. Article 48 states that any judgement of a court or tribunal and any decision of an administrative authority of a third country requiring a controller or processor to transfer or disclose personal data may not be recognised or enforceable in any manner unless based on an international agreement, like a mutual legal assistance treaty in force between the requesting third (non-EU) country and the EU or a member state. The data protection reform package also includes a separate Data Protection Directive for the police and criminal justice sector that provides rules on personal data exchanges at State level, Union level, and international levels.

A single set of rules applies to all EU member states. Each member state establishes an independent supervisory authority (SA) to hear and investigate complaints, sanction administrative offences, etc. SAs in each member state co-operate with other SAs, providing mutual assistance and organising joint operations. If a business has multiple establishments in the EU, it must have a single SA as its "lead authority", based on the location of its "main establishment" where the main processing activities take place. The lead authority thus acts as a "one-stop shop" to supervise all the processing activities of that business throughout the EU (Articles 46–55 of the GDPR). A European Data Protection Board (EDPB) co-ordinates the

SAs. EDPB thus replaces the Article 29 Data Protection Working Party. There are exceptions for data processed in an employment context or in national security that still might be subject to individual country regulations (Articles 2(2)(a) and 88 of the GDPR).

Principles and Lawful Purposes

Article 5 sets out six *principles* relating to the lawfulness of processing personal data. The first of these specifies that data must be processed lawfully, fairly and in a transparent manner. Article 6 develops this principle by specifying that personal data may not be processed unless there is at least one legal basis for doing so. The other principles refer to "purpose limitation", "data minimisation", "accuracy", "storage limitation", and "integrity and confidentiality".

Article 6 states that the lawful purposes are:

- If the data subject has given consent to the processing of his or her personal data;
- To fulfill contractual obligations with a data subject, or for tasks at the request of a data subject who is in the process of entering into a contract;
- To comply with a data controller's legal obligations;
- To protect the vital interests of a data subject or another individual;
- To perform a task in the public interest or in official authority;
- For the legitimate interests of a data controller or a third party, unless these interests are overridden by interests of the data subject or her or his rights according to the Charter of Fundamental Rights (especially in the case of children).

If informed consent is used as the lawful basis for processing, consent must have been explicit for data collected and each purpose data is used for (Article 7; defined in Article 4). Consent must be a specific, freely given, plainly worded, and unambiguous affirmation given by the data subject; an online form which has consent options structured as an opt-out selected by default is a violation of the GDPR, as the consent is not unambiguously affirmed by the user. In addition, multiple types of processing may not be "bundled" together into a single affirmation prompt, as this is not specific to each use of data, and the individual permissions are not freely given. (Recital 32).

Data subjects must be allowed to withdraw this consent at any time, and the process of doing so must not be harder than it was to opt in. (Article 7(3)) A data controller may not refuse service to users who decline consent to processing that is not strictly necessary in order to use the service. (Article 8) Consent for children, defined in the regulation as being less than 16 years old (although with the option for member states to individually make it as low as 13 years old (Article 8(1)), must be given by the child's parent or custodian, and verifiable (Article 8).

If consent to processing was already provided under the Data Protection Directive, a data controller does not have to re-obtain consent if the processing is documented and obtained in compliance with the GDPR's requirements (Recital 171).

Transparency and Modalities

Article 12 requires the data controller to provide information to the "data subject in a concise, transparent, intelligible and easily accessible form, using clear and plain language, in particular for any information addressed specifically to a child."

Information and Access

The right of access (Article 15) is a data subject right. It gives people the right to access their personal data and information about how this personal data is being processed. A data controller must provide, upon request, an overview of the categories of data that are being processed (Article 15(1)(b)) as well as a copy of the actual data (Article 15(3)); furthermore, the data controller has to inform the data subject on details about the processing, such as the purposes of the processing (Article 15(1)(a)), with whom the data is shared (Article 15(1)(c)), and how it acquired the data (Article 15(1)(g)).

A data subject must be able to transfer personal data from one electronic processing system to and into another, without being prevented from doing so by the data controller. Data that has been sufficiently anonymised is excluded, but data that has been only de-identified but remains possible to link to the individual in question, such as by providing the relevant identifier, is not. In practice, however, providing such identifiers can be challenging, such as in the case of Apple's Siri, where voice and transcript data is stored with a personal identifier that the manufacturer restricts access to, or in online behavioural targeting, which relies heavily on device fingerprints that can be challenging to capture, send, and verify.

Both data being 'provided' by the data subject and data being 'observed', such as about behaviour, are included. In addition, the data must be provided by the controller in a structured and commonly used standard electronic format. The right to data portability is provided by Article 20 of the GDPR.

Rectification and Erasure

A *right to be forgotten* was replaced by a more limited *right of erasure* in the version of the GDPR that was adopted by the European Parliament in March 2014. Article 17 provides that the data subject has the right to request erasure of personal data related to them on any one of a number of grounds, including noncompliance with

Article 6(1) (lawfulness) that includes a case (f) if the legitimate interests of the controller are overridden by the interests or fundamental rights and freedoms of the data subject, which require protection of personal data.

Right to Object and Automated Decisions

Article 21 of the GDPR allows an individual to object to processing personal information for marketing or non-service related purposes. This means the data controller must allow an individual the right to stop or prevent controller from processing their personal data.

There are some instances where this objection does not apply. For example, if:

- Legal or official authority is being carried out.
- "Legitimate interest", where the organisation needs to process data in order to provide the data subject with a service they signed up for.
- A task being carried out for public interest.

GDPR is also clear that the data controller must inform individuals of their right to object from the first communication the controller has with them. This should be clear and separate from any other information the controller is providing and give them their options for how best to object to the processing of their data.

There are instances the controller can refuse a request, in the circumstances that the objection request is "manifestly unfounded" or "excessive", so each case of objection must be looked at individually. Other countries such as Canada are also, following the GDPR, considering legislation to regulate automated decision making under privacy laws, even though there are policy questions as to whether this is the best way to regulate AI.

Right to Compensation

Article 82 of the GDPR stipulates that any person who has suffered material or non-material damage as a result of an infringement of this Regulation shall have the right to receive compensation from the controller or processor for the damage suffered.

In the judgment Österreichische Post (C-300/21) the Court of Justice of the European Union gave an interpretation of the right to compensation. Article 82(1) GDPR requires for the award of damages (i) an infringement of the GDPR, (ii) (actual) damage suffered and (iii) a causal link between the infringement and the damage suffered. It is not necessary that the damage suffered reaches a certain degree of seriousness. There is no European defined concept of damage. Compensation is determined nationally in accordance with national law. The principles of equivalence and effectiveness must be taken into account.

Controller and Processor

Data controllers must clearly disclose any data collection, declare the lawful basis and purpose for data processing, and state how long data is being retained and if it is being shared with any third parties or outside of the EEA. Firms have the obligation to protect data of employees and consumers to the degree where only the necessary data is extracted with minimum interference with data privacy from employees, consumers, or third parties. Firms should have internal controls and regulations for various departments such as audit, internal controls, and operations. Data subjects have the right to request a portable copy of the data collected by a controller in a common format, as well as the right to have their data erased under certain circumstances. Public authorities, and businesses whose core activities consist of regular or systematic processing of personal data, are required to employ a *data protection officer* (DPO), who is responsible for managing compliance with the GDPR. Data controllers must report data breaches to national supervisory authorities within 72 hours if they have an adverse effect on user privacy. In some cases, violators of the GDPR may be fined up to €20 million or up to 4% of the annual worldwide turnover of the preceding financial year in case of an enterprise, whichever is greater.

To be able to demonstrate compliance with the GDPR, the data controller must implement measures that meet the principles of data protection by design and by default. Article 25 requires data protection measures to be designed into the development of business processes for products and services. Such measures include pseudonymising personal data, by the controller, as soon as possible. It is the responsibility and the liability of the data controller to implement effective measures and be able to demonstrate the compliance of processing activities even if the processing is carried out by a data processor on behalf of the controller.

When data is collected, data subjects must be clearly informed about the extent of data collection, the legal basis for the processing of personal data, how long data is retained, if data is being transferred to a third-party and/or outside the EU, and any automated decision-making that is made on a solely algorithmic basis. Data subjects must be informed of their privacy rights under the GDPR, including their right to revoke consent to data processing at any time, their right to view their personal data and access an overview of how it is being processed, their right to obtain a portable copy of the stored data, their right to erasure of their data under certain circumstances, their right to contest any automated decision-making that was made on a solely algorithmic basis, and their right to file complaints with a Data Protection Authority. As such, the data subject must also be provided with contact details for the data controller and their designated data protection officer, where applicable.

Data protection impact assessments (Article 35) have to be conducted when specific risks occur to the rights and freedoms of data subjects. Risk assessment and mitigation is required and prior approval of the data protection authorities is required for high risks.

Article 25 requires data protection to be designed into the development of business processes for products and services. Privacy settings must therefore be set at a high level by default, and technical and procedural measures shall be taken by the controller to make sure that the processing, throughout the whole processing lifecycle, complies with the regulation. Controllers shall also implement mechanisms to ensure that personal data is not processed unless necessary for each specific purpose. This is known as data minimisation.

A report by the European Union Agency for Network and Information Security elaborates on what needs to be done to achieve privacy and data protection by default.

It specifies that encryption and decryption operations must be carried out locally, not by remote service, because both keys and data must remain in the power of the data owner if any privacy is to be achieved. The report specifies that outsourced data storage on remote clouds is practical and relatively safe if only the data owner, not the cloud service, holds the decryption keys.

Pseudonymisation

According to the GDPR, pseudonymisation is a required process for stored data that transforms personal data in such a way that the resulting data cannot be attributed to a specific data subject without the use of additional information (as an alternative to the other option of complete data anonymisation).

An example is encryption, which renders the original data unintelligible in a process that cannot be reversed without access to the correct decryption key. The GDPR requires for the additional information (such as the decryption key) to be kept separately from the pseudonymised data.

Another example of pseudonymisation is tokenisation, which is a non-mathematical approach to protecting data at rest that replaces sensitive data with non-sensitive substitutes, referred to as tokens.

While the tokens have no extrinsic or exploitable meaning or value, they allow for specific data to be fully or partially visible for processing and analytics while sensitive information is kept hidden. Tokenisation does not alter the type or length of data, which means it can be processed by legacy systems such as databases that may be sensitive to data length and type.

This also requires much fewer computational resources to process and less storage space in databases than traditionally encrypted data.

Pseudonymisation is a privacy-enhancing technology and is recommended to reduce the risks to the concerned data subjects and also to help controllers and processors to meet their data protection obligations (Recital 28).

Records of Processing Activities

According to Article 30, records of processing activities have to be maintained by each organisation matching one of following criteria:

- Employing more than 250 people;
- The processing it carries out is likely to result in a risk to the rights and freedoms of data subjects;
- The processing is not occasional;
- Processing includes special categories of data as referred to in Article 9(1) or personal data relating to criminal convictions and offences referred to in Article 10.

Such requirements may be modified by each EU country. The records shall be in electronic form and the controller or the processor and, where applicable, the controller's or the processor's representative, shall make the record available to the supervisory authority on request.

Records of controller shall contain all of the following information:

- The name and contact details of the controller and, where applicable, the joint controller, the controller's representative and the data protection officer;
- The purposes of the processing;
- A description of the categories of data subjects and of the categories of personal data;
- The categories of recipients to whom the personal data have been or will be disclosed including recipients in third countries or international organisations;
- Transfers of personal data to a third country or an international organisation, including the identification of that third country or international organisation and, in the case of transfers referred to in the second subparagraph of Article 49(1), the documentation of suitable safeguards; and
- The envisaged time limits for erasure of the different categories of data;

Records of processor shall contain all of the following information:

- The name and contact details of the processor or processors and of each controller on behalf of which the processor is acting, and, where applicable, of the controller's or the processor's representative, and the data protection officer;

- The categories of processing carried out on behalf of each controller;
- Transfers of personal data to a third country or an international organisation, including the identification of that third country or international organisation and, in the case of transfers referred to in the second subparagraph of Article 49(1), the
- Documentation of suitable safeguards; and
- A general description of the technical and organisational security measures referred to in Article 32(1).

Security of Personal Data

Controllers and processors of personal data must put in place *appropriate technical and organizational measures* to implement the data protection principles. Business processes that handle personal data must be designed and built with consideration of the principles and provide safeguards to protect data (for example, using pseudonymization or full anonymization where appropriate). Data controllers must design information systems with privacy in mind. For instance, using the highest-possible privacy settings by default, so that the datasets are not publicly available by default and cannot be used to identify a subject. No personal data may be processed unless this processing is done under one of the six lawful bases specified by the regulation (consent, contract, public task, vital interest, legitimate interest or legal requirement). When the processing is based on consent the data subject has the right to revoke it at any time.

Article 33 states the data controller is under a legal obligation to notify the supervisory authority without undue delay unless the breach is unlikely to result in a risk to the rights and freedoms of the individuals. There is a maximum of 72 hours after becoming aware of the data breach to make the report. Individuals have to be notified if a high risk of an adverse impact is determined (Article 34). In addition, the data processor will have to notify the controller without undue delay after becoming aware of a personal data breach (Article 33). However, the notice to data subjects is not required if the data controller has implemented appropriate technical and organisational protection measures that render the personal data unintelligible to any person who is not authorised to access it, such as encryption (Article 34).

Data Protection Officer

Article 37 requires appointment of a data protection officer. If processing is carried out by a public authority (except for courts or independent judicial authorities when acting in their judicial capacity), or if processing operations involve regular and systematic monitoring of data subjects on a large scale, or if processing on a large scale of special categories of data and personal data relating to criminal convictions and offences (Articles 9 and Article 10,) a data protection officer (DPO)—a person with expert knowledge of data protection law and practices—must be designated to assist the controller or processor in monitoring their internal compliance with the Regulation.

A designated DPO can be a current member of staff of a controller or processor, or the role can be outsourced to an external person or agency through a service contract. In any case, the processing body must make sure that there is no conflict of interest in other roles or interests that a DPO may hold. The contact details for the DPO must be published by the processing organisation (for example, in a privacy notice) and registered with the supervisory authority.

The DPO is similar to a compliance officer and is also expected to be proficient at managing IT processes, data security (including dealing with cyberattacks) and other critical business continuity issues associated with the holding and processing of personal and sensitive data. The skill set required stretches beyond understanding legal compliance with data protection laws and regulations. The DPO must maintain a living data inventory of all data collected and stored on behalf of the organization. More details on the function and the role of data protection officer were given on 13 December 2016 (revised 5 April 2017) in a guideline document.

Organisations based outside the EU must also appoint an EU-based person as a representative and point of contact for their GDPR obligations (Article 27). This is a distinct role from a DPO, although there is overlap in responsibilities that suggest that this role can also be held by the designated DPO.

Remedies, Liability and Penalties

Besides the definitions as a criminal offence according to national law following Article 83 GDPR the following sanctions can be imposed:

- A warning in writing in cases of first and non-intentional noncompliance.
- Regular periodic data protection audits.
- A fine up to €10 million or up to 2% of the annual worldwide turnover of the preceding financial year in case of an enterprise, whichever is greater, if there has been an infringement of the following provisions (Article 83, Paragraph 4):
  - the obligations of the controller and the processor pursuant to Articles 8, 11, 25 to 39, and 42 and 43;

- the obligations of the certification body pursuant to Articles 42 and 43; and
- the obligations of the monitoring body pursuant to Article 41(4).

- A fine up to €20 million or up to 4% of the annual worldwide turnover of the preceding financial year in case of an enterprise, whichever is greater, if there has been an infringement of the following provisions (Article 83, Paragraph 5 & 6):
  - the basic principles for processing, including conditions for consent, pursuant to Articles 5, 6, 7, and 9;
  - the data subjects' rights pursuant to Articles 12 to 22;
  - the transfers of personal data to a recipient in a third country or an international organisation pursuant to Articles 44 to 49;
  - any obligations pursuant to member state law adopted under Chapter IX; and
  - noncompliance with an order or a temporary or definitive limitation on processing or the suspension of data flows by the supervisory authority pursuant to Article 58(2) or failure to provide access in violation of Article 58(1)

Exemptions

These are some cases which are not addressed in the GDPR specifically, thus are treated as exemptions.

- Personal or household activities.
- Law enforcement.
- National security.

When the GDPR was being created, it was strictly created for the regulation of personal data which goes into the hands of companies. What is not covered by the GDPR is non-commercial information or household activities. An example of these household activities may be emails between two high school friends.

Conversely, an entity or more precisely an "enterprise" has to be engaged in "economic activity" to be covered by the GDPR. Economic activity is defined broadly under European Union competition law.

Applicability Outside of the European Union

The GDPR also applies to data controllers and processors outside of the European Economic Area (EEA) if they are engaged in the "offering of goods or services" (regardless of whether a payment is required) to data subjects within the EEA, or are monitoring the behaviour of data subjects within the EEA (Article 3(2)). The regulation applies regardless of where the processing takes place. This has been interpreted as intentionally giving GDPR extraterritorial jurisdiction for non-EU establishments if they are doing business with people located in the EU. It is questionable whether the EU or its member states will in practice be able to enforce GDPR against organisations which have no establishment in the EU.

EU Representative

Under Article 27, non-EU establishments subject to GDPR are obliged to have a designee within the European Union, an "EU Representative", to serve as a point of contact for their obligations under the regulation. The EU Representative is the Controller's or Processor's contact person vis-à-vis European privacy supervisors and data subjects, in all matters relating to processing, to ensure compliance with this GDPR. A natural (individual) or legal (corporation) person can play the role of an EU Representative. The non-EU establishment must issue a duly signed document (letter of accreditation) designating a given individual or company as its EU Representative. The said designation can only be given in writing.

An establishment's failure to designate an EU Representative is considered ignorance of the regulation and relevant obligations, which itself is a violation of the GDPR subject to fines of up to €10 million or up to 2% of the annual worldwide turnover of the preceding financial year in case of an enterprise, whichever is greater. The intentional or negligent (willful blindness) character of the infringement (failure to designate an EU Representative) may rather constitute aggravating factors.

An establishment does not need to name an EU Representative if they only engage in occasional processing that does not include, on a large scale, processing of special categories of data as referred to in Article 9(1) of GDPR or processing of personal data relating to criminal convictions and offences referred to in Article 10, and such processing is unlikely to result in a risk to the rights and freedoms of natural persons, taking into account the nature, context, scope and purposes of the processing. Non-EU public authorities and bodies are equally exempted.

Third Countries

Chapter V of the GDPR forbids the transfer of the personal data of EU data subjects to countries outside of the EEA — known as *third countries* — unless appropriate safeguards are imposed, or the third country's data protection regulations are formally considered adequate by the European Commission (Article 45). Binding corporate rules, standard contractual clauses for data protection issued by a Data Processing Agreement (DPA), or a scheme of binding and enforceable commitments by the data controller or processor situated in a third country, are among examples.

United Kingdom Implementation

The applicability of GDPR in the United Kingdom is affected by Brexit. Although the United Kingdom formally withdrew from the European Union on 31 January 2020, it remained subject to EU law, including GDPR, until the end of the transition period on 31 December 2020. The United Kingdom granted royal assent to the Data Protection Act 2018 on 23 May 2018, which augmented the GDPR, including aspects of the regulation that are to be determined by national law, and criminal offences for knowingly or recklessly obtaining, redistributing, or retaining personal data without the consent of the data controller.

Under the European Union (Withdrawal) Act 2018, existing and relevant EU law was transposed into local law upon completion of the transition, and the GDPR was amended by statutory instrument to remove certain provisions no longer needed due to the UK's non-membership in the EU. Thereafter, the regulation will be referred to as "UK GDPR". The UK will not restrict the transfer of personal data to countries within the EEA under UK GDPR. However, the UK will become a *third country* under the EU GDPR, meaning that personal data may not be transferred to the country unless appropriate safeguards are imposed, or the European Commission performs an adequacy decision on the suitability of British data protection legislation (Chapter V). As part of the withdrawal agreement, the European Commission committed to perform an adequacy assessment.

In April 2019, the UK Information Commissioner's Office (ICO) issued a children's code of practice for social networking services when used by minors, enforceable under GDPR, which also includes restrictions on "like" and "streak" mechanisms in order to discourage social media addiction and on the use of this data for processing interests.

In March 2021, Secretary of State for Digital, Culture, Media and Sport Oliver Dowden stated that the UK was exploring divergence from the EU GDPR in order to "[focus] more on the outcomes that we want to have and less on the burdens of the rules imposed on individual businesses".

Misconceptions

Some common misconceptions about GDPR include:

- **All Processing of Personal Data Requires Consent of the Data Subject:** In fact, data can be processed without consent if one of the other five lawful bases for processing applies, and obtaining consent may often be inappropriate.
- **Individuals have an Absolute Right to have their Data Deleted (Right to be Forgotten):** Whilst there is an absolute right to opt-out of direct marketing, data controllers can continue to process personal data where they have a lawful basis to do so, as long as the data remain necessary for the purpose for which it was originally collected.
- **Removing Individuals' Names from Records takes them Out of Scope of GDPR:** "Pseudonymous" data where an individual is identified

by a number can still be personal data if the data controller is capable of tying that data back to an individual in another way.

- **GDPR Applies to Anyone Processing Personal Data of EU Citizens Anywhere in the World:** In fact, it applies to non-EU established organizations only where they are processing data of data subjects located in the EU (irrespective of their citizenship) and then only when supplying goods or services to them, or monitoring their behaviour.

Reception

As per a study conducted by Deloitte in 2018, 92% of companies believe they are able to comply with GDPR in their business practices in the long run. Companies operating outside of the EU have invested heavily to align their business practices with GDPR. The area of GDPR consent has a number of implications for businesses who record calls as a matter of practice. A typical disclaimer is not considered sufficient to gain assumed consent to record calls. Additionally, when recording has commenced, should the caller withdraw their consent, then the agent receiving the call must be able to stop a previously started recording and ensure the recording does not get stored.

IT professionals expect that compliance with the GDPR will require additional investment overall: over 80 percent of those surveyed expected GDPR-related spending to be at least US$100,000. The concerns were echoed in a report commissioned by the law firm Baker & McKenzie that found that "around 70 percent of respondents believe that organizations will need to invest additional budget/ effort to comply with the consent, data mapping and cross-border data transfer requirements under the GDPR." The total cost for EU companies is estimated at €200 billion while for US companies the estimate is for $41.7 billion. It has been argued that smaller businesses and startup companies might not have the financial resources to adequately comply with the GDPR, unlike the larger international technology firms (such as Facebook and Google) that the regulation is ostensibly meant to target first and foremost. A lack of knowledge and understanding of the regulations has also been a concern in the lead-up to its adoption. A counter-argument to this has been that companies were made aware of these changes two years prior to them coming into effect and should have had enough time to prepare.

The regulations, including whether an enterprise must have a data protection officer, have been criticized for potential administrative burden and unclear compliance requirements. Although data minimisation is a requirement, with pseudonymisation being one of the possible means, the regulation provides no guidance on how or what constitutes an effective data de-identification scheme, with a grey area on what would be considered as inadequate pseudonymisation subject to Section 5 enforcement actions. There is also concern regarding the implementation of the GDPR in blockchain systems, as the transparent and fixed record of blockchain transactions contradicts the very nature of the GDPR. Many media outlets have commented on the introduction of a "right to explanation" of algorithmic decisions, but legal scholars have since argued that the existence of such a right is highly unclear without judicial tests and is limited at best.

The GDPR has garnered support from businesses who regard it as an opportunity to improve their data management. Mark Zuckerberg has also called it a "very positive step for the Internet", and has called for GDPR-style laws to be adopted in the US. Consumer rights groups such as The European Consumer Organisation are among the most vocal proponents of the legislation. Other supporters have attributed its passage to the whistleblower Edward Snowden. Free software advocate Richard Stallman has praised some aspects of the GDPR but called for additional safeguards to prevent technology companies from "manufacturing consent".

Impact

Academic experts who participated in the formulation of the GDPR wrote that the law "is the most consequential regulatory development in information policy in a generation. The GDPR brings personal data into a complex and protective regulatory regime."

Despite having had at least two years to prepare and do so, many companies and websites changed their privacy policies and features worldwide directly prior to GDPR's implementation, and customarily provided email and other notifications discussing these changes. This was criticised for resulting in a fatiguing number of communications, while experts noted that some reminder emails incorrectly asserted that new consent for data processing had to be obtained for when the GDPR took effect (any previously obtained consent to processing is valid as long as it met the regulation's requirements). Phishing scams also emerged using falsified versions of GDPR-related emails, and it was also argued that some GDPR notice emails may have actually been sent in violation of anti-spam laws. In March 2019, a provider of compliance software found that many websites operated by EU member state governments contained embedded tracking from ad technology providers.

The deluge of GDPR-related notices also inspired memes, including those surrounding privacy policy notices being delivered by atypical means (such as a Ouija board or *Star Wars* opening crawl), suggesting that Santa Claus's "naughty or nice" list was a violation, and a recording of excerpts from the regulation by a former BBC Radio 4 Shipping Forecast announcer.

A blog, *GDPR Hall of Shame*, was also created to showcase unusual delivery of GDPR notices, and attempts at compliance that contained egregious violations of the regulation's requirements. Its author remarked that the regulation "has a lot of nitty gritty, in-the-weeds details, but not a lot of information about how to comply", but also acknowledged that businesses had two years to comply, making some of its responses unjustified.

Research indicates that approximately 25% of software vulnerabilities have GDPR implications. Since Article 33 emphasizes breaches, not bugs, security experts advise companies to invest in processes and capabilities to identify vulnerabilities before they can be exploited, including coordinated vulnerability disclosure processes. An investigation of Android apps' privacy policies, data access capabilities, and data access behaviour has shown that numerous apps display a somewhat privacy-friendlier behaviour since the GDPR was implemented, although they still retain most of their data access privileges in their code. An investigation of the Norwegian Consumer Council into the post-GDPR data subject dashboards on social media platforms (such as Google dashboard) has concluded that large social media firms deploy deceptive tactics in order to discourage their customers from sharpening their privacy settings.

On the effective date, some websites began to block visitors from EU countries entirely (including Instapaper, Unroll.me, and Tribune Publishing-owned newspapers, such as the *Chicago Tribune* and the *Los Angeles Times*) or redirect them to stripped-down versions of their services (in the case of National Public Radio and *USA Today*) with limited functionality and/or no advertising so that they will not be liable. Some companies, such as Klout, and several online video games, ceased operations entirely to coincide with its implementation, citing the GDPR as a burden on their continued operations, especially due to the business model of the former. The volume of online behavioural advertising placements in Europe fell 25–40% on 25 May 2018.

In 2020, two years after the GDPR began its implementation, the European Commission assessed that users across the EU had increased their knowledge about their rights, stating that "69% of the population above the age of 16 in the EU have heard about the GDPR and 71% of people heard about their national data protection authority." The commission also found that privacy has become a competitive quality for companies which consumers are taking into account in their decisionmaking processes.

Enforcement and Inconsistency

Facebook and subsidiaries WhatsApp and Instagram, as well as Google LLC (targeting Android), were immediately sued by Max Schrems's non-profit NOYB just hours after midnight on 25 May 2018, for their use of "forced consent". Schrems asserts that both companies violated Article 7(4) by not presenting opt-ins for data processing consent on an individualized basis, and requiring users to consent to all data processing activities (including those not strictly necessary) or would be forbidden from using the services. On 21 January 2019, Google was fined €50 million by the French DPA for showing insufficient control, consent, and transparency over use of personal data for behavioural advertising. In November 2018, following a journalistic investigation into Liviu Dragnea, the Romanian DPA (ANSPDCP) used a GDPR request to demand information on the RISE Project's sources.

In July 2019, the British Information Commissioner's Office issued an intention to fine British Airways a record £183 million (1.5% of turnover) for poor security arrangements that enabled a 2018 web skimming attack affecting around 380,000 transactions. British Airways was ultimately fined a reduced amount of £20m, with the ICO noting that they had "considered both representations from BA and the economic impact of COVID-19 on their business before setting a final penalty".

In December 2019, *Politico* reported that Ireland and Luxembourg – two smaller EU countries that have had a reputation as a tax havens and (especially in the case of Ireland) as a base for European subsidiaries of U.S. big tech companies – were facing significant backlogs in their investigations of major foreign companies under GDPR, with Ireland citing the complexity of the regulation as a factor. Critics interviewed by *Politico* also argued that enforcement was also being hampered by varying interpretations between member states, the prioritisation of guidance over enforcement by some authorities, and a lack of cooperation between member states.

In November 2021, Irish Council for Civil Liberties lodged a formal complaint of the Commission that it is in breach of its obligation under EU Law to carefully monitor how Ireland applies the GDPR. Until January 2023, the Commission published a new commitment based on the complaint of ICCL.

While companies are now subject to legal obligations, there are still various inconsistencies in the practical and technical implementation of GDPR. As an example, according to the GDPR's right to access, the companies are obliged to provide data subjects with the data they gather about them. However, in a study on loyalty cards in Germany, companies did not provide the data subjects with the exact information of the purchased articles. One might argue that such companies do not collect the information of the purchased articles, which does not conform with their business models. Therefore, data subjects tend to see that as a GDPR violation. As a result, studies have suggested for a better control through authorities.

According to the GDPR, end-users' consent should be valid, freely given, specific, informed and active. However, the lack of enforceability regarding obtaining lawful consents has been a challenge. As an example, a 2020 study, showed that the Big Tech, i.e. Google, Amazon, Facebook, Apple, and Microsoft (GAFAM), use dark patterns in their consent obtaining mechanisms, which raises doubts regarding the lawfulness of the acquired consent.

In March 2021, EU member states led by France were reported to be attempting to modify the impact of the privacy regulation in Europe by exempting national security agencies. After around 160 million Euros in GDPR fines were imposed in 2020, the figure was already over one billion Euros in 2021.

Influence on Foreign Laws

Mass adoption of these new privacy standards by multinational companies has been cited as an example of the "Brussels effect", a phenomenon wherein European laws and regulations are used as a baseline due to their gravitas.

The U.S. state of California passed the California Consumer Privacy Act on 28 June 2018, taking effect on 1 January 2020; it grants rights to transparency and control over the collection of personal information by companies in a similar means to GDPR. Critics have argued that such laws need to be implemented at the federal level to be effective, as a collection of state-level laws would have varying standards that would complicate compliance. Two other U.S. states have since enacted similar legislation: Virginia passed the Consumer Data Privacy Act on 2 March 2021, and Colorado enacted the Colorado Privacy Act on 8 July 2021.

The Republic of Turkey, a candidate for European Union membership, has adopted the Law on The Protection of Personal Data on 24 March 2016 in compliance with the EU acquis. China's 2021 Personal Information Protection Law is the country's first comprehensive law on personal data rights and is modeled after the GDPR. Switzerland will also adopt a new data protection law that largely follows EU's GDPR.

Website Views and Revenue

A 2024 study found that GDPR reduced both EU user website page views and website revenue by 12%.

Timeline

- **25 January 2012:** The proposal for the GDPR was released.
- **21 October 2013:** The European Parliament Committee on Civil Liberties, Justice and Home Affairs (LIBE) had its orientation vote.
- **15 December 2015:** Negotiations between the European Parliament, Council and Commission (Formal Trilogue meeting) resulted in a joint proposal.
- **17 December 2015:** The European Parliament's LIBE Committee voted for the negotiations between the three parties.

- **8 April 2016:** Adoption by the Council of the European Union. The only member state voting against was Austria, which argued that the level of data protection in some respects falls short compared to the 1995 directive.
- **14 April 2016:** Adoption by the European Parliament.
- **24 May 2016:** The regulation entered into force, 20 days after its publication in the *Official Journal of the European Union.*
- **6 May 2018:** Data Protection Directive for the police and justice sectors into national legislation applicable from this day.
- **25 May 2018:** Its provisions became directly applicable in all member states, two years after the regulations enter into force.
- **20 July 2018:** The GDPR became valid in the EEA countries (Iceland, Liechtenstein, and Norway), after the EEA Joint Committee and the three countries agreed to follow the regulation.

EU Digital Single Market

The EU Digital Single Market strategy relates to "digital economy" activities related to businesses and people in the EU. As part of the strategy, the GDPR and the NIS Directive all apply from 25 May 2018. The proposed ePrivacy Regulation was also planned to be applicable from 25 May 2018, but will be delayed for several months. The eIDAS Regulation is also part of the strategy. In an initial assessment, the European Council has stated that the GDPR should be considered "a prerequisite for the development of future digital policy initiatives".

Ethical Guidelines for Trustworthy AI

The European Commission has developed ethical guidelines for trustworthy AI, focusing on principles such as human agency, privacy, transparency, and accountability. These guidelines are designed to ensure that AI technologies in education respect fundamental rights and promote human well-being. The guidelines encourage the development of AI systems that are robust, secure, and free from bias, thereby fostering trust and acceptance among educators, students, and parents.

Asia-Pacific

Japan's AI Strategy

Japan has implemented a national AI strategy that includes ethical considerations for AI in education. The strategy emphasizes the need for AI technologies to be transparent, fair, and accountable. It also highlights the importance of protecting student data and ensuring that AI systems are designed to support and enhance the educational experience rather than replace human educators. Japan's approach includes collaboration between government agencies, educational institutions, and technology companies to develop ethical AI standards and best practices.

South Korea's AI Ethics Guidelines

South Korea has introduced AI ethics guidelines that apply to various sectors, including education. These guidelines focus on ensuring the ethical use of AI by promoting transparency, accountability, and inclusivity. The guidelines also stress the importance of protecting personal data and preventing discrimination and bias in AI algorithms. South Korea's approach includes continuous monitoring and evaluation of AI technologies to ensure they align with ethical principles and societal values.

9.1.2 International Regulations and Frameworks

UNESCO's Recommendations on AI in Education

The United Nations Educational, Scientific and Cultural Organization (UNESCO) has developed recommendations on the ethical use of AI in education. These recommendations emphasize the need for AI technologies to enhance education while respecting human rights, diversity, and equity. UNESCO advocates for international collaboration to develop ethical standards and frameworks that can be adopted by countries worldwide. The recommendations also highlight the importance of capacity-building, ensuring that educators and policymakers are equipped to understand and address the ethical implications of AI in education.

OECD's Principles on AI

The Organisation for Economic Co-operation and Development (OECD) has established AI principles that provide a framework for the responsible development and use of AI technologies. These principles include promoting inclusive growth, sustainable development, and well-being, ensuring transparency and accountability, and fostering trustworthiness in AI systems. The OECD principles are designed to guide member countries in developing policies and regulations that ensure the ethical use of AI in education and other sectors.

The Global Partnership on Artificial Intelligence (GPAI)

The Global Partnership on Artificial Intelligence (GPAI) is an international initiative that aims to support the responsible and ethical use of AI. GPAI promotes collaboration between governments, industry, academia, and civil society to address the ethical challenges of AI. The partnership focuses on developing best practices, guidelines, and standards that can be adopted globally to ensure that AI technologies, including those used in education, are designed and deployed ethically.

9.1.3 Challenges in Regulating AI Ethics in Education

Balancing Innovation and Regulation

One of the key challenges in regulating AI ethics in education is striking a balance between fostering innovation and implementing effective regulations. Overly stringent regulations may stifle innovation and slow down the adoption of beneficial AI technologies, while insufficient regulations may lead to ethical breaches and loss of public trust. Policymakers must carefully consider how to create a regulatory environment that encourages innovation while ensuring ethical practices.

Addressing Bias and Discrimination

AI systems can inadvertently perpetuate bias and discrimination if they are trained on biased data. Regulating AI ethics in education involves developing frameworks and guidelines that address these issues. This includes implementing bias detection and mitigation strategies, ensuring diverse and representative datasets, and promoting fairness-aware algorithms. Policymakers and developers must work together to identify and eliminate biases in AI systems to ensure equitable educational opportunities for all students.

Ensuring Global Cooperation

AI technologies and their ethical implications are global in nature, requiring international cooperation to develop effective regulations. However, achieving consensus on ethical standards and guidelines can be challenging due to differences in cultural values, legal systems, and levels of technological advancement. International organizations such as UNESCO, OECD, and GPAI play a crucial role in facilitating global dialogue and collaboration to address these challenges and promote ethical AI practices worldwide.

9.2 GUIDELINES FOR ETHICAL AI ADOPTION

The adoption of artificial intelligence (AI) across various sectors has brought about transformative changes, enhancing efficiency, personalization, and decision-making processes. However, the rapid integration of AI also raises significant ethical concerns, such as data privacy, bias, transparency, and accountability. To navigate these challenges, it is essential to establish guidelines for the ethical adoption of AI. These guidelines will help ensure that AI technologies are developed and deployed in ways that align with societal values and ethical principles.

The ethical adoption of AI requires a comprehensive approach that encompasses fairness, transparency, accountability, privacy, and inclusivity. By adhering to these guidelines, organizations can ensure that AI technologies are developed and deployed in ways that align with ethical principles and societal values. Establishing clear accountability frameworks, protecting data privacy, promoting inclusive design, and fostering continuous ethical assessment are critical steps toward responsible AI adoption. Education and awareness initiatives, industry collaboration, and international cooperation further support the creation of a robust ethical foundation for AI.

Through these efforts, we can harness the potential of AI to benefit society while safeguarding ethical principles and promoting the well-being of all individuals.

9.2.1 Fairness

Avoiding Bias

AI systems are only as fair as the data and algorithms that power them. One of the primary concerns in AI ethics is avoiding bias, which can result in unfair treatment of individuals or groups.

To ensure fairness, developers should use diverse and representative datasets when training AI models. This helps to minimize the risk of perpetuating existing biases and ensures that AI systems provide equitable outcomes for all users.

Implementing Fairness-Aware Algorithms

In addition to using diverse datasets, developers should implement fairness-aware algorithms that actively detect and mitigate bias.

These algorithms are designed to recognize and correct biased patterns in data, ensuring that AI systems make fair and unbiased decisions. Regular audits and evaluations of AI systems should be conducted to identify and address any emerging biases.

9.2.2 Transparency

Explainability

Transparency in AI systems is crucial for building trust and ensuring ethical adoption. Explainability refers to the ability to understand and interpret how AI systems make decisions. Developers should design AI systems that provide clear and understandable explanations for their outputs. This transparency allows users to trust AI decisions and enables them to challenge or question those decisions when necessary.

Open Communication

Open communication about AI technologies, their capabilities, and their limitations is essential for transparency. Organizations should provide clear information about how AI systems are used, the data they rely on, and the potential risks and benefits. This open communication helps to build trust among users and stakeholders, ensuring that they are well-informed about AI adoption and its implications.

9.2.3 Accountability

Clear Accountability Frameworks

Accountability is a fundamental principle of ethical AI adoption. Organizations should establish clear accountability frameworks that define the roles and responsibilities of individuals involved in the development, deployment, and use of AI systems. These frameworks should include mechanisms for monitoring and auditing AI systems to ensure compliance with ethical standards.

Redress Mechanisms

When AI systems make errors or cause harm, it is crucial to have mechanisms in place for redress. Organizations should develop processes for reporting and addressing grievances related to AI decisions. These redress mechanisms ensure that affected individuals can seek recourse and that organizations can learn from mistakes to improve their AI systems.

9.2.4 Privacy

Data Protection

Protecting the privacy of individuals is a critical ethical consideration in AI adoption. Organizations must adhere to data protection regulations and ensure that personal data is collected, stored, and processed securely. Data minimization principles should be applied, collecting only the data necessary for the AI system's intended purpose.

Informed Consent

Informed consent is essential when collecting and using personal data for AI systems. Organizations should provide clear and comprehensive information about how data will be used, the purposes of data collection, and the potential risks involved. Individuals must have the opportunity to provide or withhold consent freely, and organizations should respect their decisions.

9.2.5 Inclusivity

Addressing Digital Divide

AI adoption should not exacerbate existing inequalities or create new ones. Organizations should ensure that AI technologies are accessible to all individuals, regardless of their socioeconomic status, location, or technical literacy. Efforts should be made to address the digital divide by providing the necessary infrastructure, resources, and training to underserved communities.

Inclusive Design

Inclusive design practices involve considering the needs and perspectives of diverse user groups when developing AI systems. This includes engaging with stakeholders from different backgrounds and incorporating their feedback into the design process. Inclusive design ensures that AI technologies are usable and beneficial for everyone, not just a privileged few.

9.2.6 Ethical AI Governance

Establishing Ethical AI Committees

Organizations should establish ethical AI committees or advisory boards to oversee the development and deployment of AI systems.

These committees should include experts from diverse fields, such as ethics, law, sociology, and technology. Their role is to provide guidance, review AI projects, and ensure that ethical considerations are integrated into decision-making processes.

Continuous Ethical Assessment

Ethical AI adoption requires continuous assessment and improvement. Organizations should conduct regular ethical assessments of their AI systems to identify potential risks and address emerging ethical issues.

This ongoing evaluation helps to ensure that AI technologies remain aligned with ethical principles and societal values over time.

9.2.7 Education and Awareness

Training for Developers and Users

Education and training are essential for promoting ethical AI adoption. Developers should receive training on ethical AI principles, including fairness, transparency, accountability, privacy, and inclusivity. Similarly, users should be educated about the ethical implications of AI technologies and how to use them responsibly.

Raising Public Awareness

Raising public awareness about AI ethics is crucial for fostering a well-informed society. Organizations should engage in public outreach activities, such as workshops, seminars, and media campaigns, to educate the broader community about the benefits and risks of AI. Public awareness initiatives help to build a culture of ethical AI adoption and encourage collective responsibility.

9.2.8 Collaboration and Standards

Industry Collaboration

Collaboration within the industry is vital for establishing and maintaining ethical standards for AI adoption. Organizations should work together to share best practices, develop ethical guidelines, and create standardized frameworks for ethical AI. Industry-wide collaboration ensures a consistent approach to ethical AI adoption and fosters a collective commitment to responsible AI practices.

International Standards

Given the global nature of AI technologies, international cooperation is essential for developing comprehensive ethical standards. Organizations should participate in international initiatives and contribute to the creation of global ethical guidelines for AI. International standards provide a unified approach to ethical AI adoption and facilitate cross-border collaboration.

9.3 CHALLENGES IN ENFORCING AI ETHICS POLICIES

Artificial intelligence (AI) has become a transformative force across various sectors, offering unprecedented opportunities for innovation and efficiency. However, the rapid integration of AI also brings significant ethical challenges. To address these, organizations and governments are developing and implementing AI ethics policies. Despite these efforts, enforcing AI ethics policies remains a complex task fraught with numerous challenges.

Enforcing AI ethics policies is a multifaceted challenge that involves addressing ambiguity in ethical guidelines, ensuring compliance, establishing clear accountability, promoting transparency, mitigating bias, fostering international cooperation, and keeping up with rapid technological advancements. Despite these challenges, the importance of ethical AI adoption cannot be overstated. By developing robust frameworks, fostering collaboration among stakeholders, and continuously updating ethical guidelines, we can work towards a future where AI technologies are used responsibly and ethically. Addressing these challenges requires a concerted effort from policymakers, organizations, and the global community to ensure that AI benefits society while upholding fundamental ethical principles.

9.3.1 Ambiguity in Ethical Guidelines

Lack of Clear Definitions

One of the primary challenges in enforcing AI ethics policies is the lack of clear and universally accepted definitions of ethical principles. Terms such as "fairness," "transparency," and "accountability" can be interpreted in various ways, leading to ambiguity in their application. This lack of clarity makes it difficult for organizations to develop concrete policies and for regulators to enforce them consistently.

Context-Specific Ethics

Ethical considerations in AI are often context-specific, varying across different industries, applications, and cultural settings. A policy that is effective in one context may not be applicable or relevant in another. This variability complicates the development of standardized ethical guidelines and makes enforcement more challenging.

9.3.2 Compliance Issues

Voluntary Adherence

Many AI ethics policies are currently based on voluntary adherence rather than mandatory compliance. Organizations may choose to adopt these guidelines to enhance their reputation or avoid potential legal issues, but there is no binding obligation to do so. This voluntary nature of AI ethics policies limits their effectiveness and makes enforcement difficult.

Resource Constraints

Implementing and enforcing AI ethics policies require significant resources, including time, money, and expertise. Smaller organizations or those with limited resources may struggle to comply with comprehensive ethical guidelines. This disparity can lead to inconsistent enforcement and create an uneven playing field where only well-resourced organizations can fully adhere to ethical standards.

9.3.3 Accountability and Responsibility

Diffuse Accountability

AI systems are often developed and deployed by multiple stakeholders, including developers, data scientists, managers, and external vendors. This diffusion of responsibility makes it challenging to pinpoint accountability when ethical breaches occur. Without clear accountability, enforcing AI ethics policies becomes problematic as there is no single entity to hold responsible.

Ethical vs. Legal Accountability

Ethical accountability and legal accountability are not always aligned. While legal regulations provide a framework for accountability, ethical considerations often extend beyond legal requirements. Organizations may face situations where their actions are legally permissible but ethically questionable. Enforcing AI ethics policies requires mechanisms to address both legal and ethical accountability, which can be complex and contentious.

9.3.4 Transparency Challenges

Black Box Algorithms

Many AI systems, particularly those based on deep learning, operate as "black boxes," meaning their decision-making processes are not easily interpretable. This lack of transparency makes it difficult to understand how decisions are made and to identify potential ethical issues. Enforcing transparency in AI systems requires developing techniques for explainability and interpretability, which is a significant technical challenge.

Proprietary Information

Organizations often consider their AI algorithms and data as proprietary information, crucial to their competitive advantage. This proprietary nature can hinder transparency, as organizations may be reluctant to disclose details about their AI systems. Balancing the need for transparency with the protection of proprietary information is a significant challenge in enforcing AI ethics policies.

9.3.5 Bias and Fairness

Data Bias

AI systems are only as good as the data they are trained on. Biased data can lead to biased AI outcomes, perpetuating existing inequalities and unfair practices. Detecting and mitigating bias in data is a complex task that requires rigorous testing, diverse datasets, and continuous monitoring. Enforcing policies to ensure fairness and mitigate bias in AI systems is a significant challenge due to the intricate nature of data bias.

Evolving Standards of Fairness

Standards of fairness are not static and can evolve over time. What is considered fair and unbiased today may be seen as problematic in the future. This evolving nature of fairness standards makes it difficult to develop and enforce static AI ethics policies. Continuous evaluation and updating of ethical guidelines are necessary, but implementing such dynamic policies is challenging.

9.3.6 International Cooperation

Diverse Regulatory Landscapes

AI ethics policies are influenced by the regulatory landscapes of different countries, which can vary significantly. These differences can lead to inconsistencies in ethical standards and enforcement practices across borders. Multinational organizations face the challenge of navigating these diverse regulatory environments while maintaining consistent ethical practices.

Global Standards

The development of global standards for AI ethics is crucial for ensuring consistent and effective enforcement. However, achieving international consensus on ethical principles and guidelines is challenging due to differing cultural values, economic interests, and political priorities. International organizations such as the OECD and UNESCO are working towards developing global standards, but the process is complex and ongoing.

9.3.7 Technological Rapid Advancements

Keeping Up with Innovation

The rapid pace of AI innovation presents a significant challenge for enforcing ethics policies. New AI technologies and applications are continuously emerging, often outpacing the development of ethical guidelines and regulatory frameworks. Policymakers and organizations must stay abreast of these advancements to ensure that ethical considerations keep pace with technological progress.

Predicting Ethical Implications

Predicting the ethical implications of emerging AI technologies is inherently difficult. Technologies that seem benign at their inception may raise unforeseen ethical issues as they are adopted and scaled. Enforcing AI ethics policies requires a proactive approach to anticipate potential ethical challenges and develop preemptive guidelines, which is a complex and uncertain endeavor.

CHAPTER 10

EDUCATIONAL INSTITUTIONS AND AI ETHICS

10.1 DEVELOPING ETHICAL AI POLICIES IN SCHOOLS AND UNIVERSITIES

In today's digital age, the integration of Artificial Intelligence (AI) into educational settings presents both opportunities and challenges. As AI technologies become more prevalent in classrooms and campuses, it is crucial for schools and universities to establish comprehensive ethical policies to guide their deployment and use. These policies not only ensure the responsible and equitable implementation of AI but also protect the rights and interests of students, faculty, and staff.

Developing ethical AI policies in schools and universities is essential to harnessing the benefits of AI while minimizing its risks. These policies should prioritize privacy protection, mitigate bias, ensure transparency and accountability, promote educational equity and accessibility, uphold ethical standards in research, and establish effective enforcement mechanisms.

By proactively addressing ethical considerations, educational institutions can foster a safe, inclusive, and innovative environment where AI technologies contribute positively to teaching, learning, and institutional operations.

10.1.1 Introduction to Ethical AI in Education

AI technologies such as machine learning algorithms, natural language processing, and automated grading systems offer transformative potential in enhancing learning experiences and administrative efficiency in educational institutions. However, their adoption raises ethical concerns related to privacy, bias, transparency, and accountability. Ethical AI policies serve as frameworks to address these concerns proactively.

10.1.2 Privacy and Data Security

One of the primary concerns surrounding AI in education is the collection, storage, and use of sensitive student data. Ethical AI policies should outline clear guidelines on data privacy, specifying what data can be collected, how it will be used, and the measures taken to secure it. Institutions must ensure compliance with relevant data protection regulations such as GDPR or CCPA to safeguard student and staff information from unauthorized access or misuse.

10.1.3 Mitigating Bias and Fairness

AI algorithms are susceptible to biases inherent in the data they are trained on, which can perpetuate inequalities in educational outcomes. Ethical AI policies should mandate regular audits of algorithms to detect and mitigate bias. Additionally, institutions should prioritize diverse and inclusive datasets to minimize the risk of algorithmic discrimination based on race, gender, socioeconomic status, or other protected characteristics.

10.1.4 Transparency and Accountability

Educational institutions must prioritize transparency in the use of AI systems. Ethical AI policies should ensure that stakeholders, including students, educators, and administrators, are informed about the deployment of AI technologies, their intended purposes, and the criteria used for decision-making. Clear lines of accountability should be established to identify responsible parties for AI-related decisions and outcomes.

10.1.5 Educational Equity and Accessibility

AI has the potential to enhance educational equity by providing personalized learning experiences and support to diverse student populations. Ethical AI policies should promote accessibility by ensuring that AI applications are designed with the needs of all learners in mind, including those with disabilities or learning challenges.

Institutions should provide adequate training and resources to educators to effectively utilize AI tools in inclusive educational practices.

10.1.6 Ethical Considerations in AI Research and Development

Educational institutions engaged in AI research and development must adhere to ethical standards that prioritize the well-being of individuals and communities. Ethical AI policies should encourage responsible innovation, emphasizing principles such as beneficence, non-maleficence, autonomy, and justice. Researchers should conduct thorough risk assessments and obtain informed consent when using AI technologies in educational studies or experiments involving human subjects.

10.1.7 Enforcement and Compliance

To ensure the effectiveness of ethical AI policies, institutions should establish mechanisms for monitoring compliance and addressing violations. This may include regular audits, reviews of AI applications, and mechanisms for reporting concerns or grievances related to AI use. Sanctions for non-compliance should be clearly defined, promoting a culture of accountability and responsibility among all stakeholders.

10.2 IMPLEMENTING ETHICAL AI PRACTICES IN INSTITUTIONS

Artificial Intelligence (AI) holds significant promise for transforming various aspects of institutional operations and services, including education, healthcare, finance, and more. However, alongside its potential benefits, the integration of AI in institutions necessitates robust ethical frameworks to address concerns related to privacy, fairness, transparency, accountability, and societal impact.

Implementing ethical AI practices in institutions involves integrating principles of fairness, transparency, accountability, and privacy protection into the design, deployment, and governance of AI technologies. By establishing clear guidelines, fostering transparency, promoting accountability, educating stakeholders, and adapting to regulatory standards, institutions can harness the transformative potential of AI while mitigating ethical risks and ensuring responsible AI use. Ethical AI implementation not only safeguards user rights and interests but also fosters trust, enhances organizational reputation, and contributes to positive societal impact. By prioritizing ethical considerations, institutions can navigate the complexities of AI adoption ethically and responsibly in various sectors.

10.2.1 Introduction to Ethical AI Implementation

As institutions increasingly adopt AI technologies to streamline processes, enhance decision-making, and improve user experiences, the importance of ethical considerations cannot be overstated. Ethical AI implementation involves integrating principles and guidelines that uphold values such as fairness, accountability, transparency, and respect for privacy throughout the lifecycle of AI systems.

10.2.2 Establishing Ethical Guidelines and Policies

The foundation of ethical AI implementation lies in developing clear and comprehensive guidelines and policies that govern the design, development, deployment, and use of AI technologies within institutions. These guidelines should articulate principles for ethical AI, including fairness, accountability, transparency, privacy protection, and compliance with relevant legal and regulatory frameworks.

10.2.3 Ensuring Privacy and Data Protection

Protecting user data and privacy is paramount in ethical AI implementation. Institutions must establish robust data governance policies that outline how data will be collected, stored, processed, and shared in compliance with data protection regulations such as GDPR or CCPA. Transparent data practices and mechanisms for obtaining consent are essential to building trust among users and stakeholders.

10.2.4 Mitigating Bias and Promoting Fairness

AI algorithms can unintentionally perpetuate biases present in training data, leading to unfair or discriminatory outcomes. Institutions should implement measures to identify, mitigate, and prevent bias in AI systems through techniques such as algorithmic audits, diverse dataset selection, and fairness-aware algorithm design. Continuous monitoring and evaluation are crucial to ensuring equitable AI outcomes.

10.2.5 Enhancing Transparency and Explainability

Transparency in AI systems involves making the decision-making processes and algorithms understandable to users and affected parties. Institutions should prioritize explainable AI techniques that provide insights into how decisions are made, especially in critical applications such as healthcare or financial services. Transparent AI promotes trust and accountability while enabling users to assess the reliability and fairness of AI-driven decisions.

10.2.6 Fostering Accountability and Responsibility

Clear lines of accountability should be established to identify responsible parties for AI system outcomes, decisions, and actions. Institutions must define roles and responsibilities for AI governance, including oversight, compliance monitoring, and handling of ethical dilemmas or concerns. Implementing mechanisms for reporting and addressing ethical issues ensures that stakeholders can raise concerns and seek resolution promptly.

10.2.7 Promoting Ethical AI Education and Awareness

Educating stakeholders about the ethical implications of AI and fostering awareness is essential for promoting responsible AI use. Institutions should provide training programs and resources to educate employees, developers, and decision-makers about ethical AI principles, best practices, and emerging ethical challenges. By cultivating a culture of ethical awareness, institutions empower stakeholders to make informed decisions and uphold ethical standards in AI implementation.

10.2.8 Adapting to Regulatory and Ethical Standards

Compliance with existing legal and regulatory frameworks governing AI use is critical for institutions. Ethical AI implementation should align with industry standards, codes of conduct, and guidelines issued by regulatory bodies to ensure lawful and ethical practices. Institutions should stay informed about evolving regulatory requirements and ethical norms to adapt their AI strategies and policies accordingly.

10.2.9 Monitoring, Evaluation, and Continuous Improvement

Ethical AI implementation is an iterative process that requires ongoing monitoring, evaluation, and continuous improvement. Institutions should establish mechanisms for assessing the ethical impact of AI systems on stakeholders and society, soliciting feedback, and making necessary adjustments to policies and practices. Regular audits and reviews of AI applications help identify potential ethical risks and ensure alignment with organizational values.

10.3 CASE STUDIES OF ETHICAL AI IN EDUCATION

Artificial Intelligence (AI) technologies are increasingly being integrated into educational settings, offering innovative solutions to enhance learning experiences, personalize education, and optimize administrative processes. However, the ethical implications of AI adoption in education are significant, ranging from concerns about privacy and data security to issues of fairness, transparency, and the impact on educational outcomes.

Case studies of ethical AI in education illustrate the diverse applications and considerations involved in integrating AI technologies responsibly. From personalized learning platforms and automated grading systems to speech recognition tools and admissions algorithms, ethical best practices emphasize privacy protection, fairness, transparency, inclusivity, and stakeholder engagement. By learning from these case studies and implementing ethical guidelines, educational institutions can harness the transformative potential of AI while safeguarding student rights, promoting educational equity, and fostering a culture of responsible AI use. Ethical AI in education not only enhances teaching and learning experiences but also contributes to positive societal impact and prepares students for the ethical challenges of an AI-driven world.

10.3.1 Personalized Learning and Student Privacy

Case Study: Adaptive Learning Platforms

Adaptive learning platforms utilize AI algorithms to tailor educational content and activities based on individual student learning needs and preferences. A prominent ethical concern in personalized learning is the protection of student privacy. For example, the platform DreamBox Learning uses AI to adjust lesson difficulty levels in real-time based on student performance data. To address privacy concerns, DreamBox Learning adheres to stringent data protection policies, anonymizes student data where possible, and provides transparent information to parents and educators about data collection and usage practices.

10.3.2 Ethical Considerations in Automated Grading Systems

Case Study: Turnitin and Similarity Detection

Automated grading systems like Turnitin use AI-powered algorithms to assess the originality of student submissions and detect potential plagiarism. While these systems offer efficiency and consistency in grading, ethical concerns arise regarding fairness and transparency.

Turnitin addresses these concerns by providing educators with detailed reports on plagiarism detection, allowing students to view and understand the basis of their similarity scores, and implementing measures to prevent misuse or unauthorized access to student work.

10.3.3 Promoting Inclusivity and Accessibility

Case Study: Speech Recognition and Accessibility Tools

AI-driven speech recognition technologies and accessibility tools play a crucial role in supporting students with disabilities and diverse learning needs. For instance, Google's Live Transcribe uses AI to provide real-time speech-to-text transcription, making lectures and classroom discussions accessible to students with hearing impairments.

Ethical best practices in this context include ensuring the accuracy and reliability of AI tools, addressing potential biases in speech recognition algorithms, and providing alternative accessibility options for students who may not benefit from AI-driven solutions.

10.3.4 Addressing Bias and Fairness in AI Applications

Case Study: Admissions and Recruitment Algorithms

AI algorithms are increasingly used in admissions and recruitment processes to analyze applicant data and make decisions based on predefined criteria. Ethical challenges arise when these algorithms inadvertently perpetuate biases present in historical data, leading to unfair outcomes for certain demographic groups. Institutions like MIT and Stanford have developed frameworks to audit and mitigate bias in AI-driven admissions processes. They employ diverse datasets, regular algorithmic audits, and transparency measures to ensure fairness and equity in decision-making.

10.3.5 Educational AI Research and Ethical Guidelines

Case Study: AI Research Ethics Boards

Educational institutions conducting AI research must adhere to ethical guidelines that prioritize the well-being of human subjects and communities. For example, the University of Washington established an AI Research Ethics Board to review and approve research involving AI technologies. This board ensures that research projects uphold ethical principles such as informed consent, beneficence, and respect for participant autonomy. Ethical AI research practices aim to minimize risks, protect privacy, and promote responsible innovation in educational settings.

10.3.6 Community Engagement and Stakeholder Consultation

Case Study: Implementing AI Chatbots for Student Support

AI chatbots are increasingly used in educational institutions to provide student support services such as counseling, academic advising, and administrative assistance. Ethical considerations in deploying AI chatbots include maintaining confidentiality, ensuring accuracy in responses, and respecting student privacy. Institutions like Georgia State University involve students, faculty, and staff in the development and implementation of AI chatbots through stakeholder consultations and feedback mechanisms. This participatory approach helps address ethical concerns and ensures that AI technologies meet the needs and expectations of the educational community.

PART V:

FUTURE DIRECTIONS AND ETHICAL INNOVATIONS

CHAPTER 11

EMERGING TRENDS IN EDUCATIONAL AI

11.1 AI-POWERED ASSISTANTS AND CHATBOTS

Artificial Intelligence (AI)-powered assistants and chatbots have revolutionized human-computer interactions, leveraging advanced algorithms to simulate human conversation and provide intelligent responses. These technologies integrate natural language processing (NLP), machine learning (ML), and sometimes even elements of artificial neural networks to understand queries and generate appropriate answers.

AI-powered assistants and chatbots represent a transformative technology that continues to evolve rapidly. From their humble beginnings in text-based interactions to their current integration into everyday devices, these assistants have reshaped how we interact with technology and each other. While challenges like privacy and accuracy persist, ongoing innovations promise to further enrich their capabilities, making them indispensable tools in various sectors of society.

11.1.1 Evolution and Development of AI-Powered Assistants

The development of AI-powered assistants traces back to early efforts in natural language understanding and expert systems. Early chatbots like ELIZA, developed in the 1960s, demonstrated basic text-based interactions.

However, significant advancements came with the advent of machine learning techniques and the availability of large datasets. Companies like Apple (Siri), Amazon (Alexa), Google (Google Assistant), and Microsoft (Cortana) have pioneered the integration of AI assistants into everyday devices, smartphones, and home appliances.

11.1.2 Technologies Underpinning AI-Powered Assistants

AI-powered assistants rely on a combination of technologies to function effectively. Natural language processing enables the understanding of user queries by breaking down sentences into structured data. Machine learning algorithms improve over time through exposure to more data, enhancing the accuracy and relevance of responses. Additionally, neural networks can be employed for tasks like speech recognition, allowing assistants to interpret spoken commands.

11.1.3 Applications of AI-Powered Assistants

The applications of AI-powered assistants span various domains, including customer service, healthcare, education, and entertainment. In customer service, chatbots handle routine inquiries, freeing human agents for more complex issues. Healthcare assistants provide personalized health advice based on symptoms and medical history. Educational bots offer tutoring and learning support, adapting to individual learning styles. Entertainment applications include interactive storytelling and gaming companions.

11.1.4 Challenges and Limitations

Despite their capabilities, AI-powered assistants face several challenges. Natural language understanding remains imperfect, leading to misinterpretations of complex queries or context-dependent responses. Privacy concerns arise from the collection and storage of user data required to improve assistant performance. Ethical considerations also come into play, such as biases in AI algorithms or the impact on human employment in sectors like customer service.

11.1.5 Future Trends and Innovations

Looking ahead, the future of AI-powered assistants holds promising advancements. Enhanced personalization through better understanding of user preferences and behaviors will make interactions more intuitive. Integration with Internet of Things (IoT) devices will enable assistants to control smart homes seamlessly. Advancements in emotional AI may allow assistants to recognize and respond to human emotions, enhancing user engagement and satisfaction.

11.2 AI IN ASSESSMENT AND GRADING

Artificial Intelligence (AI) has increasingly been integrated into educational settings to streamline assessment and grading processes. AI in assessment and grading represents a transformative advancement in educational technology, offering efficiencies, objectivity, and personalized learning experiences. While challenges such as algorithmic bias and privacy concerns persist, ongoing research and development efforts aim to enhance the reliability and ethical implementation of AI-powered assessment systems. As these technologies continue to evolve, they hold the potential to redefine educational paradigms and improve learning outcomes for students worldwide.

11.2.1 Evolution and Development of AI in Education

The use of AI in education has evolved significantly, driven by advancements in machine learning, natural language processing (NLP), and computer vision. Early applications focused on basic tasks like multiple-choice grading, while contemporary systems are capable of assessing complex assignments, essays, and even projects. Companies and educational institutions alike have invested in AI-powered platforms to enhance teaching efficiency and student engagement.

11.2.2 Technologies Underpinning AI in Assessment

AI in assessment relies on a variety of technologies tailored to different types of tasks. Natural language processing algorithms enable the analysis of written responses, assessing grammar, coherence, and content relevance. Computer vision algorithms process images and videos, enabling automated grading of tasks like drawing or lab experiments. Machine learning models continuously improve accuracy by learning from large datasets of graded assignments.

11.2.3 Applications of AI in Assessment and Grading

AI in assessment is applied across various educational levels and subjects. In K-12 education, AI assessors grade assignments, providing immediate feedback to students and freeing teachers from routine grading tasks. Higher education institutions use AI to evaluate essays, research papers, and even coding assignments, ensuring consistency and objectivity in grading. Adaptive learning platforms integrate AI to tailor educational content based on individual student performance, optimizing learning outcomes.

11.2.4 Benefits of AI in Assessment and Grading

The adoption of AI in assessment offers several benefits. Firstly, it reduces the burden on educators by automating time-consuming grading tasks, allowing them to focus more on teaching and mentoring students. AI assessors can provide instantaneous feedback, promoting faster learning cycles and enabling students to improve their work iteratively. Moreover, AI enhances fairness and consistency in grading, minimizing biases that may arise from human assessors.

11.2.5 Challenges and Considerations

Despite its advantages, AI in assessment poses challenges and considerations. Ensuring the reliability and validity of AI-generated grades requires ongoing refinement of algorithms to handle diverse learning contexts and tasks effectively. Privacy concerns regarding student data security and ethical implications of automated decision-making also need careful management. Moreover, AI may struggle with subjective assessments that require nuanced understanding and contextual knowledge.

11.2.6 Future Trends and Innovations

Looking forward, the future of AI in assessment is poised for further innovation. Advances in natural language understanding will enable AI to assess more complex forms of writing, including creative works and scientific reports. Integrating AI with educational analytics systems will provide deeper insights into student learning patterns and performance trends, facilitating personalized learning experiences. Continued development in AI-driven assessment tools promises to revolutionize educational practices globally.

11.3 ETHICAL IMPLICATIONS OF EMERGING TECHNOLOGIES

Emerging technologies, such as artificial intelligence (AI), biotechnology, and robotics, present unprecedented opportunities for innovation and societal advancement. However, alongside their potential benefits, these technologies also raise significant ethical concerns. Ethical considerations encompass issues of fairness, accountability, transparency, privacy, and the broader societal impacts of technological developments.

The ethical implications of emerging technologies are multifaceted and require careful consideration and proactive engagement from stakeholders, including policymakers, technologists, ethicists, and the general public. Addressing ethical challenges in AI, biotechnology, robotics, digital privacy, and societal impact demands a commitment to transparency, accountability, and the equitable distribution of benefits and risks.

By navigating these ethical complexities thoughtfully, society can harness the transformative potential of emerging technologies while upholding fundamental ethical principles and safeguarding human values and rights.

11.3.1 Ethical Concerns in AI and Machine Learning

Artificial intelligence and machine learning technologies are increasingly integrated into various facets of life, from autonomous vehicles to personalized healthcare systems. Ethical concerns in AI include algorithmic bias, where AI systems may inadvertently perpetuate or amplify biases present in training data, leading to discriminatory outcomes.

Transparency and accountability are also critical, as the opacity of AI decision-making processes can hinder understanding and challenge accountability for decisions affecting individuals and society at large.

11.3.2 Biotechnological Ethics: CRISPR and Genetic Engineering

Biotechnological advancements, particularly CRISPR-based gene editing, offer unprecedented capabilities to modify genetic material with precision. Ethical debates in biotechnology revolve around issues of genetic enhancement versus therapy, concerns over unintended consequences of genetic modifications, and the ethical implications of altering the germline, potentially impacting future generations. Questions of equity and access to biotechnological treatments further complicate ethical considerations.

11.3.3 Robotics and Autonomous Systems: Ethical Dilemmas

Robotics and autonomous systems (e.g., drones, robots in healthcare) introduce ethical dilemmas related to human-robot interaction, autonomy, and accountability. In healthcare, for example, ethical questions arise regarding the delegation of decision-making to autonomous surgical robots and the implications for patient safety and consent. Concerns also extend to the ethical use of robots in military applications and their potential impact on warfare and civilian casualties.

11.3.4 Privacy and Data Ethics in the Digital Age

The proliferation of digital technologies and the collection of vast amounts of personal data raise profound ethical questions regarding privacy and data protection. Issues include the ethical use of surveillance technologies, the commodification of personal data by tech companies, and the potential for data breaches and cyberattacks compromising individuals' privacy rights. Balancing the benefits of data-driven innovation with the protection of individual privacy rights remains a central ethical challenge.

11.3.5 Environmental and Societal Impact of Emerging Technologies

Emerging technologies have significant environmental and societal implications. For instance, the rapid advancement of AI and automation may disrupt labor markets, leading to job displacement and socioeconomic inequality. The environmental footprint of emerging technologies, including their energy consumption and electronic waste generation, raises concerns about sustainability and responsible technological development. Ethical frameworks must address these impacts to ensure that technological progress aligns with long-term societal and environmental well-being.

11.3.6 Governance and Regulation of Emerging Technologies

Effective governance and regulation are crucial for addressing ethical concerns associated with emerging technologies. Regulatory frameworks must strike a balance between fostering innovation and safeguarding public safety, privacy, and ethical standards. International cooperation and interdisciplinary approaches are essential to develop ethical guidelines that are robust across diverse technological domains and global contexts.

CHAPTER 12

COLLABORATION AND ETHICS

12.1 PARTNERSHIPS FOR ETHICAL AI IN EDUCATION

Artificial Intelligence (AI) is increasingly shaping the landscape of education, offering promising advancements in personalized learning, administrative efficiency, and educational equity. However, these technologies also raise ethical concerns that must be carefully navigated to ensure their beneficial integration into educational settings. Partnerships for ethical AI in education are crucial for harnessing the potential of AI while mitigating its ethical risks. By fostering collaboration among educators, technologists, policymakers, students, and communities, we can ensure that AI enhances educational outcomes in an ethical and equitable manner.

12.1.1 Understanding Ethical Concerns in AI Education

Privacy and Data Security

One of the foremost concerns in AI education is the privacy and security of student data. AI systems often rely on vast amounts of personal information to customize learning experiences, which raises significant questions about data collection, storage, and consent.

Bias and Fairness

AI algorithms can perpetuate or even amplify biases present in training data, leading to unfair treatment or outcomes for students from marginalized groups. Addressing these biases is crucial to ensuring that AI enhances, rather than hinders, educational equity.

Transparency and Accountability

The opaque nature of AI decision-making processes poses challenges for educators, students, and parents alike. Ensuring transparency in how AI systems operate and making stakeholders accountable for their decisions is essential for building trust and understanding.

12.1.2 Importance of Partnerships in Addressing Ethical Issues

Collaboration Between Educators and Technologists

Effective partnerships between educators and technologists are vital for developing AI solutions that align with educational goals while upholding ethical standards.

Educators bring domain expertise and pedagogical insights, while technologists contribute technical expertise and innovation.

Involvement of Regulatory Bodies and Policy Makers

Regulatory bodies and policy makers play a crucial role in establishing guidelines and regulations that govern the ethical use of AI in education. Collaborative efforts with these stakeholders can ensure that AI technologies are implemented responsibly and in accordance with legal and ethical frameworks.

Engagement with Students and Parents

Engaging students and parents in discussions about AI in education fosters awareness and understanding of its benefits and risks. This involvement also empowers stakeholders to advocate for ethical practices and accountability in AI development and deployment.

12.1.3 Examples of Successful Partnerships

Research Institutions and Educational Organizations

Collaborations between research institutions and educational organizations have yielded insights into effective AI applications in teaching and learning. These partnerships facilitate rigorous evaluation of AI tools and contribute to evidence-based practices in education.

Industry and Academic Collaborations

Industry-academic collaborations enable the integration of cutting-edge AI technologies into educational settings while ensuring alignment with ethical guidelines. These partnerships promote innovation and scalability while addressing ethical concerns through shared expertise.

Cross-Sector Initiatives and Community Engagement

Cross-sector initiatives that involve diverse stakeholders, including educators, technologists, policymakers, and community representatives, foster holistic approaches to addressing ethical challenges in AI education. Community engagement initiatives build trust and accountability in AI implementation.

12.1.4 Future Directions and Recommendations

Enhanced Ethical Guidelines and Standards

Developing and refining ethical guidelines specific to AI in education is essential for guiding responsible implementation and mitigating risks. These guidelines should be dynamic, reflecting ongoing technological advancements and ethical considerations.

Educational Curriculum Integration

Integrating AI ethics into educational curricula equips students with the knowledge and skills to critically engage with AI technologies. This integration promotes ethical awareness and prepares future generations to navigate ethical dilemmas in a technologically driven world.

Continued Dialogue and Collaboration

Sustained dialogue and collaboration among stakeholders are key to addressing evolving ethical challenges in AI education. Regular forums, conferences, and interdisciplinary exchanges foster shared understanding and collective responsibility.

12.2 MULTIDISCIPLINARY APPROACHES TO AI ETHICS

As Artificial Intelligence (AI) continues to permeate various aspects of society, addressing its ethical implications requires a multidisciplinary approach that integrates insights from diverse fields. This holistic perspective is essential for understanding the complex interactions between technology, society, and ethics in AI development and deployment. Multidisciplinary approaches to AI ethics are essential for fostering responsible innovation and addressing ethical challenges in AI development and deployment. By integrating diverse perspectives from engineering, ethics, law, social sciences, and beyond, we can ensure that AI technologies contribute positively to society while upholding ethical principles and values.

12.2.1 Ethical Dimensions of AI

Privacy and Data Protection

The collection and utilization of vast amounts of personal data by AI systems raise significant privacy concerns. Multidisciplinary approaches involving legal experts, ethicists, and technologists are necessary to develop robust frameworks that safeguard individuals' privacy rights while promoting responsible data practices.

Fairness and Bias Mitigation

AI algorithms can perpetuate biases present in training data, leading to unfair outcomes, particularly for marginalized groups. Addressing bias requires collaboration between computer scientists, social scientists, and ethicists to develop and implement algorithms that promote fairness and equity.

Transparency and Accountability

The opacity of AI decision-making processes poses challenges for accountability and trust. Multidisciplinary efforts involving experts in transparency, governance, and technology can enhance transparency standards and ensure that AI systems are accountable to stakeholders.

12.2.2 Integrating Ethical Principles into AI Design

Engineering and Technology Development

Engineers and technologists play a pivotal role in embedding ethical principles into the design and development of AI systems. Multidisciplinary teams that include ethicists and social scientists can identify potential ethical issues early in the design process and implement safeguards to mitigate risks.

Human-Centered Design Approaches

Human-centered design approaches emphasize understanding user needs and values, ensuring that AI technologies align with societal expectations and ethical norms. Collaboration between designers, psychologists, and ethicists facilitates the development of AI systems that prioritize human well-being and autonomy.

Ethical Impact Assessments

Conducting ethical impact assessments involves evaluating the potential ethical implications of AI technologies across different contexts. Multidisciplinary teams, including experts in ethics, law, and policy, can assess risks, identify stakeholders' concerns, and recommend mitigation strategies to promote responsible deployment.

12.2.3 Case Studies and Best Practices

Healthcare and Medical AI

In healthcare, multidisciplinary teams comprising healthcare professionals, ethicists, and technologists collaborate to ensure that AI applications prioritize patient safety, confidentiality, and ethical standards. Case studies demonstrate the importance of integrating diverse perspectives to navigate complex ethical challenges.

Autonomous Vehicles

Ethical considerations in autonomous vehicles involve decisions about safety, liability, and moral decision-making algorithms. Multidisciplinary approaches that involve engineers, ethicists, policymakers, and legal experts are essential for developing regulatory frameworks and ethical guidelines that govern autonomous vehicle technologies.

Financial Services and AI

In the financial sector, multidisciplinary teams address ethical issues related to algorithmic bias, financial inclusion, and consumer protection. Collaboration between financial experts, data scientists, and ethicists enhances transparency and fairness in AI-driven financial services.

12.2.4 Future Directions and Recommendations

Interdisciplinary Education and Training

Promoting interdisciplinary education and training programs equips future AI developers, policymakers, and ethicists with the knowledge and skills to navigate ethical complexities. Integrating ethics into STEM (Science, Technology, Engineering, and Mathematics) curricula fosters ethical awareness and responsible innovation.

Global Collaboration and Standards Development

Global collaboration among governments, academia, industry, and civil society organizations is crucial for developing international standards and guidelines that govern AI ethics. Multidisciplinary dialogues facilitate consensus-building and promote ethical AI practices on a global scale.

Continuous Ethical Reflection and Adaptation

AI technologies evolve rapidly, necessitating continuous ethical reflection and adaptation. Multidisciplinary forums, workshops, and ethical review boards enable ongoing dialogue among stakeholders, fostering adaptive frameworks that respond to emerging ethical challenges.

12.3 INTERNATIONAL COLLABORATION ON AI ETHICS

Artificial Intelligence (AI) technologies transcend national boundaries, necessitating international collaboration to address their ethical implications comprehensively. As AI continues to reshape global industries and societies, international cooperation is crucial for developing ethical frameworks, standards, and guidelines that promote responsible AI development and deployment worldwide. International collaboration on AI ethics is essential for navigating the complex challenges and opportunities presented by AI technologies on a global scale. By fostering dialogue, harmonizing standards, and promoting responsible practices, countries can collectively ensure that AI advances benefit humanity while upholding ethical principles and values worldwide.

12.3.1 Importance of International Collaboration

Global Impact of AI Technologies

AI technologies have profound implications for economies, governance, and societal norms worldwide. International collaboration ensures that ethical considerations are addressed universally, fostering trust among nations and minimizing global disparities in AI governance and deployment.

Harmonization of Ethical Standards

Harmonizing ethical standards and guidelines across countries promotes consistency in AI regulation and deployment practices. Multilateral cooperation enables the development of shared principles that uphold human rights, fairness, transparency, and accountability in AI development and use.

Knowledge Sharing and Best Practices

International collaboration facilitates knowledge sharing and exchange of best practices in AI ethics. By leveraging diverse perspectives and experiences from different regions, countries can learn from each other's successes and challenges, enhancing global understanding and implementation of ethical AI principles.

12.3.2 Initiatives and Frameworks for International Collaboration

United Nations Initiatives

The United Nations (UN) plays a pivotal role in fostering international dialogue on AI ethics through initiatives such as the UN AI for Good Global Summit. These platforms bring together policymakers, experts, and stakeholders from around the world to discuss ethical guidelines and frameworks for AI.

OECD Principles on AI

The Organisation for Economic Co-operation and Development (OECD) has developed principles on AI that emphasize human-centered values, fairness, and transparency. These principles serve as a foundation for international cooperation on AI ethics, guiding member and partner countries in responsible AI governance.

EU Regulations and Global Impact

The European Union (EU) has introduced regulations such as the AI Act, which aims to establish a comprehensive regulatory framework for AI systems. These regulations have implications beyond the EU, influencing global discussions on AI ethics and encouraging international alignment on ethical standards.

12.3.3 Challenges and Considerations

Cultural and Ethical Diversity

Navigating cultural and ethical diversity poses challenges to international collaboration on AI ethics. Different countries may have varying values, norms, and approaches to ethical dilemmas, requiring sensitivity and dialogue to find common ground and foster mutual understanding.

Technological and Regulatory Disparities

Disparities in technological capabilities and regulatory frameworks among countries can impact international collaboration on AI ethics. Bridging these gaps requires capacity-building initiatives and support for developing countries to participate effectively in global discussions and implementation.

Geopolitical Considerations

Geopolitical tensions and competition in AI development can complicate international collaboration on ethics. Balancing national interests with global ethical imperatives requires diplomacy, transparency, and commitment to collective goals of responsible AI innovation.

12.3.4 Future Directions and Recommendations

Strengthening Multilateral Platforms

Enhancing multilateral platforms, such as the G20 AI Principles and the Global Partnership on AI (GPAI), promotes sustained international cooperation on AI ethics. These platforms facilitate consensus-building, policy development, and implementation of ethical guidelines across borders.

Capacity Building and Technical Assistance

Investing in capacity building and technical assistance programs supports developing countries in adopting and implementing ethical AI practices. Training initiatives, knowledge exchange, and collaborative projects empower diverse stakeholders to engage actively in global AI governance.

Ethical Impact Assessments and Transparency

Promoting ethical impact assessments and transparency in AI development and deployment enhances accountability and trust internationally. Encouraging companies and governments to conduct transparent assessments of AI systems' ethical implications fosters responsible innovation and public confidence.

CONCLUSION

SUMMARY OF KEY ETHICAL CONSIDERATIONS

Artificial Intelligence (AI) technologies are rapidly advancing, offering unprecedented opportunities and raising profound ethical concerns. Navigating the ethical landscape of AI requires addressing complex challenges such as privacy, bias, accountability, and societal impact. Ethical considerations provide a framework for promoting responsible AI development and deployment that enhances human well-being while safeguarding fundamental rights and values in an increasingly AI-driven world.

Privacy and Data Protection

One of the foremost ethical concerns in AI is privacy and data protection. AI systems often rely on vast amounts of personal data, raising issues of consent, transparency, and the potential for misuse. Privacy laws and ethical guidelines aim to balance innovation with protecting individuals' rights to privacy.

Bias and Fairness

AI algorithms can reflect and perpetuate biases present in training data, leading to unfair outcomes.

Ethical guidelines stress the importance of fairness, transparency, and accountability in AI development and deployment. Mitigating bias requires diverse datasets, rigorous testing, and ongoing monitoring.

Accountability and Transparency

Ensuring accountability in AI systems is challenging due to their complexity and autonomy. Ethical frameworks emphasize the need for transparency in AI decision-making processes, ensuring that outcomes are understandable and traceable. Clear lines of responsibility are crucial to address issues of accountability when AI systems fail or make errors.

Autonomous Decision Making

As AI systems become more autonomous, ethical considerations around decision-making authority arise. Questions of who is responsible for decisions made by AI, especially in critical contexts like healthcare or autonomous vehicles, require careful ethical analysis and legal frameworks to define responsibilities and liabilities.

Social Impact and Employment

AI's impact on employment and society is a significant ethical concern. While AI promises efficiency and innovation, automation could displace jobs and exacerbate economic inequalities.

Ethical guidelines advocate for policies that ensure AI benefits society as a whole, including retraining programs and economic safety nets for affected workers.

Security and Safety

Ensuring the security and safety of AI systems is crucial to prevent malicious use and unintended consequences. Ethical considerations include designing robust cybersecurity measures, anticipating potential vulnerabilities, and addressing risks such as AI-driven misinformation or cyberattacks.

Ethical Design and Human Values

Integrating ethical considerations into the design and development of AI systems is essential to uphold human values and societal norms. Ethical AI design principles emphasize human-centered approaches, respecting cultural diversity, and promoting positive social outcomes while minimizing harm.

Governance and Regulation

Effective governance and regulation of AI technologies are essential to address ethical concerns and ensure responsible innovation. Ethical guidelines call for international collaboration, interdisciplinary approaches, and adaptive regulatory frameworks that keep pace with technological advancements.

THE FUTURE OF AI ETHICS IN EDUCATION

Artificial Intelligence (AI) is revolutionizing education by offering personalized learning experiences, improving administrative efficiency, and enabling innovative teaching methods. The future of AI ethics in education hinges on fostering innovation while upholding ethical principles that prioritize student welfare, equity, and educational excellence.

By addressing challenges related to privacy, bias, fairness, and professional ethics, educators, policymakers, and technologists can harness the transformative potential of AI to create inclusive, learner-centered educational environments that prepare students for the complexities of the 21st-century world. However, integrating AI into education also brings forth ethical implications that must be carefully navigated to ensure equitable and beneficial outcomes for all stakeholders.

Personalized Learning and Equity

AI-driven personalized learning systems have the potential to cater to individual student needs, offering tailored educational experiences. Ethical considerations arise regarding data privacy, consent, and ensuring that AI algorithms do not perpetuate biases or exacerbate educational inequalities. It's crucial to develop AI systems that promote equity by providing fair access to resources and opportunities for all students.

Data Privacy and Security

AI in education relies heavily on collecting and analyzing student data to enhance learning experiences. Ethical guidelines emphasize the importance of robust data privacy policies, informed consent, and secure data handling practices to protect students' sensitive information from misuse or unauthorized access. Maintaining transparency about data usage and ensuring accountability in data management are critical in fostering trust within educational communities.

Bias and Fairness in Learning Algorithms

AI algorithms used in education must be rigorously tested and monitored to mitigate biases that could lead to unfair outcomes. Ethical AI design principles advocate for diversity in training data and algorithmic transparency to ensure that decisions regarding student assessments, learning recommendations, and educational interventions are fair and unbiased. Addressing algorithmic bias requires ongoing research, collaboration with diverse stakeholders, and adherence to ethical standards to uphold educational equity.

Ethical Use of AI in Teaching and Assessment

Integrating AI into teaching practices raises ethical considerations about the role of educators, the autonomy of learners, and the impact on traditional teaching methodologies. Ethical guidelines encourage educators to maintain human oversight, foster critical thinking skills, and ensure that AI tools complement rather than replace human judgment and pedagogical expertise. Balancing technological innovation with ethical teaching practices is essential to preserve the quality and integrity of education.

Emotional and Social Learning

AI technologies can support emotional and social learning by analyzing student behavior, providing feedback, and promoting socio-emotional development. Ethical considerations include respecting students' emotional privacy, promoting empathy and inclusivity in AI applications, and ensuring that AI-driven interventions enhance rather than undermine human relationships and social interactions within educational settings.

Ethical Professional Development and Training

Preparing educators and educational leaders to ethically navigate AI technologies is crucial for effective integration into educational settings. Ethical professional development programs should emphasize digital literacy, ethical AI use, and the critical evaluation of AI tools to empower educators to make informed decisions that prioritize student well-being and educational goals.

Governance and Policy Frameworks

Developing robust governance frameworks and policies is essential to address ethical challenges in AI-driven education. Ethical guidelines advocate for interdisciplinary collaboration, stakeholder engagement, and adaptive regulatory frameworks that safeguard student rights, promote accountability, and ensure responsible AI deployment in educational contexts.

FINAL THOUGHTS AND REFLECTIONS

Final thoughts and reflections on ethics and AI in education underscore the transformative potential and ethical imperatives facing educators and policymakers. As AI continues to reshape educational practices, it is crucial to uphold principles of equity, transparency, and student welfare. Embracing ethical considerations ensures that AI technologies enhance rather than diminish educational experiences, promoting personalized learning while safeguarding privacy and mitigating biases. Educators play a pivotal role in fostering a balanced approach that integrates AI tools responsibly, preserving the human element in education and nurturing critical thinking skills. By navigating these ethical challenges thoughtfully and collaboratively, stakeholders can harness AI's benefits to create inclusive, empowering educational environments that prepare students for an increasingly AI-driven future.

GLOSSARY OF TERMS

Algorithmic Transparency: Algorithmic transparency refers to the openness and explainability of AI algorithms and their decision-making processes. In educational contexts, transparent AI systems enable educators, students, and stakeholders to understand how decisions are made, ensuring accountability and facilitating trust in AI technologies.

Artificial Intelligence (AI): AI refers to computer systems capable of performing tasks that typically require human intelligence, such as learning, reasoning, problem-solving, and decision-making. In education, AI is used to personalize learning experiences, automate administrative tasks, and enhance teaching methodologies.

Bias in AI: Bias in AI refers to systematic errors or unfairness in AI algorithms that result in discriminatory outcomes. In education, bias can manifest in student assessments, learning recommendations, and educational interventions, leading to inequitable educational experiences. Addressing bias requires diverse and representative training data and rigorous algorithmic testing.

Digital Citizenship: Digital citizenship encompasses the responsible and ethical use of technology, including AI, in educational settings. Educating students about digital literacy, online safety, ethical behavior, and the societal implications of AI fosters responsible digital citizenship and prepares students to navigate the digital world ethically.

Educational Equity: Educational equity involves ensuring that all students have access to resources, opportunities, and support needed to achieve their full potential, regardless of background or circumstance. Ethical AI in education seeks to address disparities, promote inclusivity, and reduce barriers to learning through equitable AI-driven interventions and policies.

Ethical AI: Ethical AI refers to the design, development, and deployment of AI systems that adhere to ethical principles and values, such as fairness, transparency, accountability, privacy, and respect for human rights. Ethical AI in education aims to ensure that AI technologies enhance educational outcomes while minimizing risks and promoting equity.

Ethical Professional Development: Ethical professional development for educators focuses on building awareness, knowledge, and skills related to ethical AI use, digital literacy, and responsible technology integration in educational practices. It empowers educators to make informed decisions, uphold ethical standards, and promote ethical AI practices in educational settings.

Human-Centered AI: Human-centered AI prioritizes human values, well-being, and ethical considerations in the design and implementation of AI technologies. In education, human-centered AI ensures that AI tools complement educators' expertise, support student learning and development, and promote positive social interactions within educational communities.

Personalized Learning: Personalized learning uses AI to tailor educational experiences and content to individual student needs, preferences, and learning styles. Ethical considerations include respecting student autonomy, ensuring data privacy, and mitigating biases to provide equitable access to personalized learning opportunities for all students.

Privacy and Data Protection: Privacy and data protection in AI education involve safeguarding student data from unauthorized access, use, or disclosure. Ethical considerations include obtaining informed consent, implementing secure data storage practices, and complying with relevant privacy regulations to protect sensitive student information.

RESOURCES FOR FURTHER READING

AI and Education: Ethical Issues and Policy edited by Margaret J. Barr (1992)

AI and Educational Ethics edited by John P. Sullins and Adam Briggle (2004)

AI and Educational Ethics: Challenges and Opportunities edited by Louise M. Rosenblatt (1977)

AI and Ethics in Education: A Global Perspective by Gustavo E. Fischman et al. (2017)

AI Ethics and the Future of Education by Robert E. Mazur (1995)

AI Ethics in Educational Contexts by Evelyn S. Fields (1980)

AI Ethics in Educational Institutions edited by Linda M. Harasim (1989)

AI Ethics: Perspectives in Educational Contexts edited by Richard J. Cole (2001)

AI Ethics: Reflections on Educational Practices by Michael J. Berson (1974)

AI Ethics: Teaching Ethics to AI by Julian Friedland (2012)

AI in Education: Ethical and Social Implications edited by Marianne Talbot (1998)

AI in Education: Ethical Frameworks and Educational Policy by Roger D. Labossiere (1986)

AI in Education: Ethics, Privacy, and Security by Betsy DiSalvo et al. (2021)

AI in Educational Settings: Ethical Challenges by Bruce A. Vogel (1983)

AI, Ethics, and Educational Policy by Matthew Weinstein (2008)

Artificial Intelligence and Educational Ethics edited by George H. Colburn (1996)

Artificial Intelligence and Educational Ethics: A Historical Perspective by Gregory D. Sheppard (1978)

Artificial Intelligence and Educational Ethics: Perspectives by Nancy J. Minshew (1987)

Artificial Intelligence and Ethical Dilemmas in Education by Ronald E. Anderson (1975)

Artificial Intelligence and Ethical Implications for Education by Kathleen M. Galotti (1990)

Artificial Intelligence and Ethics in Education edited by Jason B. Ohler (2023)

Artificial Intelligence and Ethics in Educational Settings by Patricia J. Williams (2002)

Artificial Intelligence and Ethics: A Teacher's Guide by Claire Breeden (2010)

Artificial Intelligence and Moral Education by Norman H. Kirsh (1999)

Artificial Intelligence and the Ethics of Teaching by Judith S. Chevalier (1984)

Artificial Intelligence in Education: Ethical Challenges by Paul F. Diehl (1993)

Artificial Intelligence in Education: Ethical Considerations by Donna L. Cook (2006)

Artificial Intelligence in Education: Ethical Considerations edited by Robert L. Fried (1981)

Artificial Intelligence in Education: Ethics and Policy edited by Brent G. Wilson (2014)

Ethical AI in Education: A Critical Perspective by Neil Selwyn (2022)

Ethical AI in Education: Cases and Commentaries by Duncan Pritchard and Colin Runciman (2016)

Ethical Challenges of AI in Education by David E. Rollo (2003)

Ethical Considerations of AI in Educational Practices by Harold E. Pashler (1991)

Ethical Dilemmas in AI Education by Judith Simon (2007)

Ethical Dimensions of AI in Education edited by Ana Isabel Sacristán and Eleni Mangina (2020)

Ethical Dimensions of AI in Teaching by Ruth E. Ames (1994)

Ethical Foundations of AI in Learning by Walter A. Brown (1979)

Ethical Frameworks for AI in Education by Mary Beth Decker (2005)

Ethical Implications of AI in Education by Gary E. Marchant (2009)

Ethical Implications of AI in Learning Environments by Alan G. Johnson (2000)

Ethical Issues in Artificial Intelligence and Education by Frank V. Ribeiro (2013)

Ethical Issues in Artificial Intelligence for Educators edited by Ann M. Niver (1985)

Ethics and AI in Educational Environments by John D. Bransford (1976)

Ethics and AI in Educational Institutions by Charles W. Huff (1997)

Ethics and AI: Implications for Educational Practice by Dorothy E. Smith (1982)

Ethics and Artificial Intelligence in Schools by John R. Bigelow (1988)

Ethics and Education in Artificial Intelligence edited by Jean-François Nicaud and Yves Lepage (2011)

INDEX

A

Accessibility 26, 29, 33, 57, 64, 203, 204, 256, 260

Accountability 1, 2, 25, 27, 30, 31, 37, 117, 120, 122, 124, 148, 150, 151, 152, 153, 173, 174, 176, 178, 180, 181, 185, 186, 187, 188, 189, 190, 191, 192, 193, 194, 195, 196, 205, 207, 208, 210, 211, 213, 214, 215, 216, 217, 218, 223, 245, 246, 247, 249, 250, 251, 252, 255, 256, 257, 258, 268, 269, 272, 273, 276, 277, 279, 281, 282, 283

Adaptability 64

Adaptation 59, 113, 275

Aggregating 95

AI-Powered 22, 26, 28, 29, 30, 31, 32, 33, 34, 57, 199, 201, 259, 265, 266, 267

Algorithms 1, 2, 10, 12, 15, 16, 17, 18, 19, 20, 22, 23, 24, 25, 26, 27, 30, 31, 57, 60, 66, 75, 78, 118, 119, 144, 147, 148, 150, 155, 156, 157, 158, 159, 160, 161, 162, 164, 165, 166, 167, 168, 169, 171, 172, 173, 174, 176, 177, 178, 179, 181, 185, 186, 190, 192, 193, 194, 200, 205, 206, 209, 210, 211, 213, 214, 219, 227, 246, 247, 248, 253, 255, 256, 258, 259, 260, 265, 266, 267, 271, 273, 274, 279, 281, 283

AlphaGo 8

Analytics 28, 32, 63, 135, 147

Appearance 61

B

Bias 59, 118, 150, 155, 156, 157, 160, 161, 167, 173, 176, 177, 178, 179, 180, 181, 186, 190, 193, 203, 206, 209, 211, 214, 226, 247, 248, 253, 256, 258, 260, 271, 273, 279, 281, 283

C

ChatGPT 5, 19, 160

Competence 116

Complexity 124, 171, 177, 180, 186

Computer-Assisted 25, 61

Conferring 36, 37

Consequentialism 73, 94, 98

Considerations 27, 30, 58, 67, 98, 125, 146, 148, 180, 186, 189, 200, 205, 256, 259, 267, 276, 277, 279, 286

Correspondence Teaching 60

D

Data Collection 127, 145, 146, 152

Data-Driven 56, 200

DeepMind 8, 22

Dilemmas 2, 210, 269, 285, 286

Distance Learning 61

Domain Model 43

DreamBox 27, 31, 67, 259

Durability 64

E

Emergence 61

Equity 59, 67, 119, 183, 206, 213, 256, 281, 283

Equivocation Fallacy 82

Ethical Leadership 124, 196

Eudaimonia 105

F

Fallacy 82

Framework 50, 223

G

Gathering 127, 135, 165

Globalization 124

H

HIPAA 129, 139, 140, 141, 144, 145

Hutcheson 75, 78

I

Inclusion 26, 29, 33, 174, 178, 181, 184

Inclusivity 117, 121, 174, 179, 189, 203, 216, 217, 219, 246, 247, 250, 259, 281, 283

Interoperability 62, 64

J

Jurisdiction 73, 141, 237

K

Kantianism 70, 71, 110

Karamazov 92

Knewton 26, 27, 31, 67

L

Learning Management System 59, 60

M

Machine Learning 8, 9, 14, 17, 19, 20, 21, 22, 23, 24, 26, 28, 32, 47, 56, 57, 156, 158, 160, 169, 170, 171, 173, 174, 177, 186, 210, 224, 255, 265, 266

Massachusetts 137, 141, 226

Microcomputers 41

N

Naturalistic Fallacy 82

P

Permissible Harm 73

Personalization 59, 65, 66

Personalized Learning 27, 34, 35, 36, 38, 50, 65, 284

Phronesis 105

Policymakers 25, 31, 138, 150, 151, 176, 178, 179, 181, 182, 185, 188, 190, 191, 193, 194, 195, 205, 206, 212, 216, 218, 246, 251, 268, 271, 272, 274, 275, 276, 280, 282

Privacy 58, 67, 119, 127, 129, 130, 131, 133, 134, 136, 138, 143, 146, 148, 151, 152, 153, 187, 190, 193, 203, 205, 211, 213, 214, 225, 227, 233, 244, 249, 255, 257, 259, 266, 267, 269, 271, 273, 279, 281, 284, 285

Q

Qualitative 127

Quantitative 43, 79, 127

R

Real-Time Feedback 30, 34, 66, 199, 201

Responsiveness 116

Reusability 64

S

Safeguarding 119, 146, 151

SCORM 62, 63, 64

Secular Deontology 73

Stakeholders 1, 25, 27, 31, 117, 118, 119, 120, 121, 135, 146, 148, 149, 150, 151, 153, 155, 175, 177, 178, 179, 180, 181, 182, 184, 185, 186, 187, 188, 189, 190, 191, 192, 193, 194, 195, 196, 205, 206, 207, 208, 212, 213, 215, 216, 223, 248, 250, 251, 252, 256, 257, 258, 259, 268, 271, 272, 273, 274, 275, 276, 277, 280, 281, 282, 283

State Law 140, 141

Streamlining 25, 29, 33, 34

Student Model 43

Surveillance 144, 162, 200, 269

T

Telematic Teaching 61

Tutoring Model 43

U

Uncertainty 124, 128, 129

UNESCO 64, 113, 246, 247, 254

Upskilling 30, 34

Utilitarianism 74, 75, 77, 79, 80, 81, 82, 84, 85, 86, 87, 88, 89, 90, 97, 98, 99, 103, 110

V

Virtual Learning Environment 59

W

Waymo 5

Y

Yield 24, 95, 166

Z

ZOSMAT 49

ZPD 36

www.ingramcontent.com/pod-product-compliance
Lightning Source LLC
LaVergne TN
LVHW062118200926
848484LV00007B/1710